-AN-
ENCYCLOPEDIA OF
CLAIMS,
FRAUDS, AND
HOAXES OF
THE OCCULT AND
SUPERNATURAL

OTHER BOOKS BY THE AUTHOR

The Truth about Uri Geller
Houdini: His Life and Art
Flim-Flam!
Test Your ESP Potential
The Faith Healers
The Magic World of the Amazing Randi
The Mask of Nostradamus
James Randi: Psychic Investigator
Conjuring

AN ENCYCLOPEDIA OF CLAIMS, FRAUDS, AND HOAXES OF THE OCCULT AND SUPERNATURAL

James Randi's Decidedly Skeptical
Definitions of Alternate Realities

EXPOSED BY

JAMES RANDI

ST. MARTIN'S PRESS · NEW YORK

Design by Jessica Shatan

LIBRARY OF CONGRESS CATALOGING IN PUBLICATION DATA

Randi, James
The encyclopedia of claims, frauds, and hoaxes of the occult and the supernatural
/James Randi
    p.   cm.
    Includes bibliographical references and index.
    ISBN 0-312-10974-1
    1. Occultism—Encyclopedias. 2. Parapsychology— Encyclopedias.
  3. Supernatural—Encyclopedias. 4. Occultism—Controversial literature.
  5. Parapsychology—Controversial literature.
    I. Title.
BF1407.R36 1994
133'.03--dc20   94-6707
                                                    CIP

First edition: May 1995
10 9 8 7 6 5 4 3 2 1

What is wanted is not the will to believe but the wish to find out, which is the exact opposite.

—BERTRAND RUSSELL

DEDICATION

This book is gratefully and humbly dedicated to a sizable group of genuine friends. In recent years, I have been taken to court by my opposition, who apparently found that they could not successfully attack my lifework but could seriously occupy me with depositions, interrogatories, and the many other legal processes. This has, I must admit, caused me to take much of my time away from the subjects I've been investigating, and the financial burden has been very ruinous, as well.

As this situation developed, from the sidelines stepped a large number of my colleagues and friends, who came to my rescue not only by establishing a fund to support my legal fight, but also by attracting the attention of a myriad of good folks who joined them in contributing research facilities, services, hard cash, and much love when I was in great need of all those commodities. I cannot thank them all individually, but certainly Dick Smith, Penn & Teller, the Denmans, Jacques Theodore, Patti Maslinoff, Bob Steiner, Michael Shermer—to name only a few—marched right beside me as I went into battle.

And along came a troop of lawyers who decided that my cause was a just one. In New York, Michael Kennedy and Greg Lenihan took up one case, and in Baltimore, Diane Lank, several more Michaels, Lynette Phillips, Vera and Susan, Erik and Lamar—all troops under the Piper & Marbury banner—went into battle to defend me on another case because they felt, rightly or wrongly, that it was a good thing to do. On the sidelines, Brenton Ver Ploeg provided enthusiastic battle cries and advice.

It wasn't all battle, either. There was much empathy, genuine concern, and reassurance from my team as I danced the strange judicial tango with often hostile partners. I was unfamiliar with the steps, making my way over a strange dance floor and in constant danger of hitting a bump or hole that I'd not been warned about. That I survived—very nicely, I must add—is due largely to my voluntary guides.

In the process, I learned the usual "lawyer jokes," some of which I had originally heard as "psychic jokes" and all of which were tolerated by my teammates. If I ever offended in this respect, I know that I've already been forgiven.

I hope I may continue to have the respect of these good people, and I assure them that they have earned my respect and my love.

The assistance of Dr. Ray Hyman of Eugene, Oregon, in editing this manuscript, making useful suggestions and eliminating some potential blunders, is gratefully acknowledged.

And as always, my sincere affection for José Luis Alvarez, a colleague who has stood by me through so many difficult times and has understood my problems when they seemed insurmountable. I cannot imagine how it could have been without his caring.

CONTENTS

FOREWORD

et me declare my interest right away. I've been an awestruck
fan of Randi's ever since I saw him, trussed hand and foot,
hanging upside down from the jib of a crane, a hundred feet
above Niagara Falls. I could hardly bear to watch as he emulated
his hero, Houdini, and extricated himself from this awkward
predicament.

Somewhat less hazardously, Randi has also appeared on my TV
series, "Arthur Clarke's World of Strange Powers," demonstrating
how psychic surgeons, spoon-benders, and mind-readers achieve
their effects. Before my incredulous eyes, he has performed feats
which I can't explain to this day, and would have been forced to
accept as demonstrations of paranormal abilities, did I not have his
solemn assurance that they weren't....

Perhaps Randi's *Encyclopedia* should be issued with a mental
health warning, as many readers—if they are brave enough to face
unwelcome facts—will find some of their cherished beliefs totally
demolished. Unfortunately, it is just those who need this treatment
most urgently, who may be incapable of benefiting from Randi's
witty account of popular delusions, past and present.

As we approach the end of this terrible century, the *fin de siècle*
phenomenon that seems to afflict such periods is becoming more
and more apparent. Some of its manifestations are helpful—witness the (on the whole) beneficial changes in international politics,
above all the end of the Cold War. Yet at the same time we are confronted by a rising tide of irrationality, and belief in superstitious
nonsense, which once seemed mercifully extinct.

So I am particularly glad to see that Randi trounces the "New
Agers." In one sense, of course, every age renews itself, as indeed it
should. But the nitwits currently parrotting this slogan seem unable

to understand that *their* "New Age" is exactly the opposite, being about a thousand years past its sale date.

How I wish that Randi's *Encyclopedia* could be in every high school and college library, as an antidote to the acres of mind-rotting rubbish that now litter the bookstands! "Freedom of the press" is an excellent ideal, but as a distinguished jurist once said in a similar context, "Freedom of speech does not include freedom to shout 'Fire!' in a crowded theatre." Unscrupulous publishers, out to make a cheap buck by pandering to the credulous and feebleminded, are doing the equivalent of this, by sabotaging the intellectual and educational standards of society, and fostering a generation of neobarbarians.

Of course, sometimes the headlines of such rags as the *National Prevaricator* are so ridiculous that not even the most moronic could take them seriously. Was it my imagination, or did I really see one which said ALIENS FROM OUTER SPACE IN US CONGRESS? Well, that would certainly explain a great deal....

Perhaps the most entertaining section of this *Encyclopedia* is the appendix giving forty-nine of the countless "End of the World" pronouncements that have been made over the last two thousand years. It is beyond belief that, even though the confident predictions of the "prophets" are invariably refuted, many of their dupes continue to have faith in them—and have even founded religions, some still in existence today, which have managed to conceal their disreputable origins. I cannot help thinking, as we approach the year 2000, that the time is ripe to establish an "End-of-the World-of-the-Month-Club."

But this sort of insanity should not be a matter for humor; it can lead to appalling tragedies when disillusioned cultists, as has happened several times recently, kill not only themselves, but their innocent children, when the Trumpets of the Lord fail to sound on schedule.

I am a little disappointed that Randi doesn't deal with one of my pet hates—Creationism, perhaps the most pernicious of the intellectual perversions now afflicting the American public. Though I am the last person to advocate laws against blasphemy, surely nothing could be more antireligious than to deny the evidence so clearly written in the rocks for all who have eyes to see! Can anyone *really* believe that God is responsible for a cruel and pointless hoax, by forging billions of years of prehistory? It is indeed a national tragedy that millions of children have been prevented from appreciating the awesome scale—in time as well as space—of our wonderful universe, owing to the cowardice of politicians and school boards. But I am delighted to know that Hollywood, of all places, has now undone much of the damage. Thank you once again, Steven, for *Jurassic Park*.

And although the Catholic Church is—very rightly—castigated by Randi for many of its past crimes, at least the Pontifical Academy endeavored to put the record straight when it announced (and I quote) "We are convinced that masses of evidence render the application of the concept of Evolution to Man and the other primates beyond serious dispute."

Scanning the *Encyclopedia* is not only informative, but highly entertaining. However, it cannot fail to leave thoughtful readers somewhat depressed, and inclined to answer with a resounding negative the question, "Is there intelligent life on Earth?"

Well, we can be cheered by the knowledge that Randi provides at least one specimen.

—ARTHUR C. CLARKE
Colombo, Sri Lanka

INTRODUCTION

This volume is designed to provide a guide to the many subjects that are usually included in the "supernatural" category. The reading public has been poorly served by previous similar catalogs, which, having often been compiled by undiscriminating and rather naive authors, can fail to give a complete and accurate picture of the subjects handled. Unquestioning belief in every sort of unproven claim of magical, occult, and mystical notions, fueled by what seems to be a missionary zeal, has guided other writers. This can give students only the affirmative view of subjects that have often actually been long ago disproved. Important negative evidence has frequently been omitted and/or de-emphasized in other books in order to support a positive finding for matters that have stirred the interest and imagination of our species ever since the first human began to wonder about something that seemed just beyond understanding.

As U.K. writer Lewis Jones has warned when discussing what constitutes a proper book of this format:

> The lesson is for readers: In a standard definition of the word *encyclopedia*—a work that contains information on all branches of knowledge—be particularly wary of the term *information*. The expression "tabloid encyclopedia" may not be quite the contraction you thought it was.

The earliest attempts to explain mysterious matters took a religious direction, and those solutions have largely given way today to a myriad of cults, movements, fashionable gurus and half-baked philosophical notions with varying degrees of fascination that seem to provide more attractive and more easily digestible answers to the questions than those offered by hard thought and research.

Though it is not widely accepted or even well known to the public, it is a fact that no occult, paranormal, psychic, or supernatural claim has ever been substantiated by proper testing. In 1988, a very comprehensive survey of the best evidence for these claims conducted by the National Research Council concluded that:

> despite a 130-year record of scientific research on parapsychology, our committee could find no scientific justification for the existence of phenomena such as extra sensory perception, mental telepathy, or "mind over matter" exercises.

To properly evaluate these claims, it is not enough merely to gather huge amounts of anecdotal material in support of the avowed powers and events, and correct testing methods are not always obvious to the inexperienced observer. For these reasons, some amateurs have come up with results that they believe, erroneously, are sufficient to establish the existence of psychic or magical powers.

One very substantial source of such material has been Lewis Spence's 1920 *An Encyclopaedia of Occultism*, a puzzling mixture of straight history, wild speculation, credulous acceptance, and mild reservation. Spence quoted almost every account he could find, from lists of angels' names to lengthy descriptions of thoroughly discredited stories and theories. Few matters that came to Spence's attention failed to be accepted and listed, though he managed to avoid including evidence that might oust colorful subjects from his book.

Though the fact is that easily designed and conducted tests of supernatural powers are available to science, wishful thinking and data searching (exploring for and selecting out positive data and/or omitting negative data) long ago invaded the labs of the paranormalists, giving further headaches to responsible, serious researchers who honestly want good data to be gathered—positive or negative. At present, there are no replicated positive data available to support paranormal claims.

Replication by conjurors of such wonders as spoon bending, clairvoyance, precognition, psychokinesis, and levitation (long established as items in the conjuring repertoire) cannot prove anything about claims of real paranormal performance—except that it can easily be mirrored, exactly, by means of trickery. An audience of average intelligence and average powers of observation *can* be deceived. Scientists, with their specially tuned and therefore limited perceptions, are often more easily misled by those who would deceive them, and frequently deceived by their own eagerness for reportable findings.

The onus of proof is on the paranormalists and the other believers to establish their case, without resorting to special pleading and exceptions to standard expectations of scientific rigor, which the conjurors—understandably—often require in order to succeed at their performances. The conjurors are entertainers, bringing delight to the public, not leading them to actually believe the impossible, and they should not have to prove anything except their value as entertainers. Conjuring is an ancient and honored profession.

The casual reader, or one not already familiar with the field, will in effect be stepping through the looking glass of Lewis Carroll when he or she turns these pages. The world of the paranormalists is a very, very different one from the real one.

Psychics, cult members, and fringe-science folks often say that their claims and ideas cannot be examined by regular rules and means that would be considered acceptable in any other discipline. They have developed their own jargon to describe their unique gifts, much of it borrowed from scientific terminology and stealing validity by that appropriation. They sometimes disagree with one another so markedly that only one of them can be right, and all may be wrong. Logic, rational thought, and common sense are tools they seem unfamiliar with, and even cursory examination shows that their claims are very unlikely to be true. Most importantly, these folks insist that their tenets can only be properly examined by persons who believe them—in advance of any examination—and who do not hold any skepticism concerning the subject. That is not a condition under which the truth is apt to reveal itself.

Subjects listed here are those that have been recognized to fall under the headings of paranormal, supernatural, or occult, along with a miscellany of other items that are included because:

1. They are unlikely to be true
2. They have poor or nonexistent supporting evidence
3. They are clearly magical in nature, or
4. They are myth-based

Such subjects are often used to support theories and ideas that are more legitimately listed. While subjects such as "auras" and "ESP" clearly fall into the category of parapsychology, others like the "Davenport brothers" and "Transcendental Meditation" are only peripherally connected, but add to a better understanding of the main subjects. Cross-indexing indicates to the reader how to obtain more in-depth understanding of each subject.

I have tried valiantly to avoid pontificating in the preparation of this volume. If personal attitudes—rather than factual delineations—invade the subjects, please forgive the intrusion. Long familiarity with these subjects naturally gives rise to a certain cast of mind, which doubtless will be apparent. I trust that the text does not in any way incorrectly describe the subjects, and opinions are, I hope, clearly discerned, apart from a recitation of the facts and the fallacies involved.

Some of the definitions contained here have been drawn from my previous writings, somewhat edited to suit this format. For in-depth treatments of some subjects, readers may wish to refer to my previous books.

I have emphasized certain words in the text by printing them in bold type, indicating that the reader will be further informed by referring to those subjects, as well. Emphasized subjects such as **Dr. Joseph Banks Rhine** can be found properly listed as, **Rhine, Dr. Joseph Banks.**

If I sound rather less than credulous concerning some subjects, that is due to long-term familiarity with the field. I may not offer soft and gentle treatment where it is not deserved. Some notions are just too childish to merit kindness.

~AN~
ENCYCLOPEDIA OF
CLAIMS,
FRAUDS, AND
HOAXES OF
THE **OCCULT** AND
SUPERNATURAL

A

Abaris Said to be the teacher of **Pythagoras**, Abaris was a **magician** of Scythia, an ancient culture on the north shore of the Black Sea. He claimed to possess a golden arrow, given to him by Apollo, by means of which he could travel through the air and become invisible. It is not clear how this was supposed to be accomplished, but such details are unimportant in comparison with the basic claim.

Abaris is said to have lived without eating or drinking. This, coupled with the fact that his pupil Pythagoras is supposed to have stolen his golden arrow, must have resulted in a certain dissatisfaction with his life.

Abdelazys (also Alchabitius) A tenth-century Arabian astrologer whose book on **astrology**, *Alchabitius cum commento*, was first published in Latin in 1473, and then in 1503 in Venice. The book is no clearer or more useful than any other book on the subject. It is merely old.

Abominable Snowman Known in various localities by names such as Yeti, Bigfoot, Meh-Teh, and Sasquatch, this unsubstantiated creature is said to be seven to ten feet tall, with feet twice the size of a human's, and with a noticeably disagreeable aroma. It has been reported in Tibet, Nepal, China, Siberia, Canada, and the U.S. Northwest.

In 1832, a report from the U.K. representative in Nepal described a hirsute creature who reportedly had attacked his servants. The natives called the beast "rakshas," which means **"demon."** This appears to be the first report of the Snowman made by a Westerner.

An impressive report was made by mountaineers who crossed a Himalayan glacier in 1951 and photographed giant footprints measuring thirteen by eighteen inches. However, tracks left in snow tend to enlarge when exposed to direct sun, and this may well explain many of the accounts of Snowman tracks, since smaller tracks of native animals tend to spread under warmth.

Other tracks found in Canada and the United States are the admitted results of hoaxers, even though the "experts" called in have sometimes validated the artifacts as genuine tracks of an unknown species. A short piece of movie film made in 1967 by Roger Patterson at Bluff Creek, California, appears to show a female Bigfoot casually walking away from the camera. The film has been hotly contested over the years and is the best of all the evidence ever offered.

It is possible that Patterson himself was hoaxed; the figure he saw and filmed might have been a person in costume. In the 1968 film *2001: A Space Odyssey*, most viewers were not aware that the apes shown were actors in costume holding real baby chimpanzees. The 1989 film *Gorillas in the Mist* used actors in costumes that were totally convincing. The Patterson figure is nowhere nearly as good as those representations, though we cannot expect that a genuine Bigfoot must move like an ape, and it may very well move like a human dressed in an uncomfortable costume.

While the existence of such a creature is not at all impossible, two elements speak against it: First, there would need to be a very considerable number of them available to maintain the gene pool and to thus ensure survival of the species; it is difficult to imagine that a population of such a large animal could so successfully avoid detection. Second, the fact remains that to date, not one bit of material evidence (hair, skin, bones, droppings) of this creature has ever been produced, though a chimpanzee scalp

was once offered and is still occasionally brought up by devotees of this fascinating legend.

abracadabra This is the name of the supreme deity of the Assyrians. It is also a **magical** word often appearing on an **amulet,** and first mentioned by the third-century physician Quintus Severus Sammondicus. It is often seen in the configuration of a diminishing triangle:

```
A B R A C A D A B R A
A B R A C A D A B R
A B R A C A D A B
A B R A C A D A
A B R A C A D
A B R A C A
A B R A C
A B R A
A B R
A B
A
```

It was believed that certain evils would diminish and vanish in the same way the word did. The word was often used by conjurors as an exclamation at the culmination of a trick. Now not so often employed, and in any case totally ineffective.

See also **charm.**

Abraham the Jew (1362?-1460?) An **alchemist/magician** from Mayence, a town west of Koblenz, Germany. He came from a family of magicians and traveled through Austria, Hungary, Greece, Constantinople, Arabia, Palestine, and Egypt, where he met and studied with a mentor magician, Abra-Melin. He finally settled in Würzburg, Germany, where he married.

He performed his wonders before

Henry VI of England, Pope John XXIII (the first one), and Emperor Sigismund of Germany.

A tome supposed to have been written by Abraham titled *The Book of the Sacred Magic of Abra-Melin, as delivered by Abraham the Jew unto his son Lamech*, tells the reader how to "excite tempests," have visions, "retain familiar spirits," raise the dead and walk under (not on) water. Instructions on how to summon these convenient powers are followed by observations on "comedies, operas and all kinds of music and dances." All these abilities are said to be attained by means of the **kabala**.

Abraham was intolerant of other magi, believing himself—and his hero, Abra-Melin—to be the only performers worth consideration. This is a common delusion among such folks.

Abra-Melin Teacher of **Abraham the Jew**, which see above.

Abrams, Dr. Albert (1863-1924) The consummate quack, Abrams was a medical graduate of the University of Heidelberg (in 1893) who moved to the United States to become a professor of pathology at Stanford University, a post he held for five years. Then he developed a diagnostic idea he called "spondylotherapy" which consisted of striking the vertebrae with a hammer. This rather alienated him from his colleagues at Stanford, and perhaps from some of his patients as well.

Abrams left Stanford and began teaching spondylotherapy to other physicians for a fee of $200. Next he originated the idea of diagnosing disease by means of a sealed, scientific-looking black box he called the Dynamizer. This device, he said, worked at any distance by analyzing a drop of the patient's blood and, he said, could even determine the religious affiliation of the patient! Many persons, including some doctors, believed him.

Soon, for a healthy fee, Abrams was broadcasting cures to his patients by radio waves through another quack device he called the Omnipotent Oscilloclast. Other varieties of these boxes were named the Biodynamometer and the Reflexophone. His customers actually took all this seriously and paid well for his services.

Abrams's various boxes were available for rental by would-be instant healers, but were thoroughly sealed up. The agreement was that the renter could not examine the innards of the device. When a few skeptics did open the boxes, they found simple wiring, a few resistors, a small motor that only made a humming noise, and nothing that could in any way perform a diagnosis or "broadcast" or even produce radio waves.

Investigators even sent Abrams drops of red ink in place of blood, but he was still able to find human diseases in the samples. A spot of chicken blood brought back a diagnosis of cancer, malaria, diabetes, and two different venereal diseases. The chicken, it appeared, had gone through an unusual existence in its life of just less than one year.

The American Medical Association called Abrams the "dean of twentieth century charlatans." He died wealthy in 1924, leaving an estate of millions of dollars.

See also **George De la Warr** and **Ruth Drown**.

Abraxas (also Abracax or Abrasax.) The supreme god of the **Gnostics**, pictured with the head of a king and with serpents for feet. Also, Abraxas is a Gnostic "word of power" and a divine name with magical significance. Vulgar rumor has it that it was once used as a trade name for a household cleaner made by Proctor & Gamble, but was quickly withdrawn from the market after **Bible** thumpers raised their usual din about **Satanism**.

actorius A stone found in the gizzard of a capon, worn as an **amulet**, or **charm**, to bring courage, though due to surgical intervention, capons are not generally known for their courage. This is simply a concretion of various mineral substances, and can be defined as an avian pearl. Not in demand as a gemstone.

acupressure—*see* acupuncture.

acupuncture The (probably mythical) Chinese ruler known as the Yellow Emperor (Huang-ti, circa 2704 B.C.-?) is said to have brought the bow and arrow, writing, the water well, shoes, and the calendar to his subjects. It is said that he also wrote a medical manuscript, *Nei Jing*, that is still used by modern healers.

Repeating material that was considerably older, the book postulated a theoretical fluid/gas/plasma labeled **qi** (pronounced *chee*). The study of this substance or influence is known as **qi gong** (pronounced *chee gung*). The qi is believed to circulate through the body by means of pathways called **meridians**. There are twelve or fourteen major meridians. (Since dissection of the body was forbidden in the old Chinese culture, it was probably the veins and arteries that they occasionally saw following catastrophic accidents, which they mistook for these conduits for the qi.)

A great number of "acupuncture points" are specified on the body, and very fine needles, traditionally of gold or silver, inserted into these points on a properly oriented (north-south) patient and twiddled about rapidly be-tween the fingers, are said to bring about analgesic, anesthetic, or curative effects.

One form of acupuncture uses only the ear, which is regarded as a **homunculus**. Needles are inserted into various specific parts of the ear that represent parts of the entire body. A doctor in California has developed a staple-in-the-ear treatment that he claims will help patients lose weight, stop addictions, and serve in various other helpful ways. Many very fat drug addicts swear that this system works.

A form of the art in which finger

pressure is substituted for the needles is known as acupressure, also called, "shiatsu." This form is understandably more popular than the needle version.

Adalbert An eighth-century French mystic who was fond of giving away parings of his nails and locks of his hair to his disciples and admirers. He said an **angel** had given him various holy **relics,** but it is not known whether those mementos included nail parings or locks of hair.

Adalbert always carried with him a letter from Jesus Christ that he said had been delivered to him by St. Michael. Church officials finally lost all patience with him for borrowing their miracles and threw him into prison, where he died.

Adam In the *Bible*, the First Man. He was mated to Eve, the First Woman. Their sons were Cain and Abel. In a Talmudic legend, however, Adam's first wife was Lilith and she bore him **demons.** Parenthood, it seems, is an uncertain art fraught with various problems.

Adamantius A Jewish physician, circa A.D. 300, who espoused the study of **physiognomy** (reading character from facial features) and wrote copiously on the subject in Greek. The first translation of his work (in French) was published in Paris in 1556, and then in a 1780 book titled *Scriptores Physiognomoniae veteres.* Perhaps by design, no portrait of Adamantius survives by which we might determine his own character.

Adamski, George (1891-1965) A traveling wine salesman of Greek origin who brought the subject of UFOs to world-wide attention with his wild tales of having traveled into outer space with extraterrestrials. Tales of his having oversampled his wares are not substantiated.

The Adamski books *Flying Saucers Have Landed* (1953), *Inside the Space Ships* (1955), and *Flying Saucers Farewell* (1961), which described civilizations on the planets Venus, Mars, and Saturn, are still in print in several languages and are still extolled by believers. This, even though we now know that the physical scenarios described by Adamski are quite impossible.

Facts seldom interfere with belief.

adept As a noun, the word refers to a person said to be skilled at using **magical** or **occult** powers as a result of studying various practical mystical techniques. Adepts are also known by great names like the Great White Brotherhood, Mahatmas, Rahats and Rishis. A chela is an apprentice to an adept. The profession is not taught at most centers of learning. Not yet, that is.

As an adjective, the word denotes one with the abilities of an adept.

Adoni (also Adonai) A title substituted by the Hebrews for "Jehovah" to avoid pronouncing or even writing the latter word, which is supposed to be so holy and powerful that it brings punishment upon the one who utters it. No evidence exists that any such calamity visits a transgressor, and in fact the reader may repeat the word endlessly out loud without fear of penalty. However, people may think you strange, and no guarantees are given.

Aetherius Society (1919–) The Reverend Dr. Sir George King (none of the three titles are verified) says he was contacted in 1954 by The Master Aetherius—some sort of **adept**—from the planet Venus and was told to become the Voice of Interplanetary Parliament.

The result was the Aetherius Society, which met regularly at one time in Caxton Hall, London. It is now an international movement, holding regular meetings in which an entity known as "Mars, Sector Six" introduces the faithful to the Master Aetherius, who is, we are told, 3,496 years old, more or less. A journal, *Cosmic Voice*, is published by the society to bring news of the thriving civilization on Venus to the population of Earth.

George King says he has met Jesus Christ, Lord Buddha, and Saint Peter, all of whom now speak to and through him. Another entity named Saint Goo-Ling is also heard from occasionally.

The society teaches that a race of intelligent fish living underwater on the far away planet Garouche are trying to suck the air away from Earth, thus killing all terrestrial life, but not the marine life; the undersea creatures, it is claimed, obtain their oxygen from the water, which is supplied from an unknown source. This naive view of basic biology is embraced by the society.

The fact that Venus cannot sustain a civilization (the surface being at an average temperature of 860°F/460°C, far above the melting point of lead) and the failure of King's confident prediction that mankind would never land on the Moon—among other claims and notions—has brought the wisdom of the Master Aetherius into some doubt, yet the society flourishes, perhaps because of these adversities, not in spite of them.

One of the favorite harmless but useless activities of the society is charging up devices known as "spiritual batteries." This is accomplished by spending seven hundred "prayer-hours" standing before strange boxes and gesturing at them, being careful not to overcharge them, of course. The belief is that these batteries will hold their charges for ten thousand years.

aetite — *see* **bezoar.**

afreet In oriental mythology, the **spirit** of a dead person, often a **demon.** To be avoided.

Age of Aquarius — *see* **astrology.**

AGLA An acronym formed from *"Aieth Gadol Leolam Adonai"* (God is great forever), used by kabalists to invoke **demons.** Effectiveness not scientifically determined but doubtful.

Agpaoa, Tony (Antonio C. Agpaoa, 1939-1982) Agpaoa is the **quack** who began the still-popular **psychic surgery** craze in the Philippine

Islands, attracting thousands of persons annually to his center in Baguio, the most beautiful area in all the Islands. In some cases, he actually performed simple surgical services, removing cysts and draining infected areas; the rest, mostly very spectacular procedures in which his hands appeared to plunge into the body, were the usual **conjuring** tricks.

On one occasion, Tony was being driven in his gold-plated Mercedes when he fell ill and asked to be rushed via private chartered jet to San Francisco, where his appendix was removed. When his small son also needed medical care, Tony took him to the United States for medical help, but the boy did not survive the hospital stay.

In 1968 Agpaoa visited the United States for the third time, performing his sleight-of-hand act for patients who paid well for the service. Then he was arrested in Detroit and charged with medical fraud. Choosing not to answer the charges, he skipped his $25,000 bail and fled back to the Philippines.

Agpaoa died in 1982 of what the Manila newspapers referred to as "rich living" and was interred in a glass coffin, for some unknown reason.

Agrippa (Henry Cornelius Agrippa Von Nettesheim, 1486-1535) A noted German intellectual and mystic born in Cologne, Agrippa became a member of the court of Maximilian I, king of Germany, at an early age. Though otherwise an

Cornelius Agrippa, a sixteenth-century mystic who had a great influence on the supernatural beliefs of his day.

astute student, he became fascinated by an early form of **numerology** and the **kabala**, and he subsequently taught this idea at several universities. Strangely enough, he was opposed to **astrology.**

At age twenty-four, Agrippa wrote a three-volume book, *On Occult Philosophy*, which attempted to reconcile natural phenomena and **occult** lore. His concept of religion seems to have been an amalgam of Christian, neo-Platonic, and kabalistic ideas. The book was not published for another two decades, finally seeing print in 1531.

One of Agrippa's genuine contributions to knowledge was the observation that a person's thoughts and attitudes can affect the physical condition of the body, a possible suggestion of what was to become the science of psychology.

Endless claims of valor on the field of battle, intimate acquaintance with royalty, diplomatic appointments, court positions, and

The kabalistic seal of Cornelius Agrippa

heroic military accomplishments were made by Agrippa, and some may even be true.

Tales of **sorcery** and general occult practices also surround the Agrippa legend. He is said to have used various methods of **scrying** and **divination**, to have called up **spirits** and **demons**, and to have a great black dog named Monsieur as a **familiar**. These rumors got him into major trouble with various ecclesiastic powers of his day, and he came into serious conflict with the **Holy Inquisition**. For this clash and for various debts he was imprisoned several times, but always managed to buy his way out.

He died poverty-stricken at the age of forty-nine in Grenoble, France.

Akashic records (also *akasic*.) The word akashic is derived from the Sanskrit expression *akasha*, meaning a theoretical universal medium of some sort. This can be loosely compared to what science once presumed was the "ether" or medium through which electromagnetic forces operated. These insubstantial substances are unsubstantiated.

The "records" are supposed to contain data on *everything* that has

ever happened, *is* happening, or ever *will* happen in the entire universe, much like IRS records. This idea was adopted, preached, and popularized by **H.P. Blavatsky** as part of the **Theosophy** religion. Presently, the notion is reflected in the "holistic" view held by the **new agers**.

Many **psychics** have said they somehow obtained their information from these records, particularly **Edgar Cayce** and **Rudolf Steiner**. The claim is impossible to examine.

Akkadian-Chaldean inscriptions From the seventh century B.C. in the reign of Assurbanipal, these documents from the Royal Library of Nineveh are among the oldest purely **magical** writings known. They consist mostly of **exorcisms** against all sorts of evil. No more use now than they were then, but fascinating as historical records of Man's eternal fascination with such notions.

Aksakof, Alexandre (1832-1880?) A very rich Russian **spiritualist** and statesman who, with nothing better to do, brought **mediums Henry Slade** and **Eusapia Palladino** to Russia. At his urging, a Russian Scientific Committee was established to investigate spiritualistic claims, but it failed to produce any valuable work.

Albertus Magnus (1205-1280?) He was Albert of Cologne, a wellborn Christian philosopher and Dominican who for a short time served as a bishop. He defended the writings of Aristotle in accordance with church doctrine, wrote about and experimented with **alchemy,** and theorized on **magic.** It was rumored that he had discovered the **philosopher's stone** and that he could control the weather. He was a very prolific writer.

It was said that he had spent thirty years to produce what we today would call an android, a figure of brass in the shape of a man, with the power of speech. We are told that it was destroyed by **St. Thomas Aquinas** because its answers to his questions puzzled him.

Albert's actual and potentially useful work consisted of discussions of herbal remedies, the effect of which, because of the intellectual limitations of his time, he could not differentiate from magic.

Alchabitius – *see* Abdelazys.

alchemy & **alchemists** Beginning about the year 100 and reaching its flower in medieval times, alchemy was an art based partly upon experimentation and partly upon **magic.** Early investigators of natural processes centered their search on a mythical substance they knew as **philosopher's stone** (the expression *stone* refers to any general mineral substance) which was supposed to possess many valuable attributes such as the power to heal, to prolong life, and to change base metals into precious metal—such as gold. This substance was eagerly—and understandably—sought after, and the rich folks of the day sponsored alchemists who promised them the stone in the same way that today's

wealthy will court and support inventors of **perpetual motion machines** and those who claim mystic powers. Expectations of success were then, and are now, equally and perpetually futile.

The three general aims of the alchemists—transmuting base metals into gold, prolonging life indefinitely, and manufacturing artificial life—failed to be met. Very few alchemists obtained any success of any kind at all, but friar **Nicolas Flamel** (1330-1418) of Paris, who claimed to have found the secret of transmutation, is said to have died very rich. In the year 1400, the cautious Henry IV of England passed a

Alchemists preparing a distillate.

Nicolas Flamel, an alchemist who was said to have made wondrous discoveries, and who did die rich.

law against the "art of multiplication," which meant creating gold or silver by alchemy. If it took place, Henry wanted in on it. A subsequent Henry, the Sixth, took a different tack in 1455 when he granted four commissions to scoundrels who assured him they could produce all sorts of gold.

But along the way, alchemists made many genuinely valuable contributions to knowledge, though such fundamental discoveries as the chemical elements and the manner in which they form compound substances escaped them. Their basic "elements" were fire, air, earth, and water, and they believed that all substances were combinations of sulfur, mercury, and common salt, which they said were themselves composed of the four "elements."

In modern times, there was great excitement among those who still clung to belief in alchemy when it was determined that all real elements are composed of the same particles (electrons, protons, neutrons) in different ratios; the immediate assumption was that the long-sought process of transmutation was at last possible. True, elements are now transmuted, an

atom at a time, by high-energy bombardment with subatomic particles, but this is as similar to the notions of the alchemists as space flight by rocket is to attaining earth orbit on a pogo stick.

Eventually, when the nonsense and misinformation were boiled out of alchemy, it became chemistry. *See also* **elements** and **Paracelsus.**

Alexander (mentalist, 1880-1954) Billed in 1900 as "The Man Who Knows," Claude Alexander did a regular oriental-style magic act in the first half of his stage show, but regardless of the high quality of his conjuring, the audience was impatiently waiting for his question-answering second half.

Dressed in a turban and oriental robes, Alexander asked that questions be written out by his audience on slips of paper, which were then folded up, collected, and spread out on a table before the artist. He held each in turn to his forehead, appeared to divine what the question was, and then provided an appropriately veiled and provocative answer. In spite of the obvious fact that he was a conjuror and trickster, the audience ate up his every word and wanted more. This constitutes both a tribute to his skill and an indication of the great lack of judgment on the part of the spectators.
See also **one-ahead method.**

alfridarya — *see* **astrology.**

Alpha Project — *see* **psychokinete.**

Althotas — *see* **Cagliostro.**

American Society for Psychical Research (ASPR) Founded in 1885 in Boston by the psychologist William James to study and record supernatural, **occult**, and, particularly, **survival-after-death** claims, and modelled after the **Society for Psychical Research** (SPR) in London, the ASPR became independent of the SPR in 1905. It underwent many political crises and changed leadership and locality many times. The secretary in 1887 was Richard Hodgson, a leading investigator of psychic claims.

It is currently headquartered at 5 West 73rd Street, New York City, NY, 10023, and has an adequate library and study facilities where members pursue various chimerae.

amulet (From the Arabic *hamulet,* meaning, "that which is suspended.") A **charm** (*which see*) designed more for protection than for conferring power or strength, which is the function of the **talisman**. Now often made of plastic and sold in spooky shops or at airport souvenir stands to nervous passengers. Usually worn on a cord or chain about the neck.

ancient astronauts There is a theory that thousands of years ago, civilizations from other star systems visited Earth and gave early Man information to assist in his development. The idea seems to be that folks used to be pretty slow-witted and had to have help to develop such clever stuff as the wheel, bricks, and cudgels.

Evidence has been offered by many writers, particularly by best-seller **Von Däniken** and none of it is convincing when the actual facts are determined and examined even casually. The theory is presently promoted by tabloid newspapers, sensationalist journals, UFO periodicals, and other fringe-science entities, but holds little interest for serious researchers.

angel In theology, a being just below the gods in rank. Whether angels have gender or any sensual interests or abilities has been a matter of some interest to philosophers and the intrusively curious. And, surprisingly enough, at no place in the j are angels' wings even mentioned. Those appendages seem to have been simply invented by medieval artists, and the attractive idea was picked up and used by everyone since, no questions asked.

The head of the angels is Michael, an archangel who rules over Anael, Gabriel, Oriphiel, Raphael, Samuel, and Zachariel. The position is for life, and Michael is immortal.

Angels of Mons On September 29, 1914, the London *Evening News* published a charming fiction story by Arthur Machen titled "The Angels of Mons." The story told of the patron saint of England, St. George, appearing at the Battle of Mons, Belgium (August 23, 1914), in company with a troop of thoroughly English **angels** wielding longbows and raining arrows on the enemy, thus aiding the British troops in their retreat from that famous encounter.

The story was so attractive that it was distributed internationally and was soon being treated as fact. Some veterans of Mons even began saying that they had personally seen the angels at the battle.

Today the legend is still believed due to its uncritical, periodic revival and the restatement and improvement of the tale by journalists, and mystics cite it to prove the support of God for the Forces of Good.

anima mundi   The "soul of the world" idea accepted by mystics like **Paracelsus** and many others. It is an expression of the concept that there is a sort of all-pervading **spirit** that is the "vital force" behind all life and energy.

See also **animal magnetism.**

animal magnetism   The conviction that the life process itself has a measurable "substance" to it is common to many cultures. This term has come to be used, inaccurately, as a catchall one for the mystics' "life force," **anima mundi** or "élan vital." It loosely resembles the oriental idea of **qi** as well. The specific term was developed by **Anton Mesmer** to explain the force he believed was at work to bring about the **hypnotic**/hysterical effects he induced in his subjects.

This is a somewhat different though equally imaginary entity from that referred to by **Christian Scientists** as **M.A.M.** (for "malicious animal magnetism") which their founder, **Mary Baker Eddy**, believed was poisoning her, transmitted into her body by her enemies. It appears that she adopted the idea from Phineas Parker Quimby, a "magnetic healer," the originator of the wild theories upon which Christian Science is based.

ankh   Egyptian hieroglyph, also known as the "looped cross," representing the glyph for "life." A large stone or metal figure of that shape was often shown being carried in the right hand of Egyptian gods. The smaller version is often worn as an **amulet** or **charm**, and is just as effective as any other such device.

anthropomancy   A useless system for determining the future by tearing open living human beings and examining their entrails. The slightly more acceptable variety of this is **augury**, in which a bird is the victim. Anthropomancy, at least, is not known to be currently in use.

Anthroposophy   A philosophy developed by Hungarian architect/ artist/occultist **Rudolf Steiner** (1861-1925) that consisted of ideas very similar to those of **H.P. Blavatsky**, whose **Theosophical** movement Steiner had embraced in 1899. In 1902 he became secretary of the German branch of the Theosophical movement, but by 1913 he had broken with them and had formed his own group.

A true mystic, Steiner claimed, as Blavatsky had, to be able to consult the **Akashic Records**. He discovered **spirits** of all sorts everywhere and determined whether they were beneficial or malevolent. He was a devout believer in **astrology**, a trait he shared with the German poet Goethe, of whom he was a great admirer. He edited Goethe's nature writings for publication.

Steiner's architectural designs, very distinctive indeed, are organic in appearance and can be found in many locations in Germany and the Scandinavian countries. The pleasant, natural lines and features of his designs are truly beautiful and appealing.

In 1919, he developed the Steiner Schools (in some parts of the world known as Waldorf Schools, named after the German brand of cigarette known as Waldorf-Astoria) to teach his ideas such as "bio-dynamic agriculture" and "eurythmics," a method of dance intended to portray music by movement. His educational method encourages children to seek out nature spirits and to merely observe, rather than closely examine or test, situations. Steiner came up with the notion that humans live their lives in seven-year cycles, and his educational plan is geared to that idea.

To whatever extent the schools adapt Steiner's teachings on a more realistic and useful basis, the Steiner Schools treat retarded children through their clinics (known as Campbell Villages) that are supported by the system.

Apollonius of Tyana (A.D. 3-98. Also known as Balinus.)

A Greek philosopher/mystic, contemporary with Jesus Christ, who is said to have traveled as far as India in search of **magical** knowledge. He studied the ideas of **Pythagoras** and

was credited with **prophecy**, raising the dead, invisibility, **bilocation**, and other miracles, and his disciples claimed that after his own death, he rose, alive, and ascended bodily into heaven. In Asia Minor, temples were dedicated to him as a minor god.

However, most of the detailed information on Apollonius comes from the writer Philostratus, and his rendition is generally believed to be pure fiction.

applied kinesiology

This is a claimed diagnostic technique also known simply as AK. It consists of having the subject stand with a test substance in one hand, while the other arm is stretched straight out from the side of the body. The operator places his palm upon the outstretched arm and presses down with a certain force, attempting to depress the arm and judging the degree of the force required to accomplish this effect. He then compares it with the amount of force needed to depress the arm when the test substance is not being held by the subject in the other hand, or when a "bad" substance is held.

It is claimed that when a harmful substance is being held, the arm depresses easily; when a beneficial or harmless substance is present, the force needed is much greater, since the body is now not weakened by the **vibrations** of the negative substance.

The effect observed is entirely due to the expectations of the operator, and this can clearly be shown by appropriate "blind" testing procedures, in which the operator is kept ignorant of the expected result. As evidence that the AK idea is pure **sympathetic magic**, it is enough to know that promoters claim that while refined sugar can be clearly shown in a very dramatic manner to be a "bad" substance by this method when actual sugar is placed in the hand, the same strength of effect is also brought about by simply having the subject hold a scrap of paper with the word "sugar" or the chemical formula $C_{12}H_{22}O_{11}$ (sucrose) written on it in place of the actual substance. Believers in AK have no problem rationalizing the absurdity of such a claim.

In the United States, in response to our increasing demand for nonsense, expensive courses are now being offered to doctors and dentists in which AK is taught to them as a diagnostic tool, and many otherwise sensible medical professionals have taken these courses and have accepted the effect as genuine.

AK has been tested thoroughly, and has always been found useless.

apport (Incorrectly, aport) A substance or object said to be transferred from one physical location to another without passing through normal space-time. The process of "beaming up" in science fiction would satisfy this definition—so far, an entirely mythical notion.

In **spiritualism**, an apport is any object or substance brought into the séance room by apparently supernatural forces. Even scents perceived by the **sitters** are said to be evidence of apports. **Lamar Keene**, a reformed spiritualist from the Florida area, said of this "evidential" material:

> I just bought cheap stuff from the local stores, took off the stickers and took it in to the séance. It didn't need any sleight-of-hand at all. I just threw it all up in the air when the lights were out, and the sitters scrambled to get some of it. Everyone was happy!

See also **asport**.

aquilaeus — *see* **bezoar**.

Aquinas, St. Thomas (1225?-1274) A remarkable Christian philosopher known as Doctor Angelicus, who expressed himself extensively on theology, metaphysics, and mysticism. His *Summa Theologica* is one of the basic writings of Christianity. As with all such important historical figures, a certain mythology has developed about his life story, and certain sections of the *Summa Theologica* are the work of writers who took over when Aquinas died before completing it.

See also **Devil** *and* **witchcraft**.

Arcanum, The Great The mysterious, all-encompassing "secret" that is said to explain and permit all **magical** forces, powers, and knowledge to be achieved. Not known to have been revealed to anyone, as of this writing.

archangel It is popularly believed that there are two orders of **angels**: ordinary, standard angels, and the archangels, sort of super-angels. In the *Bible*, however, only two references are made to the higher rank. At one point, Michael is called an archangel, and later it says that at a certain moment, "the Lord shall descend from heaven . . . with the voice of the archangel." It is thus unclear what the rank means, though archangels are doubtless just as real as regular angels.

In the *Koran*, four archangels are listed: Gabriël, in charge of revelations, Michael, the warrior, Azraël, who brings death, and Azrafil, whose only function appears to be standing by with a huge horn to sound the Last Trump.

In the *Bible*, archangel Michael is described as a militant sort who slays a dragon, is called a "prince," is in charge of human virtue, and is in command of nations. A busy angel.

ARE — *see* **Association for Research and Enlightenment.**

Arigó, José (1918-1971) Brazilian José Pedro de Freitas took the name Arigó when he achieved fame in 1950 as a **native healer**. He claimed to be able to operate on the human body without making incisions, though in some cases he did use a simple, unsterilized pocketknife. Arigó said he had the spirit of "Dr. Adolfus Fritz" whispering in his right ear. This German "medical student" is supposed to have died in the 1800s, though there is no trace of evidence that such a person ever existed.

Arigó would hand out illegibly scribbled prescriptions to his patients. The only person who could read these was his brother-in-law, who fortunately owned the local pharmacy and thus filled all prescriptions produced by Arigó. A medical team headed by **Dr. Andrija Puharich**, admittedly unable to understand the prescriptions, issued a statement saying that Arigó—an uneducated man—had never made an error in the issuing of a prescription or in the name of a registered trade name of a drug. That incredible statement was offered as proof of the validity of Arigó's claims.

Though it was reported that patients felt no pain or discomfort when operated on by Arigó, Puharich's own films show them reacting very strongly to incisions to excise simple boils and lipomas.

Arigó was convicted in Brazil of the illegal practice of medicine in 1957, was then pardoned, and was again convicted in 1964. He died in a truck accident at the age of fifty-three.

Armageddon Although commonly used as a designation for the **end of**

the world, this name actually applies to a real geographical location in Israel near Mount Carmel, about five miles from the coastal city of Haifa. It was the site of several important battles in ancient history.

According to the predictions of St. John in *Apocalypse*, a battle between good and evil will take place there at some unspecified time, producing a river of human blood "to the height of a horse's bridle" for a distance of two hundred miles. Assuming that (a) *all* the blood were to be drained from each victim's body at the same moment, that (b) the "river" is only ten feet wide and does not flow at all, and that (c) the horse is rather small, it would mean that some three hundred sixty million persons would have to be slaughtered during this battle, all simultaneously. Since the area cannot itself hold that number of persons standing shoulder to shoulder, it appears that St. John's figures are poorly arrived at. But perhaps that is one of the properties of a miracle.

Arnold, Kenneth A private pilot who reported that he had seen nine flying "saucer-shaped" objects while in his private plane near Mount Rainier on June 24, 1947. This gave rise to the expression "flying saucer" and started the UFO craze, which is still very much with us, like the common cold.

Artephius A Hermetic magician of the twelfth century, often confused with **Apollonius of Tyana**. He is said to have lived more than 1,025 years, at which age he wrote *The Art of Prolonging Life*. His own longevity was claimed to be accomplished by **demonic** aid. Sure.

Arthur (King) Probably a totally mythical warrior/monarch/hero of Britain who is said to have reigned about A.D. 500. Arthur's legend is closely tied to the equally imaginary magician **Merlin**.

There is some chance that the Arthur story may be based on that of a former Roman soldier, or on his eventual successor named Artorius. However, this area of early English history is quite uncertain, and much of it appears to have been created to satisfy prominent myths.

Artorius — *see* **Arthur**.

ascended master An **adept** or saint who teaches from another **astral plane** of existence by means of direct voice messages, dreams, or visions experienced by mystics. A doubtful premise.

asiza In African Dahomey, spirits that live in the forests and grant **magical** powers to humans.

Asmodeus The king of the **demons** in Hebrew mythology, with three heads, goose feet, and a snake's tail. He can reveal to men the hidden treasures of the earth and can make them invisible. His queen is Lilith. *See also* **Adam**.

asport The opposite phenomenon of **apport**. In this case, objects already present at the **séance** will vanish. Often it is valuable objects that vanish in the dark room and are not seen again by their owners.

ASPR — *see* **American Society for Psychical Research.**

Association for Research and Enlightenment (ARE) Headquartered in Virginia Beach, Virginia, the ARE was founded in 1931 by **Edgar Cayce** (1877-1945). It is dedicated to perpetuating Cayce's teachings on spiritual healing, **reincarnation** and other notions. The center boasts a comprehensive library and a conference center associated with Atlantic University. The ARE promotes herbal remedies, baths, and fasting as methods to cure ailments, in the manner prescribed by Cayce.

astral body Said to be a duplicate of the human physical body, but composed of much "finer" matter than the denser, "real" body. It is supposed to experience the feelings on behalf of the physical body, and to communicate these matters to it. It leaves the physical body during sleep, or as a result of trauma such as injury or drug use. This notion appears to satisfy most of the questions about dreaming, death, or hallucination, without offering any proof or appeal other than the convenience of such an invention and the resulting lack of requirement for applied thought and/or research.

astral plane One of the fuzzy "places," levels, or dimensions said by occultists to exist in parallel with the real world. A plane is often inhabited by **demons, spirits,** or other unworldly entities. Oz and Wonderland may be equivalents.

astral projection Traveling out of the body via **astral planes,** a notion probably derived from the experience of highly colorful and memorable dreams.

astrological sign — *see* **astrology, horoscope,** *and* **zodiac.**

astrology The actual beginnings of astrology are lost in history. From the Old Babylonian period (1800-1700 B.C.) we have the first records of attempts to correlate such simple, basic problems as famine, death, or war with the positions of the stars and planets. These records were kept over a wide range of territory, from what is now Turkey to Iraq and Iran. The "Venus Tablets of Ammisaduqa," recording the motions of the planet Venus, were themselves copies of earlier observations made in the time of King Ammisaduqa, tenth ruler of the First Dynasty of Babylon, circa 1626 B.C.

In the earliest times, **omens** derived from astronomical observations were applied solely to the rulers or to matters of public welfare; it was some time before other, ordinary individuals were permitted, by law, to have forecasts made for them. In Rome, astrology was so popular at one period that Caesar Augustus (63 B.C. – A.D. 14) forbade its use as too dangerous to the proper conduct of government.

Astrology was, in its beginnings,

a genuine search for knowledge—an attempt to find, in the configurations of the stars and planets, some meaning for humans that might enable them to ascertain something about the future, as if that future were written, obscurely but gloriously, in the heavenly patterns that nightly present themselves to observers.

Only five planets—Mercury, Venus, Mars, Jupiter, and Saturn—were known to the early observers. Since they were named after gods and were believed to represent the actual bodies of the gods, the movements of those objects against the background of mythical figures represented by the constellations seemed important. It was that relationship of god to "sign" that was the basis for the notion that the fortunes of humanity were to be found by examining the night skies.

There were two divisions to astrology at first. Horary astrology dealt with measuring motions of the stars and planets and thereby predicting their configurations. This division eventually grew into **astronomy.** Horary astrology was essential for performing the second type, judiciary astrology, the popular aspect that offered—and still offers—predictions and trends to the clients.

Such a notion is seductive because it seems to make life simpler. It attributes everything from interpersonal relationships to the destiny of nations to the stars. It appears to eliminate the understandable confusion offered by life, confusion created both by the advances of new

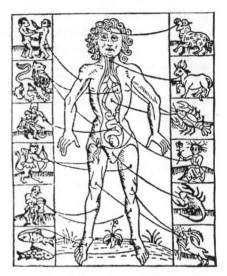

A medieval illustration of the correspondences between astrological signs and parts of the human body.

technology and by highly specialized knowledge that are beyond the reach and comprehension of the average person, and it seems to remove the need for personal responsibility, handing it all over to fate but allowing a glimpse into the future that might provide some advantage.

Today, though we now understand much more about the true nature of the starry universe, many individuals still cling to the medieval notion that earthly events in their individual lives may be predicted from observations of the skies performed by experienced—and perhaps inspired—practitioners of astrology.

This belief even extends into governmental offices, as in India, where in all walks of life astrology is taken quite seriously, to the point that a prominent Indian science adviser once complained to the American ambassador to India that a primary problem for his department was that they lacked a sufficient staff of competent astrologers. Even in the U.S. White House, a president and his first lady were actually arranging their official and personal schedules in accordance with the calculations of an astrologer who was retained by them. Prince Charles of England, a devout believer in many strange matters, has had his birth sign (Scorpio) worked into the design of his crown that he wears as Prince of Wales.

Astrology has invariably failed to meet not only the practitioners' expectations, but any other simple test of the most basic effect, though the contrary is widely claimed by the believers.

"Sun Sign" astrology—the kind that is found in the newspaper columns—may say that for one-twelfth of the entire population of the world, today is "a good day to pursue new fashion ideas" or that another twelfth of humanity will find this a day to "act boldly on property investments." These probabilities would apply whether the reader is a Maori lawyer, an Irish fisherman, or a Peruvian geologist.

Opinions on astrology have been offered by persons all through literature and the arts. The philosopher/physician Maimonides (1135-1204) in his *Responsa I*, said, "Astrology is not a science; it is a disease." Francesco Guicciardini (1483-1540), a papal adviser, wrote:

How happy are the astrologers if they tell one truth to a hundred lies, while other people lose all credibility if they tell one lie to a hundred truths.

The Italian pundit was flying in the face of his boss, who was, along with so many of his fellow popes, dependent on resident astrologers to provide him with advice.

Dr. Erika Bourguignon, professor of anthropology at Ohio State University, refers to astrology as "a pseudoscience and a divinatory art," and Sir John Maddox, editor of the science journal *Nature*, has commented on astrology as it was dealt with in his publication:

. . . one of the things we have published on astrology a few years back was a very carefully done study in California with the collaboration of 28 astrologers from the San Francisco area and lots of subjects—118 of them altogether—and lunar charts were made by the astrologers. It turned out that the people couldn't recognize their own charts any more accurately than by chance . . . and that seems to me to be a perfectly convincing and lasting demonstration of how well this thing works in practice. My regret is that there's so many intelligent, able people wasting their time and, might I say, taking other people's money, in this hopeless cause.

(Sir Maddox was referring to the project of Dr. Shawn Carlson of San Diego, which tested astrology and was reported in *Nature*.)

Though the Sun enters the sign Aquarius once every year, the **new** agers announced that in the 1960s the world entered the Age of Aquarius, though it is not clear, as with most notions of these folks, just what that means.

The formal though perfunctory opposition of religion to astrology originates with the possibility that if one's fate is already determined in the stars, sin cannot exist because it is thus not a voluntary action. This is explained by some astrologers by the statement, "Astrology impels but does not compel."

A form of astrology that says that each planet governs the life of a person for a certain number of years is known as "alfridarya." "Asterism" is a variety that deals only with the fixed stars, ignoring the sun and planets.

Though astrologers in general only claim to be able to predict the coming of disasters, those in Cambodia (called "horas") are believed to also be able to avert them.

See also **horoscope** and **zodiac**.

astronomy The genuine science that developed from **astrology**. Astronomy deals with the stars and planets and everything about them, such as their relative motions, composition, and distance. The Earth is included only so far as it enters into the cosmic scene as a planet. Astronomy has a long history of dependable, accurate forecasts, placing it among the royalty of sciences.

athame The black consecrated knife used, particularly by Western witches, and by others, to trace out the **magic circle** for invoking **demons**.

Atlantis In his 1882 book *Atlantis, the Antediluvian World*, onetime lieutenant governor of Minnesota, U.S. congressman, and senator Ignatius Donnelly (1831-1901) revived interest in a fabulous "lost continent" first described by Plato (circa 427-347 B.C.) as having existed in the Atlantic Ocean area "beyond the Pillars of Hercules" (the Strait of Gibraltar) over ten thousand years ago. The reference is found in both of Plato's dialogues, *Timaeus* and *Critias*. The entire continent, about as large as Europe, along with its highly developed civilization, was destroyed in a night and a day by an explosion and resulting tidal wave, said Plato.

The story, which Plato said originated in Egypt, just may be based on an actual cataclysm such as the one suggested by evidence discovered at the island of Santorini, north of Crete. It appears that about 1500 B.C. there was a volcanic explosion that should have decimated the area, and though that event does not satisfy the geographical location, copying errors might account for the differences. No evidence exists for a mid-Atlantic continent, and in fact we now know much more about the actual topography of the ocean bottoms, and Atlantis is simply not there.

It is interesting to note that Donnelly was also the genius who developed the notion that by examining Shakespeare carefully for a secret cipher, he had proven that someone else—**Sir Francis Bacon**—wrote the bard's work. It is a favorite crackpot idea still pursued by dilettantes who have tired of other fashionable conspiracy schemes.

See also **Bimini road.**

augury A tool for **prophecy,** the word derived from the Latin *avium garritus,* meaning "speech of birds."

While prophecy in general often makes use of substances and objects such as dice, **Tarot cards,** or sky clouds to determine the future, augury is most specifically concerned with the appearance and arrangement of the revealed entrails of unfortunate birds, as well as the flight patterns of the more fortunate ones.

In the latter system, the augur (the person who has this specialized wisdom) marks out with a wand the area of the sky in which he has chosen to observe the flight patterns, then divides that area into two left-and-right segments. If the birds fly to the left, it's bad news; to the right, good. When the omens appear satisfactory, the augur utters "*Addixit,*" Latin for "All right."

Augury is not at all a satisfactory process and is particularly unpopular with birds.

See also **anthropomancy** and **divination.**

aura One **new age** claim that has received a great deal of attention involves the notion that humans are surrounded by some sort of a glow or "field" that is invisible to all but gifted psychics. The aura is of variable size, quality, and color, and occurs mainly surrounding the head, according to the aura seers.

The variables are said to be indications of character, health, and emotions. Colors are particularly important:

> Pink means affection.
> Bright red means anger.
> Dark red means passion and sensuality.
> Yellow means high intellectual activity.
> Orange means selfishness, pride, and ambition.
> Brown means greed.
> Green means many, many different things.
> Blue means religion and devotion.
> Purple means psychic ability and occult power.

In representations of Christian and Buddhist saints and other holy figures, the halo shown probably indicates the aura. When it surrounds the whole body, it is known as the aureola.

Numerous tests of the existence of this phenomenon have proved negative.

aureola — *see* **aura.**

automatic writing A claimed phenomenon similar to that of the **Ouija board.** The operator holds a pen or pencil which is then said to move independently across a sheet of paper and write out messages from other living persons, from deceased persons, or from unknown discarnate entities.

The "Martian Alphabet" developed by Swiss spirit medium Hélène Smith during her automatic writing.

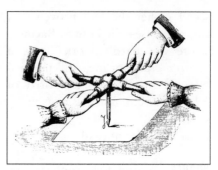

An "automatic writing" device similar to the ouija board, held by two to four persons whose unconscious movements cause it to produce writing.

This idea has been popular with **spiritualists** from the beginning of that religion, and one Swiss **spirit medium** named Hélène Smith (née Catherine-Elise Müller, 1863?-?) even invented an entire written language which she used to relate details of Martian civilization to her **sitters**. Psychologist Theodore Flournoy examined Mlle. Smith's claims and found that this language was very similar to French, using the same syntax. Mlle. Smith's native tongue was French.

Also known as "psychography." *See* **ideomotor effect** *and* **planchette**.

Avenger bombers — *see* **Bermuda triangle**.

Azoth — *see* **philosopher's stone**.

~ B ~

Backster, Cleve Mr. Backster is a polygraph (lie detector) expert who hooked up a houseplant to his instruments and discovered that even thinking about fire caused the graph to "nearly jump off the page." He even claimed that electrically connecting two containers of yogurt resulted in rudimentary "communication" between the yogurts, but *only* if the two were from the same original culture.

Backster's basic claim is that plants can communicate with one another, can read the minds of humans, and can experience emotions like fear, joy, and sorrow. This was described in the 1973 book *The Secret Life of Plants*. Since plants do not have a central nervous system, this seems unlikely to be true.

Inspired by Backster's book, Eldon Byrd, then an employee of the U.S. Department of the Navy, developed a project for funds to conduct experiments with seaweed aimed at training the plant to react to danger, thus warning naval divers.

To date, no one—not even the U.S. Navy—has taken Backster's claims seriously enough to establish a Society for Prevention of Cruelty to Plants, nor has there been any effort to legislate humane methods of chopping broccoli or making applesauce.

Bacon, Sir Francis (1561-1626) Sir Francis is generally given credit for having prepared the intellectuals of his day for the scientific method of investigating. He was a person of remarkably clear perception and observation who refused any sort of emotional acceptance of unproven ideas. He said:

> Such is the way of superstition, whether in astrology, dreams, omens, divine judgements or the like; wherein men, having a delight in such vanities, mark the events where they are fulfilled, but where they fail, though they happen much oftener, neglect and pass them by.

Bacon's work was the direct cause of the establishment of the Royal Society, which was essentially founded to pursue his methods. His major work, among many, was *Novum Organum.*

Bacon, Roger (1214-1292 or 1294) The English Franciscan monk Roger Bacon (nicknamed Doctor Mirabilis, "The Admirable

Doctor") was a noted medieval advocate of experimentation and observation as a means to learning, an advanced idea for that time in history. It was said that he built a bronze head that spoke and answered questions, but such canards are often circulated about persons of accomplishment.

Bacon was probably the greatest scientific mind of his time, even before science was delineated and organized, albeit hobbled by the religious restrictions of intellectual exercise under which he necessarily labored.

In about 1240 he also briefly described the tricks of the **conjurors** of his time and declared them to be harmless amusements. His learned opinion on tricks was largely ignored, and conjurors continued to be persecuted by ignorant secular and ecclesiastic authorities as minions of **Satan**.

Bacon adopted the prophecies of Joaquim of Flore (see Appendix II, year 1260) but this and his credulous belief in **astrology** and other forms of mysticism aside, he was a genuine contributor to knowledge.

Balinus — see **Apollonius of Tyana**.

band writer — see **thumb writer**

banshee (Derived from the Celtic "ben" for "woman," and "sighe" for "fairy.") A female Irish family ghost. Usually dressed in ratty white robes and with tangled hair over her skinny shoulders, the banshee wails, knocks, and carries on loudly just before the death of one of the fam-

ily. One can only imagine how she carries on *after* the death.

The Scottish version is known as a *benshie* or *benshee* or the *bodach glay*, meaning "gray specter."

barau In Polynesia, the name for a **sorcerer**.

bat A relatively harmless flying mammal. Since most varieties are nocturnal, the unfortunate creature has been assigned various evil characteristics and powers. The discovery of the South American vampire bat gave credence among the credulous to the legend of the human **vampire**.

In Germany, it was once believed that one who wore the left eye of a bat as a **talisman** would become invisible; since many persons were seen wearing such an object, the belief died out rather quickly.

Beelzebub The Lord of the Flies is represented pictorially as a gigantic fly. He is a prince of **demons**, and the Canaanites dedicated a large temple to his worship. He was known to the Cyreneans as Achor. Beelzebub is also one of the alternate names of **Satan**.

Beloff, Dr. John (1920-) A well-known U.K. **parapsychologist**, Dr. Beloff was appointed trustee of the **Koestler** Foundation (after Arthur Koestler, 1905-1983), and in 1984 he established the Koestler chair of parapsychology at Edinburgh University. He was president of the **Parapsychological Association** in 1972 and in 1982. He has contributed substantially to the **psi** literature.

Dr. Beloff has affirmed his belief in such **mediums** as Eva Carrière, Margery and Florence Cook, based on descriptions in the literature of their work.

Following the Alpha Project (*see* **psychokinete**) in 1982, Dr. Beloff was the only parapsychologist who took advantage of the suggestion that an experienced, competent **conjuror** be consulted in cases of experiments where deception might be possible. The resulting exposure of a **cheating** subject saved his lab from pursuing further work with that subject, who has now taken up reading **Tarot cards**.

One of John Beloff's books is titled *Psychological Sciences* (1974).

Bender, Hans (1907-1991) Impressed by the results of a **Ouija board** session when he was seventeen, Hans Bender became interested in **psi** and eventually was appointed the first chairman of the Department of **Parapsychology** at the Albert-Ludwig University in Freiburg, Germany. This effectively brought Germany into the world of psi, a mixed blessing. Bender worked with parapsychologist **Wilhelm Tenhaeff** (1894-1981), performed experiments with the **psychic Gerard Croiset**, and certified it all as genuine.

For his unquestioning acceptance of psi, Bender came in for a great deal of criticism from his colleagues in science, who referred to him as *der Spukprofessor* ("spook professor"). He also accepted the spoon bending of **Uri Geller** as a genuine example of **psychokinesis**.

Shortly before he died, it was discovered that Bender did not have the doctorate that he had claimed all his life and that in his extensive writings on psi, he had ignored very well established evidence against the phenomena and had greatly enhanced the facts and figures in favor of it. It appeared that Bender was requiring his readers to believe that everything of which he himself was convinced was factual. His work and writings are now no longer taken seriously.

Bermuda Triangle (also Devil's Triangle) A huge triangle formed by the islands of Bermuda and Puerto Rico, and the city of Fort Lauderdale, Florida, is said to be an area of profound danger for anyone or anything venturing into it. It was first so designated by a writer for *Argosy* magazine.

The whole legend began in December 1944 when five Avenger bombers of the U.S. Navy were lost while on a routine training mission out of the Fort Lauderdale air base. A sensational 1974 book by Charles Berlitz, *The Bermuda Triangle*, brought this supposed mystery to the attention of the public.

The Berlitz book, written thirty years after the loss of the bombers, contained invented details, distorted and exaggerated figures and descriptions, and even fabricated radio conversations that were claimed to have taken place between the naval pilots and the Fort Lauderdale air base. The event

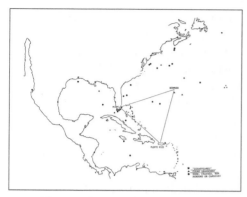

As can be seen from this map, the majority of the disasters said to be attributed to the dreaded Bermuda triangle are well away from that area, and explanations are not difficult to arrive at.

was not that unusual, if the invented details are ignored, and as evidence for any sort of mystery in the triangle, the Avenger bombers matter is a very poor example, but it remains as the event most quoted by the believers.

Other ships that are said to have vanished in the area either did not exist, or sank or capsized in other areas—even in the Pacific or Mediterranean—or went down due to perfectly ordinary and well understood causes.

The Bermuda Triangle, an area subject to violent storms and rough seas, does produce problems, but no more than any other similar area anywhere in the world. There is no need to ascribe supernatural or even unusual causes to any losses that occur there. Unless, of course, you want to sell lots and lots of books.

Bernadette Soubirous — *see* Soubirous, Bernadette

Besant, Annie — *see* Blavatsky, H.P.

bezoar A reddish stone found in the entrails of animals, usually a concretion like a kidney stone. It is also said to be extracted from an aged toad's head. Used as a powerful **amulet** or **charm**, particularly against poison.

The *aetite* or *aquilaeus* is a similar stone found in the stomach of an eagle, a hollow stone formed of iron oxide, and claimed to be able to detect a thief and to heal epilepsy. When bound to a woman's arm, they say, it prevents abortion, and fastened to her thigh, it aids in giving birth. It is actually just as effective when fastened to the father's key chain or, better still, left inside the eagle.

A bezoar being removed from the head of a toad.

In Shakespeare's play *As You Like It*, the duke says:

> The toad, ugly and venomous, wears yet a precious jewel in his head.

Which goes to show how much dukes know.

Aside from the spurious **magical** qualities ascribed to these concretions, the term *bezoar* is now properly used to designate any sort of antidote to a poison.

See **charm**.

Bible The book upon which the Christian religion is based. It is divided into the Old and the New Testaments, the former dealing with events before the time of Christ and the latter—in the four Gospels— with events of the life of Christ and the period following his death, plus events in the history of the many early Christian churches.

Early editions in English were many and varied. The Breeches Bible was so named because Genesis 3:7 refers to **Adam** and Eve preparing "breeches" from sewed-together "figge-tree leaves" upon discovering that they were naked. In the Vinegar Bible, the "Parable of the Vinegar" was given in Luke 20, rather than the "Parable of the Vineyard." A 1632 edition had the seventh commandment as "Thou shalt commit adultery." It earned the title of the "Wicked Bible."

In the reign of Henry VIII (1491-1547) it was decreed that

> . . . no woman (unless she be noble or gentle woman) no artificers [craftsmen], apprentices, journeymen, servingmen, under the degree of yeomen . . . husbandmen or labourers

could read any part of the *Bible* without danger of fines or imprisonment.

The 1611 King James Version of the book is now recognized as the authorized edition. Though in the almost four centuries since its first publication scholars have become aware of many serious discrepancies in that edition, it is still accepted as correct.

The *Bible* deals with many **magical** events, aside from the miracles

(such as **resurrection** of dead persons or multiplying food and drink) ascribed to Christ. In the Old Testament are found a number of references to the punishment of **sorcerers,** and the process of trial by ordeal appears in Numbers 5:11-13. In Jonah 1:7, we find a reference to chance being used for **divination:**

> Come, and let us cast lots, that we may know for whose cause this evil is upon us. So they cast lots, and the lot fell upon Jonah.

This process is justified and validated by another biblical passage, Proverbs 16:33, where we read:

> The lot is cast into the lap, but the whole disposing thereof is of the LORD.

This conclusion apparently still stands, despite our present better understanding of the laws of chance and probability.

A **witch** is found in Exodus 22:18. Immediately following the official amounts established for a virgin bride-price and the money penalty to be paid by the seducer of a not-yet-betrothed virgin is found the rule that:

> You shall not allow a witch to live.

The famous **Witch of Endor** was said (1 Samuel 28) to exorcise spirits, and the High Priest of the Israelites carried with him two magical stones called Urim and Thummim that enabled him to **prophesy.**

In Genesis 20:3, 31:23, and 37:5; Job 33:15; Numbers 12:6; and 1 Kings 3:5, **sorcery** is referred to, and at least twenty methods of foretelling the future are described in the book.

Bigfoot —*see* Abominable Snowman.

bilocation A person, object, or definition existing in two places at the same time. **Cagliostro** is said to have exhibited this power. Saint Anthony of Padua (1195-1231) and **Padre Pio** (1887-1968) were others who claimed it. The **conjuror** Pinetti (1750-1800) apparently drove out of the gates of Paris at two different places at the same moment. An impossible phenomenon.

bilocation A person, object, or definition existing in two places at the same time. **Cagliostro** is said to have exhibited this power. Saint Anthony of Padua (1195-1231) and **Padre Pio** (1887-1968) were others who claimed it. The **conjuror** Pinetti (1750-1800) apparently drove out of the gates of Paris at two different places at the same moment. An impossible phenomenon.

Bimini road Beginning in 1968, when an interesting pattern of natural rock was discovered underwater off the coast of Bimini, occultists began claiming that the formation was actually a road built on the site of the lost continent of **Atlantis** and thus was strong evidence for the existence of this mythological place.

The "road" is actually the now-submerged former coastline of the island and is made of beach rock, a concretion of shells and other debris formed in modern times. This fragile material tends to fracture in more or less straight lines and then at

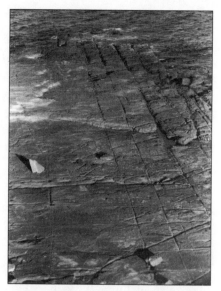

This shows part of the coast of eastern Australia and a "beach rock" formation that appears to be man-made but is quite natural. It is the same formation found just off the coast of Bimini.

right angles to those fractures, resulting in a pattern of large fragments resembling an area of paving stones. Such natural formations, also referred to as tessellated pavement, are extremely common along the eastern shore of Australia, and almost entirely around Tasmania, where they are plainly exposed to view along the coast. For a hundred miles along the coast of Venezuela there is a similar undersea formation.

Perhaps Atlantis was much, much larger than we'd thought.

biorhythms A notion originated in the 1890s by German doctor Wilhelm Fliess (1859-1928), biorhythm theory says that three cyclical influences are set in motion at the moment of birth, and that by charting these cycles it can be determined which days are propitious and which not. Fliess originally postulated only two cycles, but later a third was added.

The three cycles—physical, emotional, and intellectual—are respectively 23, 28, and 33 days in length, and a day when any curve crosses the zero line (a node) is a "critical" day. When two nodes coincide, it is said to be an especially dangerous day. As for *three* nodes, well, don't ask. The triple-critical will occur for everyone at the age of fifty-eight years and sixty-eight days, which should produce a plethora of deaths at this point, but no such actuarial bump has ever been noticed. Then, at the age of just more than 116 years, four months, and a couple of weeks, the *second* triple-critical arrives. If one has lived through the first, this crisis should definitely do one in.

Followers of this modern form of **prophecy** look assiduously for correlations between the theory and actual fact, and of course are thus able to find many such relationships which they believe support the theory. Such a process is the antithesis of scientific research.

Studies in which control groups were established have shown that there is no value to the theory. It is a form of magic and pseudoscience.

Bishop, Washington (Wellington) Irving

(1856-1889) This American **mentalist** was famous for his **blindfold drive** and other astounding feats. A mountebank who learned his trade as an assistant to John Randall Brown, a newspaperman who specialized in "**muscle reading**," Bishop flourished in the 1880s.

He started his career working with the famous **spiritualist** act of **Anna Eva Fay**, first functioning as her manager. Then in 1876 he chose to expose her methods in the New York *Daily Graphic* newspaper and at that point he began doing his own show.

At first Bishop denied the existence of any paranormal powers, then apparently decided that the easier path was with the fakers, and he became a "real" psychic overnight.

Bishop is credited with originating the blindfold drive trick (in 1885) in which the performer is able to navigate in a vehicle while his eyes are covered. Bishop used a horse and carriage, while modern practitioners depend on an automobile.

One of Bishop's favorite routines, copied from Brown, was to have a fictitious murderer, a weapon, and a victim chosen from among the audience members while he was out of the area. Upon his return he would identify all three. He performed this and other mysteries in the United States and in Britain, with great success.

In Britain he made great but spurious claims of wealth, even turning over the proceeds of several performances (less "expenses") to charitable causes. His pretensions of riches were part of his pose, apparently to attract huge fees for specialized projects in which he tried to become involved.

John Randall Brown originated the act that Washington Irving Bishop was to bring to a point of perfection. Brown was a newspaper reporter who performed only as an amateur.

It was also in Britain, however, that he lost a lawsuit brought against him by the famous conjuror J. N. Maskelyne, who objected to his claims of genuine psychic power. This provoked libelous remarks from the American, and J.N. promptly sued him, winning the case and driving Bishop from England to escape paying the £10,000 penalty.

Bishop was fond of claiming that he'd been tested by scientists, but when the conditions for the tests were not of his own making, he failed. When challenged to do specific feats that he claimed he could do with regularity, he either refused to be tested or switched tests or the conditions for the tests, and only then succeeded. His claim was that he did not understand his own powers, but when a newspaper editor named Charles Howard Montague

learned to do Bishop's act, successfully duplicating a drawing made by one of his audience, he declared:

> Mr. Bishop would have us infer that he does not know how he does it. I know how I do it, and I am rather of the opinion that his self-consciousness [self-awareness] is not a great way behind my own. It is very difficult for me to believe that so expert a student of the sensations of other people should be so poor a pupil in his own case.

Bishop chided Montague for failing to recognize that "Almighty God" had given him his abilities, and questioned Montague's belief in a deity, as if that discredited his interference. But Montague was unfazed, proceeding to perform the Bishop act for many large audiences, always denying that any supernatural forces were at work.

After numerous marriages and bouts with alcohol and drugs and almost every excess available to him, Bishop died suddenly in New York at age forty-three. His demise had a certain macabre mystery about it, since he had said that he was subject to cataleptic fits and might thus be buried alive if not carefully examined after his apparent passing. A dramatic "swoon" following his stage performance was not uncommon for him, and he claimed that several times he'd come close to being sliced up by doctors about to perform autopsies on his still-living body.

His mother, a rather overly dramatic, raving sort of woman who some years earlier had thrown herself into her husband's grave as he was being lowered to his final rest, made wild accusations in the press about her son having been autopsied while not yet dead, but nothing was proven. The event provided journalists with marvelous stories for decades and is still occasionally resurrected.

Black Art principle In conjuring this principle is used—for one thing—to produce the illusion of floating objects. It is done by covering supports and personnel in black material and operating against a black backdrop. The idea is said to have been developed and first used by illusionist Max Auzinger about 1875. The luminous trumpets, tambourines, and other objects used by some **spiritualists** during dark **séances** similarly appear to be floating due to the same optical effect. Dealers in supplies for spirit mediums sell a variety of devices to be used with this method. *See also* **Nelson, Robert.**

black arts — *see* black magic.

black boxes — *see* **Dr. Albert Abrams, George De la Warr,** and **Ruth Drown.**

black magic A form of **magic** performed for evil purposes, or in the view of religion, any magic that is not of divine origin, whether the intent is evil or not.

Lewis Spence, in his *Encyclopaedia of Occultism*, writes in reference to this subject in medieval Europe:

In Black Magic human perversity found the means of ministering to its most terrible demands and the possible attainment of its darkest imaginings. To gain limitless power over god, demon and man; for personal aggrandisement and glorification; to cheat, trick and mock; to gratify base appetites; to aid religious bigotry and jealousies; to satisfy public and private enmities; to further political intrigue; to encompass disease, calamity and death—these were the ends and aims of Black Magic and its followers.

Mr. Spence did not doubt that these "ends and aims" were attainable. However magic of any hue has not, of itself, in any way altered the history of the world or of any particle in it despite the worst or best intentions of the magi.

Black Mass Supposed to be a blasphemous version of the Catholic Mass in which the naked body of a woman (preferably a virgin, as one might imagine) is used in place of an altar. Popularly believed to be performed by **witches** at a **sabbat,** this ceremony may well be another of the totally fictitious aspects of actual **witchcraft.**

Sophisticated Parisians of the seventeenth century toyed with the idea as a diversion. It is referred to by the Marquis de Sade (Donatien Alphonse François de Sade, 1740-1814) in his novel *Justine* and that very description may have given rise to the notion that it was an actual part of witchcraft.

Those fanatics who hunted down

witches and hanged or burned them for imaginary crimes of course believed in the Black Mass. They added to the myth by inventing boiled babies, drinking blood in place of sacramental wine, and other improbable aspects. Today similar irrationalities are accepted in courts of law when evidence is given in cases involving **Satanism**.

Blackburn and Smith   In 1882 the team of Douglas Blackburn and G. A. Smith were authenticated by the **Society for Psychical Research** for their amazing **telepathic** demonstrations. Smith, blindfolded and sometimes concealed under a blanket, was able to name words that had only been shown to Blackburn and could also reproduce drawings secretly shown to Blackburn. The "experts" embraced, at last, this most welcome and undeniable evidence that supernatural forces did indeed exist.

In 1908, the investigators all having died, and Blackburn believing that Smith had also died, he revealed the methods the pair had used to perform their trickery, a hoax that had

> originated in the honest desire of two youths to show how easily men of scientific mind and training could be deceived when seeking for evidence in support of a theory they were wishful to establish.

Smith immediately showed up to complain and denied everything, but Blackburn was intent on telling the story. One example will serve to show how ingenious and original the team was. In the London *Daily News*

of September 1, 1911, Blackburn explained how, with Smith covered in blankets, he had been able to transmit to him a drawing he'd been handed by one of the experimenters. Smith was to draw on a piece of paper he had with him in the dark under the blanket, the impression he'd "telepathically" received from Blackburn, who revealed to the *News*:

> I also drew it, secretly, on a cigarette paper . . . and had no difficulty while pacing the room collecting "rapport," in transferring the cigarette paper to the tube of the brass projector on the pencil I was using. I conveyed to Smith the agreed signal that I was ready by stumbling against the edge of the thick rug near his chair.
>
> Next instant he exclaimed: "I have it." His right hand came from beneath the blanket, and he fumbled about the table, saying, according to arrangement: "Where's my pencil?"
>
> Immediately I placed mine on the table. He took it . . . under the blanket. Smith had concealed up in his waistcoat one of those luminous painted slates which in the dense darkness gave sufficient light to show the figure when the almost transparent cigarette paper was laid flat on the slate. He pushed up the bandage from one eye, and copied the figure . . .
>
> Presently Smith threw back the blanket and excitedly . . . produced the drawing . . .

Without this confession the **parapsychologists** might have today their prime case for ESP. The single example above shows how scientists can be easily deceived by simple means, having not even recorded in their reports such details as the handing over of the pencil and the stumbling on the rug since such small items seemed not to be important. As one can see, they are.

Blackmore, Dr. Susan J. (1951-) A graduate of Oxford University, Dr. Blackmore earned a Ph.D. in **parapsychology** at Surrey University. Her work consisted of ESP experiments with **Tarot cards, out-of-body** experiences (OBE), **ganzfeld tests,** and extensive work with children.

Blackmore became disillusioned with parapsychology when she obtained only negative results, sometimes in areas where other researchers had reported significant figures. She differed with some of her colleagues on their protocols, and her three books express some of those disagreements. They are *Parapsychology and Out-of-the-Body Experiences* (1978), *Beyond the Body* (1982), and *The Adventures of a Parapsychologist* (1986).

Dr. Blackmore is affiliated with many organizations in the field of parapsychology, including the **Committee for Scientific Investigation of Claims of the Paranormal** (CSICOP).

Blavatsky, Helena Petrovna (1831-1891) This woman was born Helena Von Hahn in the Ukraine. Like many **psychics**, HPB, as she was known to her disciples,

The medallion worn by H.P. Blavatsky, founder of the Theosophist religion.

claimed that as a child she had been given divine visions and had experienced magical gifts, being able to move objects by **psychokinesis.**

At seventeen, she was married to a forty-year-old general named Nikifor Blavatsky, but left him after three months and went off to Constantinople. She retained the noble name. Later in her life, she claimed that for the next few years she visited every exotic place known, was initiated into mystical orders, and finally settled in Tibet, where she contacted the "mahatmas," **adepts** who lived in caves and taught her the mysteries she was to subsequently teach. All these tales are highly doubtful.

What is known to be true is that she went from being a piano teacher to a circus bareback rider to a **spirit medium,** and she eventually was employed by the spirit medium

Daniel Dunglas Home as an assistant, where she doubtless learned some of the tricks of the trade.

At age forty, while she was operating as a spirit medium in Cairo, where she had started her Société Spirite, a great commotion arose when a long cotton glove stuffed with cotton was discovered in the **séance room,** and HPB wisely departed hastily for Paris.

Two years later, in 1873, she moved to the United States and began performing **séances** for wealthy patrons there. In 1875, in partnership with Colonel **Henry Steel Olcott,** a lawyer and writer who dealt with spiritualistic claims, she founded the **Theosophical Society.**

Theosophy became the passion and the profession of the woman who insisted upon being addressed as "Madame." She claimed to bring messages from two "masters" or "mahatmas" named Koot Hoomi and Morya. These messages were often in the form of small bits of paper that floated down from the ceiling above her. She attracted many prominent persons to the movement by her performance of these effective diversions.

In India, HPB flourished as a cult figure for several years, until a housekeeper who had formerly worked as a magician's assistant exposed the tricks by which Blavatsky had been fooling her followers. Blavatsky blustered a great deal and threatened to sue, but instead chose to leave India, and never went back.

Next in England in 1885, her tricks were exposed by the **Society for Psychical Research,** when certain pieces of **conjuring** equipment were shown to be the means by which she produced the written messages from her mahatmas, and it was revealed that she had deceived a disciple by hiring an actor wearing a dummy bearded head and flowing costume to impersonate the mahatma Koot Hoomi. The exposure did little to shake the belief of the faithful of England, who have always been tolerant of those who would take advantage of them.

Madame Blavatsky wrote several mystical books, among them *Isis Unveiled* (1877), which was shown to have been copied from previous works of other authors, and *The Secret Doctrine* (1888). A basic part of the mythology given in these books is that mankind is passing through a series of seven "root races." These are: Astrals (pure spirits), Hyperboreans (from a now-vanished continent), Lemurians (who interbred with animals and thus went bye-bye), Atlanteans (who had psychic powers and secret energy sources, but went under during a cataclysm), and the Race of Hope, the Aryans. This fifth group was seized upon by the Nazi theorists, along with the **Rosicrucian** ideas, as a basis for their racial superiority notions.

After Blavatsky's death in 1891 from Bright's disease, a disciple named **Annie (Wood) Besant** (1847/8-1933) a former militant atheist, took over Theosophy along with Charles Webster Leadbeater (1854-1934). The religion, over the ensuing years, split up into several factions, each with its own charismatic **guru**, and it has never been the same since.

Heinrich Himmler, the chief of the Nazi SS (Schutzstaffel, meaning "protection squadron"), was a devoted follower of the racial theories of Blavatsky and based the design of the SS on her teachings and on those of **Aleister Crowley** and the Templars, the band of twelfth-century knights who protected the pilgrims of the crusades.

The parent group of the Theosophists is still a minor religious movement headquartered in Adyar, India, and its activities now concentrate on social welfare.

blindfold vision This is a conjuring trick often done by **mentalists**. It consists of the performer being blindfolded—often with tape, opaque metal masks, and/or bandages—and then accomplishing various feats such as reading, writing, negotiating an obstacle course, or driving a vehicle, apparently without the use of sight. It has also been called Eyeless Vision, the name given it by Dr. Harlan Tarbell, a well-known writer on conjuring techniques.

The very effective trick has been taken up with great success by the **psychics,** who of course say that when they do it, it's not a trick.

Bluebeard (Gilles de Rais, or de Retz, also de Laval, circa 1404-1440) A French baron, a marshal of France, and a wealthy landowner, de Rais married into an even wealthier family at age sixteen. He

fought alongside **Joan of Arc** at the Battle of Orléans, then at age twenty-eight he suddenly retired from public life and began the study of **alchemy** with the intent of finding the **philosopher's stone.**

He soon gained the reputation of a **sorcerer,** taking into his service a number of rogues who promised him success in his search for untold wealth. He maintained an outward innocence and gentle attitude at the same time he was slaughtering children as sacrifices to the **demons** who he was told could satisfy his needs.

As more and more children went missing in the area, the evidence against him mounted, and he was finally arrested. At his trial in 1440 he confessed to the most heinous crimes imaginable, his confession being considerably facilitated by torture, of course. He was put to death by the **Holy Inquisition** for his crimes, one of the relatively few justified executions performed by this Holy Office. Because of his high position, de Rais was given the privilege of being strangled before he was burned. A nice touch.

He earned the name Bluebeard (*Barbe Bleue*) from his glossy black beard, and by that name he has come down through history as a character in children's stories.

Blue Book A privately published, regularly updated directory of names and pertinent information about potential **sitters,** secretly subscribed to by **spiritualist mediums** who wish to have personal data with which to impress clients. Regional versions exist, and the source is carefully guarded. The data are submitted free or sold to the publishers by practicing mediums, who obtain it from each other and from important and wealthy clients.

Individual "spirit camps" or similar communities will often keep their own private lists, formerly on index cards, but now in computer form, of persons who have visited there. Former **spirit medium** and author **Lamar Keene** describes the process in his book *The Psychic Mafia*.

Book of Coming Forth by Day, The

(*Pert Em Hru*, also known as *The Book of the Dead*.) From about four thousand years ago, the Egyptian document titled *The Book of Coming Forth by Day* was placed in the sarcophagus alongside the mummified body of an important person. This guide to the underworld, the text of which was often also drawn or inscribed on the tomb walls, was intended to instruct the **ka** (spirit) of the deceased in the proper protocol for facing the perils to be encountered after death.

In reality, it contained a long list of formulas that could be recited to ward off the penalties that might be incurred. It was a sort of Egyptian version of a Christian Indulgence, a magical system to defeat the intent of the gods or to placate them.

Before the problem of reading Egyptian hieroglyphics had been solved, a copy of this document on the original papyrus was purchased by the elders of the Mormon Church and was divinely interpreted by them to be a lost book of the *Bible* that established their religion as orthodox, a claim maintained even after it was clear that the book was no such thing. The explanation now offered by the church spokesmen is that there are really two translations of the book, one mundane and the other divine. To some people, this is not a convincing argument.

Book of the Dead, The — *see Book of Coming Forth by Day, The.*

Borley Rectory

Known as "the most haunted house in England," this very substantial residence of the parish rector, Reverend Henry Bull, was built in 1863. The first occupants of the house began reporting seeing the **ghost** of a nun, then a phantom coach and two black horses. Subsequent residents were frightened by strange whispering noises, creaks on the staircase, ringing bells, and a light that was periodically seen, from the outside, in the window of an empty upper room.

In July 1929, when the fourth resident rector moved in, he reported that in addition to the usual ghosts encountered on stairways and in hallways, **spirit** writing had appeared on the walls and pebbles were raining down on the house. He managed to bear all this for six years, then moved out. He had children.

Borley Rectory lay empty for more than a year, until the celebrated ghost hunter **Harry Price** took up residence in 1937 and arranged for colleagues to live there in shifts. The phenomena began increasing dramatically in scope and magnitude, dishes being smashed, sleepers being thrown out of bed, and strange artifacts such as a ring and an old coat "materializing" in unused rooms.

In February 1939, an upset oil lamp ignited the old home (a **poltergeist** event, perhaps?) and it was reduced to ashes. Price's investigations and reports continued, even over the ruins of the building, for several years afterward.

In 1955, the London Society for Psychical Research (SPR) issued a 180-page report following an extensive investigation of the Borley phenomena and concluded that there were no related events that could not have had rational explanations. More importantly, the report concluded that the most impressive phenomena had been produced by Harry Price himself.

One event, the light seen periodically in the upper window, was explained by the fact that it coincided with the approach of a regularly scheduled train nearby. The locomotive headlight was reflected, for a few seconds, in that window.

Still a favorite haunted house story in England, the site is visited regularly by curiosity seekers, and current phenomena are still reported to be connected with the nearby Borley Abbey.

See also **poltergeist.**

British National Association of Spiritualists — *see* Society for Psychical Research.

Brown, Rosemary This U.K. mystic claims to compose and play music under the direct spiritual contact of the **ghosts** of Beethoven, Chopin, Schubert, and other major composers. This has been referred to as composing after decomposing.

Though it has been claimed that Ms. Brown is musically "naive," she worked as a teacher of piano for years before the shades of the greats of music began to guide her fingers. Judging from the results she has demonstrated, it appears that these departed persons have, not unexpectedly, lost most of their musical skills as a result of death.

broxa A **witch/demon** of medieval times that could change shape and read the future. It flew at night and drank human blood like a **vampire.**

bunyip In Australian aboriginal lore, a roaring, hairy monster known for jumping out of water holes to terrify passers-by. Also known as the yaa-loo and the wowee-wowee, names possibly derived from the reactions of a person encountering one at a quiet water hole. It must be remembered that Australians tend to invent things (such things as the quite impossible duck-billed platypus) just to amuse themselves at the expense of gullible tourists.

Burt, Sir Cyril (1883-1971) A British psychologist who was interested in heredity and, eventually, in **parapsychology.** He was at one time an assistant to parapsychologist **Samuel G. Soal.**

It was discovered, after Burt's death, that the work on heredity for which he had been knighted was spurious, many of his sources and references having been invented to satisfy the needs of his conclusions, and it was found that he had also appropriated the work of other researchers as his own.

Burt was very supportive of parapsychological claims, and it is interesting to note that the man he first worked for, Soal, was also revealed as a **cheat** after his death.

Bandaged as shown here, the Kashmiri Kuda Bux was able to drive a car, shoot a rifle, and duplicate writing, all as a result of his clever conjuring act.

Bux, Kuda (1905-1981) A Kashmiri **mentalist** with dark, deep-set eyes and heavy eyebrows, Kuda Bux was known as "The Man with the X-Ray Eyes." He earned this title by means of his **blindfold** act. While such an act is and was commonly done by many others, Bux had a version which involved large wads of cotton placed over bread dough that filled his eye sockets and the whole thing was then bound in place with multiple layers of bandages until his head appeared to be a huge ball of cloth. He would then drive a car, duplicate handwriting or drawings, and even fire a rifle at targets indicated by a volunteer. Once, he bicycled on New York's Broadway while blindfolded, a dangerous feat even when fully sighted.

Kuda Bux first attracted international attention in 1935 by performing one of the most famous **"fakir"** stunts, walking on burning embers. He did a carefully observed **fire walk** in England and subsequently duplicated the performance in the United States outside Radio City Music Hall. It was a stunt that he was familiar with from his early days in India and Pakistan, since it was frequently executed as part of religious ceremonies in that continent.

Ironically enough, in the last years of his life Kuda Bux suffered a gradual loss of his eyesight due to glaucoma. Though his performance methods were and are well understood in the trade, he has been made into one of the Unexplained Mysteries so needed by the paranormalists to bolster their beliefs.

C

cabala — *see* kabala.

Cagliostro, Conte Alessandro (1743?-1795) Cagliostro, referred to by historian Thomas Carlyle as the "Prince of **Quacks,**" was one of the most infamous characters of the French Revolution. Said to have been born in 1743 at Palermo, Sicily, as Joseph (Giuseppe) Balsamo (a claim that has been seriously questioned, since there is only one source for it, and that a dubious one), he liked to claim that he was a **Gypsy,** which he might well have been. Since so much of his career was described by himself, it is well to treat it all with some caution. However, some aspects have been well established.

Cagliostro professed to be a count, a **magician** of the **Hermetic** school and an **alchemist.** He claimed to be accompanied by an invisible "master" named Althotas, only one of the many imaginary items invented by the count.

He began his fabulous career in Palermo in a minor way by forging a few theater tickets and a falsified will, then he robbed his uncle and was accused of a murder. At this point he decided upon a much safer way of earning money by pretending that he was able to locate gold and buried treasure for paying clients. The man who was to become Cagliostro would show gullible customers sites where he said he sensed concealed assets.

Marrying very well in Naples, Cagliostro next went into the eternal-youth business in 1780 at Strasbourg. He and his wife, Lorenza Feliciani, traveled Europe selling age-regression potions to wealthy clients, illustrating their point by claiming that Lorenza, then twenty, was actually sixty years old. They offered for sale his "spagiric food" (from the Latin *spagiricus,* meaning "chemical") as an "elixir of immortal youth." About this time Cagliostro assumed the title of Grand Copt and said that he had lived for centuries. He claimed that he had witnessed the crucifixion of Christ, but that he appeared much younger than he was as a result of regularly using his magical elixir.

Paris went wild over him, with Cardinal de Rohan, not noted for his discernment, becoming a prominent fan and supporter of the Sicilian faker. Cagliostro related fanciful stories about his conversations with **angels**, lurid accounts of his childhood discoveries of his powers, and descriptions of gigantic cities in remote parts of the earth. There were available, of course, the usual number of people who always seem ready to listen to such charlatans and to believe them. For these he made his usual promise to locate gold and jewels, taking a fee, then moving on to other locations before having to make good on his promises.

The fake count lived in high luxury, with estates all through Europe filled with treasures of every sort. He created a very fashionable secret society called the Egyptian Lodge and was consulted by statesmen and philosophers, many of whom declared him to be genuine and possessed of real magical powers. Very much in the manner adopted a century later by **H.P. Blavatsky**, founder of **Theosophy**, Cagliostro demonstrated physical marvels such as writing that appeared on slips of paper which seemed to materialize from thin air and were said to have been penned by spirits or beings from other planets.

In Paris, in 1785, Cagliostro became involved in the famous Affair of the Diamond Necklace, a scandalous event that is thought by some historians to have been an important element in precipitating the French Revolution. Cagliostro

Cagliostro, the shady figure who haunted pre-revolutionary France.

was brought to trial along with his dupe, Cardinal de Rohan. Though he defended himself cleverly and effectively against those charges, he was imprisoned in the Bastille for other reasons. Eventually released after nine months, he was ordered to leave France.

He went to England, where it seems he was no longer as welcome as before, and he was locked up in Fleet Street Prison. Fleeing through Europe and once more back in Rome, he was denounced by his wife to the **Holy Inquisition**, charged with heresy, and condemned to death, but old friends intervened. The sentence of the Inquisition was commuted by the pope and Cagliostro was imprisoned at the San Leo Prison in Urbino until his death in 1795.

Alexander Dumas' *Memoirs of a Physician* and Goethe's *Grand Cophta* [sic] are based on events in Cagliostro's incredible life.

Cagliostro obviously employed various optical and chemical methods, along with some basic sleight of hand, to produce small tricks as convincing evidence of his powers. His name was even evoked by the famous French **conjuror** Robert-Houdin to add luster to one of that master's more spectacular feats, and modern conjurors often name certain of their tricks after the Sicilian charlatan who so effectively fleeced his world for so many years.

When Cagliostro died, so essentially died a belief in genuine **sorcery,** though it peeps from out of its grave occasionally even today. The era of the admitted trickster dawned, in which audiences were no longer asked to believe that those who performed mysterious demonstrations did so with divine or demonic assistance. The real, honest conjuror stepped to the front of the stage and took a bow for skill, originality, and dedication.

cambion   The offspring of a **succubus** and an **incubus.** Obviously, a bad seed.

Cambridge investigation   In 1857, the editor of the Boston *Courier* newspaper offered a prize of $500 for the production of **spiritualistic** phenomena in the presence of three Harvard professors, Benjamin Pierce, Louis S. Agassiz, and E.N. Horsford. On June 25, 26, and 27, **séances** took place with Leah and Katherine Fox (of the famous **Fox sisters**), a "writing medium" named Mansfield, "rapping medium" Mrs. Kendrick, a George Redman, and the **Davenport brothers.** Despite this impressive array of top talent, the tests at what became known as the Cambridge investigation were total failures for the spook artists and victories for the skeptics. The spiritualist movement ascribed it all to "ignorance of the laws of mental and magnetic science" on the part of the Harvard professors.

Cardan, Giordano (circa 1501-1576) An Italian mystic, **astrologer,** physician, and talented philosopher who

believed that particularly virtuous persons could see the future and could be aware of any event in any time or place. He also believed that he was supremely virtuous.

According to legend, Cardan almost failed in his most celebrated prediction, that of his own death. He locked himself up in his home at age seventy-five, depriving himself of food in order to die at that predicted age. This demonstrates a rare dedication to one's art.

Carrière, Eva (1886-?) Born Marthe Béraud, known in the research literature as "Eva C.," and extensively examined by several prominent scientists, Carrière was famous for **materializing spirit** faces (starting in 1911) after having been searched before the **séance.** The faces that show up on the photographs—taken under conditions that she carefully controlled—are distorted and marred, hardly convincing to anyone even moderately skeptical.

It appears that her "materializations" were crude drawings on crumpled paper, items not too difficult to conceal from the kind of examination that was usually employed by researchers. In 1914, it was found that Carrière's faces closely resembled pictures found in the French fashion magazine *Le Miroir.* Certain features had been accented or altered, but the resemblance was unmistakable. The scientist/baron **Alber Von Schrenck-Notzing** came up with the marvelous rationalization that the spirit faces, rather than being the results of trickery, were supernaturally generated by Carrière's memories of having once read the magazine. This, he said, made them "ideoplasts" rather than ectoplasm. (Similar reasoning was recently invoked by Dr. Jule Eisenbud to explain the performances of Ted Serios. *See* thoughtography.)

In Algiers, Eva many times produced a full-figure materialization of a bearded spirit named Bien Boa, said to be an Indian who had been dead for three hundred years. A fired coachman of the medium, named Areski, was exposed as the actor performing the part of Bien Boa, and Eva's career came close to ending prematurely. However, since the believers were, as usual, willing to overlook such a small peccadillo, she went back into business, this time in Paris.

The Society for Psychical Research investigated Eva C.'s work, obtained a sample of the ectoplasm she produced, and tested it. It turned out to be chewed-up paper.

cat Long associated with supernatural powers, the cat was first domesticated in ancient Egypt, where it was deified as the "Speaker of Great Words." In that culture, killing a cat was punishable by death, and an entire city, Bubastis, was built in Lower Egypt to honor cat worship. It is said that some seven hundred thousand pilgrims journeyed to Bubastis annually in May to enjoy a festival in honor of the ani-

mal and to have the privilege of feeding the feline population there. Cats were regularly mummified for burial. The cat goddess Ubasti (in Greek, "Aelurus") is seen in Egyptian religious art as a cat-headed woman.

The cat was also sacred in ancient India, and Freya was the cat goddess in Scandinavia.

Cayce, Edgar (1877-1945) A photographer who as a child began to hear voices and see visions. When he was twenty-four he began offering spiritual cures. While he said he was in a trance, Cayce diagnosed illnesses of persons he had never met, performing this task after merely being given the name and location of a patient who had written to him, in a manner similar to that practiced today by the qi gong practitioners in China. He would declare on Atlantis, reincarnation, and other similar subjects while he gave his diagnoses, using what he believed to be clairvoyant powers.

Cayce said he had been through a number of incarnations, which included a warrior of Troy, a disciple of Jesus Christ, an Egyptian priest, a Persian monarch, and a heavenly angel-like being that had been on Earth prior to Adam and Eve.

Though he had the reputation of never directly charging for his mail-order diagnoses, Cayce received large amounts of money in the form of donations. He claimed divine connections by which he was able to "have the body" of the ill person during a "trance state," a condition that was admittedly indistinguishable from sleep on occasion, sometimes even accompanied by snoring. The more than thirty thousand **readings** he did that are on file at the **Association for Research and Enlightenment** in Virginia Beach, Virginia, call for simple herbs, massage, fasting, and rather strange physical procedures that have doubtful value as remedies.

In common with most of the divinely inspired mystics, Cayce also dabbled in **prophecy**. In 1934 he declared that Poseidia (which he said was a portion of **Atlantis**) would be the first part of that fabled continent to rise again from the Atlantic. "Expect it in 1968 or 1969," he told his fans. Poseidia, his imaginary creation, did not rise, nor have any of his other prophecies been fulfilled.

But there is always hope. In his 1934 predictions, he declared in an "update on earth changes":

The earth will be broken up in the western portion of America. The greater portion of Japan must go into the sea. The upper portion of Europe will be changed as in the twinkling of an eye. Land will appear off the east coast of America. There will be the upheavals in the Arctic and in the Antarctic that will make for the eruption of volcanoes in the Torrid areas, and there will be the shifting then of the poles—so that where there have been those of a frigid or semi-tropical [sic] will become the more tropical, and moss and fern will grow. And these will begin in those periods in '58 to '98.

We have, as of this writing, the last three years of this forty-year time window in which to see these events occur.

Cazotte, Jacques (1719-1792)

In 1788, just a year before the Reign of Terror took hold in France, a mystic named Cazotte was said to have made a prediction that he and his dinner companions would all die on

Jacques Cazotte at the soiree where he announced the fates of the aristocrats under the Reign of Terror.

the guillotine or perish by suicide, a grim prophecy that came true. Since Dr. Joseph Ignace Guillotin (1738-1814), said to be one of those dinner guests, had not yet invented the device that was to bring him historical recognition, and the "prediction" has been shown to be part of a fiction (*Prophétie de Cazotte*) written and published in 1806 by author Jean de Laharpe, this fabrication is not now taken seriously by even the most zealous believers.

cereology — *see* **crop circles.**

chakra   In **Tantric** anatomy, one of several "points of power" located in the human body, to and from which **psychic** forces flow. The seven most accepted chakras are the base of the spine, a spot just below the navel,

The chakras of the human body.

the solar plexus, the heart, the throat, the brow, and the top of the head. There are three others, all located in the lower pelvis; these are not used except in **black magic,** as might be expected.

See also **Kundalini yoga.**

channeling   Beginning in about 1980, jaded celebrities began gravitating to a new notion that was actually **spiritualism** rewarmed. Instead of sitting in a darkened **séance room** holding hands and singing hymns, however, channeling consists of buying a $600 seat in a fully lit theater and listening to **gurus** expounding

the wit and wisdom of great personalities who expired as much as thirty-five thousand years ago. One of the most prominent public figures to embrace this idea was the superbly talented actress Shirley MacLaine. She chose, for a while, to support the claims of J.Z. Knight, who spoke as Ramtha, a warrior from thousands of years ago.

There are a number of other channelers in the business, such as Jach Pursel (who channels Lazarus), along with Jane Roberts and Jean Loomis (who respectively did and do Seth), Pat Rodegast (with Emmanuel), Elwood Babbitt (he does Vishnu— along with Mark Twain, Albert Einstein, William Wordsworth, Jesus Christ, and others!), and dozens of other minor actors. They are or were all essentially amateur thespians speaking in strange, strained voices with very bad impressions of foreign accents and making even stranger faces and gestures, delivering mindless pap to the gullible who can afford them.

There even is published by Barbara Bell, out of San Anselmo, California, a *Barbie Channeling Newsletter* dealing with a channeler who claims to contact the "archetypical feminine plastic essence who embodies the stereotypical wisdom of the 60s and 70s." In other words, Ms. Bell is bringing erudition from a polyethylene doll by tapping into the emotional reservoir of countless little girls who have given their devotion to Barbie. This claim seems to fit in well with the other claims made by those who contact folks from Atlantis.

Conjuror Jamy Ian Swiss has an excellent comment on channeling. He refers to it as "just bad ventriloquism. [The channelers] talk funny but their lips move."

charms The verbal version of a charm is a short verse or expression offered to confer protection or a wish. "Gesundheit!" ("Good health!") is a simple form, often said in response to a sneeze, a moment when a **demon** is said to be able to enter one's body through the nose. Also, "Good luck!" or "Bless you!" are common informal charms. In ancient Greece, the words *aski, kataski,* and *tetrax* were charm words used to ward off enchantments. A more involved, formalized charm might be termed a **prayer**.

As a material thing, a charm can be any sort of an object; a substance such as herbs or medicines contained in a bottle, bag, or vial; beads; medallions; or an **amulet** (an amulet being more specifi-cally designed to ward

Typical talismans.

off **spiritual** evil). A crucifix or a bit of hair in a locket, an **ankh,** or any number of Buddhist symbols represent commonly used charms. In the Buddhist religion, the use of an amulet is pretty well universal.

An amulet (the word derives from the Arabic for "to carry") is usually an inscribed charm of metal, stone, clay, wood, or bone, worn about the neck or otherwise carried on the person. A "hag-stone" (called a "mare-stone" in Scotland) is a bored stone worn to avert nightmares. The amulet can also be in the form of a gem, colored threads, a ring, a key, or a knot.

"Magic squares," mathematical matrices that exhibit peculiar qualities when summed, are often inscribed on amulets. An example is:

4	9	2
3	5	7
8	1	6

In this basic square, any line of three figures—vertical, horizontal, or diagonal—adds to fifteen. Such an attribute is thought to confer magical security on the bearer.

The Hebrew mezuza is another example, inscribed with the name of Jehovah, though this charm is usually affixed to a doorpost as a bar to various demons. Amulets can be specially designed as protection from the **evil eye,** imprisonment, loss of property, or other misfortunes. The figure of a scorpion covered with appropriate symbols is said to protect against nightmares, **incubi,** and **succubi.** The Triskelion, a symbol consisting of three legs bent at the knee and joined at the thigh in a circle, is said to protect against the **evil eye.** The Isle of Man incorporates the Triskelion in its heraldry.

Some amulets are designed to protect only on certain days, their potency being determined by **astrological** means. Some are merely scraps of paper with magic symbols written on them; they are crumpled up and swallowed. Amulets obtained or made at a crossroads or a burial ground are supposed to be particularly effective.

Roman sorcerers prepared amulets specifically designed to prevent or cure diseases of the eye, headaches, toothache, tumors, fevers, epilepsy, or poisonous bites. In Hindu mythology there is a powerful stone which is made into an amulet called Salagrama. Its powers are almost unlimited.

In the Middle Ages, Carmelite monks were permitted to sell "conception-billets," which are bits of consecrated paper to be placed at thresholds, attached to domestic articles, or simply swallowed to offer protection against theft or disease. Placed into a child's cradle, such a billet is believed to guard against the child being stolen by a **witch;** we don't know of any children so protected who have been reported as stolen by a witch.

Feathers from the wings of the **angel** Gabriel were sold as charms by medieval monks to fend off the plague. No record exists of a customer asking a monk how he obtained the feathers.

In his *Doctor **Faustus,*** Christopher Marlowe says of a potent charm:

> Within this circle is Jehovah's name
> Forward and backward anagram-
>   matized. . . .
> Then fear not, Faustus, to be res-
>   olute
> And try the utmost magic can per-
>   form.

And we all know what happened to Dr. Faust, don't we? Or do we?

See also **abracadabra, angel,** *and* **talismans.**

cheating (Derived from *escheator,* the term for an official who collects taxes) A process—physical, sensory, or psychological—by which psychics are able to produce for inexperienced observers the effects of genuine **psi.** When the performers are caught cheating, the officially recognized scientific researchers—known as **parapsy-chologists**—conclude that they were forced into doing so because their powers failed them or they did it unknowingly in **trance**; when the performers are *not* caught at it, *that* portion of the research is said to be genuine.

An interesting euphemism adopted by researchers is the use of the term "mixed mediumship" to refer to **mediums** who are caught at fakery, since the remainder is assumed to be the real stuff.

In his satire *Hudibras,* author Samuel Butler wrote:

Doubtless the pleasure is as great
Of being cheated as to cheat;
As lookers-on feel most delight
That least perceive a juggler's
    sleight,
And still the less they understand
The more they admire his sleight of
    hand.

Cheiro — *see* **Warner, William.**

chela — *see* **adept.**

chimera (also chimaera.) A (hopefully) mythical beast that the Greek hero Bellerophon, astride the winged horse Pegasus, is said to have slain. It was a lion up front, a serpent (or dragon) at the rear, and a goat in the middle. It had the three heads belonging to these creatures.

The term is used today to describe an unrealistic goal such as squaring the circle, **levitating** by **Transcendental Meditation,** bending a spoon by looking at it, or **parapsychology.**

chiromancy — *see* **palmistry.**

chiropractic The American Medical Association has referred to chiropractic as "an irrational, unscientific approach to disease causation." Originated in 1895 by one Daniel David Palmer, it was made into a thriving trade by his son, B.J. Palmer. The major claim of the art is that "subluxations" (misalignments of the spinal column) cause illnesses.

The various schools of chiropractic differ in what they claim can be cured by manipulating the spine, some having almost no limit (asthma, bacterial and viral infections, migraine, cancer, AIDS), while others are satisfied to relieve muscle spasms—for which such massage is probably beneficial. Some obviously renegade chiropractors sell their patients on "color therapy" in which **applied kinesiology** is used to determine the victim's sensitivity to specific colors, and they also use "polarity reversal" in which magnets are used to change the "bioenergy" field of the body. Both systems are perfect examples of expensive **quackery,** having no basis whatsoever in fact.

Chiropractors have been known to bruise and sometimes more gravely injure their customers, but often these people go right back to receive more at the hands of the operator, seeming not to learn from experience. Chiropractors are fond of pointing out that regular MDs are far from perfect, a fact that in no way validates what they themselves are doing and that appears to be only a method of misdirecting the attention of the detractor.

While there doubtless is some value to chiropractic in respect to massage relief of strains and muscle spasms, statements made by chiropractors include such howlers as specifying that a subluxation of the sixth dorsal vertebra brings about diphtheria. Such a notion is another classic example of quackery.

But having your back rubbed *does* feel good, and the pops produced by being flexed and stretched *do* sound impressive.

Christian Science/Scientists This is a religion founded by **Mary Baker Eddy** (1821-1910) in Boston in 1879, based on a theory she said she developed after she believed she was miraculously healed in 1866. She said that she had fallen on the ice and had been given three days to live, but that she healed herself solely through reading the **Bible**. However, when he was questioned about this, her doctor denied her story and under oath he repudiated the claim. This had no effect at all upon the believers.

Phineas Parkhurst Quimby (1802-1866), a "magnetic healer" whom Mrs. Eddy had studied with, was an originator of the basic idea that disease is all in the mind, a notion that Mrs. Eddy adopted as her own.

The Christian Science church does not record the date of Mrs. Eddy's death.

See also **faith healing, malicious animal magnetism.**

Christopher, Milbourne (1914-1984) Christopher was a magician and a well-known and respected writer on the subjects of **conjuring** and the **paranormal**. He also served as president of the Society of American Magicians.

Three of his books, *Milbourne Christopher's Illustrated History of Magic, Panorama of Magic,* and *Search for the Soul,* are highly recommended reading.

Christopher was heavily involved in investigations of **Lady Wonder**, the horse accepted by **Dr. Joseph Banks Rhine** as genuinely **telepathic**, and he also looked into the claims of **Uri Geller**. He was associated with the **Committee for Scientific Investigation of Claims of the Paranormal**.

Church of Christ, Scientist — *see* **Christian Science**.

clairaudience (From the French for "clear hearing") The claimed psychic power by which certain persons say they can "hear" information from **occult** sources such as **spirits**.

The voices heard by **Joan of Arc** are examples of either clairaudience or hallucination. The latter is a preferred and **parsimonious** choice.

See **clairvoyance** *and* **Doris Stokes**.

clairvoyance (From the French for "clear seeing") The claimed psychic power by which certain persons say they can "see" information about living beings or even about an insentient object or location without using the ordinary sensory means. Related to **clairaudience**. A clairvoyant—a person possessing this ability—often uses a **scrying** device to perform the act. Crystal gazing and even **tea leaf reading** can be included in this category, and each works equally well.

Clever Hans phenomenon

In 1891, a German named William Von Osten displayed to the public his horse, Clever Hans (Kluge Hans), who was apparently able to perform mathematical calculations. The horse was examined in 1904 by a committee headed by a prominent psychologist, Professor C. Stumpf. The professor reported that they could find no evidence of direct signaling, as if that were enough to endorse the wonder. People flocked to see him perform. Then Dr. Albert Moll examined the evidence and declared Hans to be a perfectly ordinary animal who was being unconsciously cued by his owner. Stumpf thereupon retracted his endorsement.

An experimenter named Oskar Pfungst, a student of Stumpf, did the really definitive tests of Hans under Stumpf's direction, and the results of those observations gave rise to the discovery of the existence of the process of involuntary/unconscious cuing now known as the Clever Hans phenomenon.

Hans was not the only horse (or other animal) to react to secret and/or unconscious cuing. There have been many such. In 1591, in England, a horse named Morocco became famous and made his owner rich. The horse called the totals on a pair of over-sized dice, added and subtracted, and pointed out letters and persons in the audience. The ani-

Contemporary illustration of Morocco, the talented mathematical, dancing horse of Elizabethan times.

mal even showed up in Shakespeare's play *Love's Labour's Lost,* Act 1, Scene 2, as "the dancing horse."

In 1927, **Dr. Joseph Banks Rhine,** considered the father of **parapsychology,** witnessed **Lady Wonder,** another horse said to have psychic powers, and though he was not convinced that the horse could calculate, he did believe it was **telepathic.** Lady Wonder's owner used toy alphabet blocks which the horse knocked over to spell out words being thought of by the spectators, but the words were always known to the owner who handled the horse. Rhine believed he had eliminated all possibilities of trickery and error, and reported:

There is left then, only the telepathic explanation, the transference of mental influence by an unknown process. Nothing was discovered that failed to accord with it, and no other hypothesis proposed seems tenable in view of the results.

Despite an investigation by **Milbourne Christopher** which indicated that the horse's owner was cuing Lady Wonder with movements of her whip, and a second, better designed set of tests of his own that produced no positive results, Rhine decided to stick with his original conclusion, offering the explanation that while the horse had once possessed ESP powers, it later lost them and trickery was resorted to.

The excellent book of Ricky Jay, *Learned Pigs and Fireproof Women,* discusses other animals who were considered miraculous.

See **cheating**.

closed medium (also *shut-eye medium*)

A term in opposition to "**open medium**." A "closed" medium does not confide in other performers or admit to them any trickery. In some cases, such a medium actually believes in his or her powers, and does not purposely perform trickery. He or she chooses to conduct business in isolation, not making use of advice or information that might be obtained from other mediums.

cold reading

Among practitioners of the **occult** arts, there is a technique known as "cold reading." When the performer is faced with an audience that is entirely strange to him, he uses this tried-and-true method of guessing names, relationships, events, and situations that might relate to audience members.

The technique is differentiated from "hot reading," which is used when the reader has obtained specific, hard information about a **sitter** and merely has to reveal it in a convincing manner. U.K. author/historian Ian Wilson looked into the methods of one **Doris Stokes,** a prominent U.K. **clairaudient,** and discovered that the people for whom she had produced "evidential" messages were people who had contacted her in advance of the show, had given her information, and had then been invited to attend her meeting. The information she'd received from them was then given back to them and embellished upon. Mrs. Stokes's work serves well as an excellent example of hot reading.

Performing cold reading by throwing out common names and hoping that someone will "link" with one of them, following up by guessing or simply asking the relationship of a name that has been selected out and "accepted" by a sitter, the medium is well on the way to convincing an unwary listener that he or she has contacted the dead.

Here's the way it's done. Suppose that a sitter has accepted the name "Mary." The medium can now say, "I want to put Mary close to you." What does this really mean? It's really a question as to whether or not Mary *is* "close to" the sitter. In the worst-case scenario, where Mary is dead, is buried in another country, was never very fond of the sitter, and was not related to him, we might uncharitably fail to recognize how close that guess was. However, a clever medium can easily rescue this seemingly bad guess by saying, "Ah, but though Mary failed to tell you of her great affection for you while she was here, she has come through tonight to remedy all that." Though it sounds hard to believe, sitters actually accept such excuses. They are more than willing to accept. And note that the reader did not *say* that Mary *was* close to the sitter; what he said was only a comment, though certainly one that begged a response.

The cold reading routine includes a number of excellent methods for extracting information from the sitter without it appearing as if the medium has actually asked for it. Comments like "Why is this person laughing?" or "She's shaking her head as if to say no" will often elicit a response. As with the "Mary" comment earlier, some questions don't appear to be questions at all: "I get this person in spirit" or "Somehow, I feel Jim was related to you or lived near you" are examples. Even more useful are those modifiers that generalize or fuzz up the statement so that it has a greater chance of being successful or of evoking an answer. Phrases like "I think that . . ." or "I feel as if . . ." or "I want to say . . ." and many other **try-ons** are used for this purpose.

Other useful techniques: The reader can say "Yes, of course," and then repeat to the sitter a fact that has just been given him, as if he knew it all along. Or he can say "Of course! I got that very strongly!" when he is given a fact that he didn't get at all. When he hears something from the sitter that

appears to "link" up, he might declare "Now we're putting it all together," even though the sitter is the one who is making it work.

The main facets of the system are:

1. Readers use such phrases as "I think . . ." (or "I don't think . . ."). This is a way of "trying on" a guess for acceptance.

2. Readers simply ask for direct, factual information from the sitter which they say is a way to "help along" the process. The sitter is usually very willing to help.

3. Readers often say that they cannot differentiate between past, present, and future events and relationships, so that there are many more possibilities for "hits."

4. Wide ranging of the sitter's imagination is not only expected by the mediums, but is encouraged. Sitters are told to be creative and try to make the reading fit.

5. There is a willing, eager collusion between the medium and the sitter, even if largely unconscious on the part of the sitter.

Cold reading isn't necessarily learned in a series of lessons. Though classes in "spiritual development" are sometimes offered by mediums and are understood, both by teacher and students, to have been designed to enhance their awareness of the **survival-after-death** philosophy, the lessons seem also to instruct the learners in how to extract certainties out of ambiguity. For example, trying to guess a word sealed in an envelope, students are encouraged to discover relationships between obscure ramblings and the word itself. A notion about walking down a road, for example, might be said to correctly relate to the concealed word "success" because "everyone seeks a path to success, and a path is a sort of road." The words used are always general in nature (*success, peace, happiness, sadness, longing, searching*) rather than more definitive words like *cat, hammer, Germany,* or *coffee.*

Most proficiency at cold reading is obtained by observing old masters of the trade and by trial and error. Methods of probing and backing up, laughing away failures and turning them into forgivable boo-boos, getting around long pauses in which the sitter fails to volunteer needed information, and blaming errors on the "poor spiritual wavelengths" all become clear with a little study.

By means of cold reading, a proficient operator can readily convince a sitter that contact with a departed person has been firmly established. That's what it's really all about. The victims of the process are constantly encouraged to think of something that can "link" the very trite but tried-and-true phrases to any deceased (or living) person or past (or present) situation they can come up with or imagine. The vague language and the inevitable modifiers (*possibly, maybe, perhaps*) often offer many easy connections that can be arrived at.

Collins, Doris (1918-) A U.K. clairvoyant/clairaudient also famed for her claimed healing powers. In a manner largely indistinguishable from that of her now-deceased colleague **Doris Stokes,** Ms. Collins uses techniques of **cold reading** to entertain her audiences, though in a markedly more commanding manner than Ms. Stokes ever managed. Most probably, Doris Collins is the U.K.'s best-known **psychic** performer.

Columbus poltergeist   In early 1984, newspapers around the world reported that genuine **poltergeist** phenomena were being experienced in the presence of a fourteen-year-old girl in Columbus, Ohio, named Tina Resch. The Columbus *Dispatch* newspaper followed the titillating story for a week, during which flying telephones, loud percussive noises, swinging and falling lamps, and other events were troubling Tina's family.

Upon investigation, it was discovered that the girl was an adopted child who wanted to discover her true parents, and she used the media attention to plead for that information. A video camera from a visiting TV crew that was inadvertently left running recorded Tina **cheating** by surreptitiously pulling over a lamp while unobserved. The other occurrences were shown to be inventions of the press or highly exaggerated descriptions of quite explainable events. Descriptions given by **parapsychologist** William Roll, who specializes in poltergeist investigations and had examined the situation in person, turned out to be of quite impossible sequences.

The case of the Columbus Poltergeist faded away after a few

months and is not now seriously discussed. In 1994 Tina Resch was sentenced to life imprisonment for the murder of her three-year-old daughter.

Committee for Scientific Investigation of Claims of the Paranormal (CSI-COP)

A Buffalo-based organization consisting of professionals in various sciences, journalists, technicians, philosophers, and other specialists such as **conjurors,** founded in 1976. Its purpose is to examine claims made in support of paranormal powers, to prepare reports on these subjects, to convene conferences and meetings, to publish the *Skeptical Inquirer* as a journal, and to encourage research on the subjects.

CSICOP is essentially a scientific group, has no religious ties, and has a strong advocacy of truth and investigation of **paranormal, occult** and supernatural reports. It began with funding from the American Humanist Association, then became totally autonomous. Numerous similar groups in twenty-four states and in twenty-five foreign countries (Argentina, Australia, Belgium, Canada, Slovakia, Estonia, Finland, France, Germany, Hungary, India, Ireland, Italy, Japan, Malta, Mexico, Netherlands, New Zealand, Norway, Russia, South Africa, Spain, Sweden, Ukraine, and United Kingdom) have sprung up, but are distinctly independent of CSICOP.

As might be expected, committed believers in the occult have chosen to distort the aims and purpose of CSICOP. For example, U.K. author Colin Wilson has described the committee as "a society to combat belief in all forms of occultism," thereby missing—perhaps purposely—the intent and value of the group.

CSICOP and the *Skeptical Inquirer* can be contacted at P.O. Box 703, Buffalo, NY 14226-0703.

Confidence Man (Also, con man)

A swindler, cheat, charlatan. A dishonest person who by charm, earnestness, guile and seeming innocence, gains the confidence of his victims and cheats them out of money or goods., or obtains an endorsement or favorable position as a result of lies and general trickery. Usually, the victim is asked to become involved in a little cheating too, during the course of the action and is thus made to look like a fool and/or a deceiver when the game is discovered. The operator of a three-shell game would also come under this label, since the eventual victim here is made to feel that he knows more about the rules of the game than the operator, and thus cannot be deceived himself.

compass trick

This simple trick, in which a magnetic compass is caused to deflect from its normal north-south orientation, can be traced back in the literature to the seventeenth century, but is obviously much older. It probably was one of the tricks discovered at just about the time the device was first constructed, much prior to Marco Polo's return from Cathay in about 1300.

The trick is accomplished by introducing almost any magnet or sufficiently massive magnetic metal (the metal need not be itself magnetized) into the proximity of the instrument. **Conjurors** have done this by concealing a magnet on the knee, in a shoe, or in the clothing and bringing it close to the compass. The hands are frequently waved about during such a demonstration, and since the movement of the needle does not correspond directly to such movements, the spectator is led to believe that a magnet is not being palmed. This is known in the trade as misdirection.

Compendium Maleficarum (*Witches Manual*)   A seventeenth-century book by Francesco Maria Guazzo that goes into great and tiresome detail on pacts made with **Satan**. Wonderful reading for masochists.

Conan Doyle, Sir Arthur (1859-1930) (Note: the family name is Conan Doyle, not simply Doyle.) Knighted for his defense of Britain's activities in South Africa, Conan Doyle was the creator of the famous fictional detective character, Sherlock Holmes.

Following the death of his son Kingsley in wartime, Sir Arthur became a firm believer in, and supporter of, **spirit mediums**. He was also a bit of a snob, and it was one reason for his credulity. Post-Victorian society, of which he was a leading product, had cataloged people according to class. Therefore, when he was confronted with the **Cottingley fairies** photos taken by two young girls, he reasoned that two adolescent females "from the artisan class" could not possibly deceive an aristocrat such as himself,

and he convinced himself that the photos were genuine. That, for him, settled the matter. And Sir Arthur Conan Doyle was not accustomed to being told that he was wrong.

His easy acceptance of such matters as **fairies** brings into question his declared faith in spirit mediums, especially because his endorsement was very instrumental in bringing legitimacy to their claims, and to **spiritualism** as a religion.

The uneasy friendship between Sir Arthur and magician **Harry Houdini,** and their serious mutual respect, was strained when the writer ascribed to Houdini genuine **psychic** powers. It seemed inconceivable to him that the magician could do what he did without resort to genuine miracles. Houdini knew quite well that what he did was simple **conjuring,** that any person could thereby be fooled, and was astonished that Sir Arthur could not recognize or admit that fact.

Sir Arthur traveled abroad preaching the claims of spiritualism, showing incredibly naive lantern slides of supposed miracles, including those of the Cottingley fairies. He faithfully continued to support spiritualism and all of its followers until his death in 1930, four years following that of Houdini.

conjureting   The claimed ability to call up **demons** and storms. Not a socially admired talent.

conjuring/conjuror   The art of seeming to perform genuine **magic** is known as conjuring, and the artist is known as a conjuror. The art has a written history dating back to a manuscript known as the Westcar Papyrus, after its 1823 discoverer, Henry Westcar. That document is currently in the Berlin State Museum. Written 3,800 to 4,000 years ago, it relates events that are said to have occurred 500 years earlier in the reign of Pharaoh Khufu, more popularly known as Cheops, probably the builder of the **Great Pyramid** at Giza, near Cairo.

The Westcar Papyrus recounts a series of tales told at the court of Cheops to the pharaoh by his sons. One story tells of Webaoner, a court magician/scholar faced with the problem of an adulterous wife who was sending expensive gifts to a townsman who had attracted her. Webaoner, it says, sculpted a small wax crocodile which then became seven cubits (twelve feet) long, dutifully swallowed the erring wife, and was once again a harmless wax model. Next is a story about a magician named Djadjaemonkh, who found a lost **amulet** by *folding* a lake! He

> placed one side of the water of the lake upon the other, and lying upon a potsherd he found the fish-shaped charm.

The papyrus then relates that a magician known as Dedi was able to reattach the head of a goose that had been cut off. To demonstrate his skills for the pharaoh, a goose was brought and decapitated. The papyrus says:

> The goose was placed on the western side of the pillared court, and

its head on the eastern side. Dedi said his magic words. The goose arose and waddled and so did its head. The one reached the other and the goose stood up and cackled. Next he caused a waterfowl to be brought, and the like was done with it. Then His Majesty caused that there be brought to him an ox, and its head was felled to the ground. Dedi said his magic words, and the ox stood up behind him with its tether fallen to the ground.

The lake-folding and wax crocodile stories are certainly not accounts of conjuring but tales of **sorcery.** However, the bird's-head-off-and-back-on-again trick and the method for doing it are well known to conjurors, though not done *quite* as described here. Where the papyrus relates that the same feat was performed with an ox, it may be simply a bit of hyperbole—not entirely unheard of in descriptions of conjuring—and quite likely to creep into the story. It must be pointed out that this document was written by a scribe from secondhand reports nearly five hundred years after the events are supposed to have taken place.

There is a continuous history of the conjuring art from the Westcar Papyrus down to the present day. Such superstars as **Harry Houdini,** John Nevil Maskelyne, Blackstone (*père et fils*), Joaquin Ayala, David Copperfield, and Siegfried & Roy have kept audiences enthralled with their skills. But conjuring is not magic and should not be mistaken for a supernatural performance, even when the conjuror chooses to misrepresent his abilities, as occasionally happens.

The art of conjuring uses sleight of hand, special equipment, secret technology, carefully learned psychological methods, and various illusionary techniques to present to the spectator—for purposes of entertainment—the same effect that would be experienced if magic were actually possible.

In the United States, the word "conjuring" is interchangeable with "magic," and conjurors are referred to as "magicians."

control — *see* **spirit guide.**

Cook, Florence Eliza (1856?-1904) Miss Cook was dismissed from a teaching job at age sixteen, then worked with several different professional **spirit mediums** who were later exposed as frauds, as she herself was when she took up the profession.

Cook's **spirit guide** was known as Katie King (a character who was to reemerge a generation later as a guide to medium **Eusapia Palladino**), and Cook was able to produce full-size, full-form **materializations** of this character, who, strangely enough, in all photographs appears to be an exact double for Cook. Never were the medium herself and Katie both seen at one time. Also, if the materialized form was not really a spirit, the part of Katie King may have been created and played by Cook's look-alike sister, also named Katie.

Sir William Crookes (*which see*) was closely associated with Cook and wrote copiously on her mediumship. Though he and other investigators employed overly intricate and cosmetically scientific systems to control Cook, and superficial accounts of their research state that such instrumentation showed no sign of trickery, the actual records disagree with such reports. Cook actually failed to satisfy the controls, and yet her supporters glossed over major problems and ignored quite positive evidence of trickery. Her sister Katie failed entirely to pass controlled tests, even to the very loose standards of those who tested her.

Eventually, following a **séance** given on May 21, 1874, Crookes seems to have abandoned his belief in Cook, though he never publicly retracted his support of her.

See also **Mary Showers.**

corn circles — *see* **crop circles.**

Cottingley fairies In 1917, two little Yorkshire girls in Bradford, England, Elsie Wright and her cousin Frances, told everyone that they had seen **fairies** in a place called Cottingley Glen, and they said that they had even taken photographs of the entities as proof of their stories. They produced five rather amateurish "fairy" photos that were widely celebrated at the time.

Author **Sir Arthur Conan Doyle,** an otherwise often levelheaded man except when it came to the supernatural, chose to accept and endorse the story told by the girls, probably because it fit in well with his belief

The Cottingley Fairy photographs were staged using cutouts prepared from illustrations in a children's book. Yet this photograph fooled Sir Arthur Conan Doyle, creator of the great detective hero, Sherlock Holmes.

system. Conan Doyle, even before he saw the photographs—and he never did meet the girls—accepted the whole tale and set about promoting the existence of fairies, elves, and other wee creatures who he firmly believed were flitting about in the woods.

Sir Arthur even took lantern slides made from the Cottingley photos abroad to America with him, as part of his lecture tour. The rights to the photos themselves were given by Elsie's mother to the **Theosophy** movement, which embraced belief in wood **sprites** and such beings. Years later, when Elsie saw a photograph of a huge church the Theosophists had built with the proceeds of sales of the photos, she grumbled that she and Frances hadn't seen a penny for their labors, while millions of pounds had been raised from their work.

Only a few years ago, the two who had perpetrated this rather delicious hoax on Conan Doyle—and, through him, on the whole world—died. They had not ever been willing to openly admit that

their photos were fakes, but along the way they dropped tantalizing hints. Elsie, the elder, admitted in 1978 that their "little joke fell flat on its face right away" and explained that, had it not been for the hopelessly unrealistic Conan Doyle seizing upon the opportunity to discover and champion yet another supernatural discovery, their photographs would have just remained "out of sight in a drawer" where her father had thrown them.

Elsie was amazed that people accepted their hoax. She wrote, "Surely you know that there can not be more than one grown up person in every five million who would take our fairies seriously." Elsie's dad, she wrote, was dismayed by it all. He asked his wife, "How could a brilliant man like Conan Doyle believe such a thing?"

The photos were prepared simply by photographing cutouts of fairies drawn by Elsie from a popular children's book, *Princess Mary's Gift Book*. Frances and Elsie thus created a hugely successful monster that lives on even today—despite the proof of trickery—in the pages of sensational journals and in books.

The great puzzle is why the Cottingley Fairy photographs were ever accepted in the first place. They are very obviously fakes, and it can easily be proven that they are. The first, and the most famous, of the five photographs shows Frances with four tiny fairies in full flight. What is often ignored is the image of a small waterfall in the background behind Frances, which Mr. Brian Coe, curator of the Kodak Museum in Harrow, England, says was registered on the film of that era only by a lengthy time exposure. However, the fairies themselves, and their fluttering butterfly wings, are very sharp and clear. That rapid motion would have required a shutter speed that was far beyond the capabilities of the camera that was used to take the picture, particularly in view of the subdued light that was present, and sufficient film speed was similarly not available. The four other photos are subject to the same kind of detection.

The British **Society for Psychical Research** (SPR)—already well organized when these photos began being publicized—took a quarter century before they examined the evidence, and in 1945—to their credit—they decided that they were now "skeptical of the reality of fairies in general and of the Cottingley Fairies in particular." Science marches on.

The *British Journal of Photography* understandably took until 1975 to even mention these photos, then in 1982 ran a series of quite devastating articles that should have effectively ended the controversy. Despite such in-depth investigative research and the very strong negative evidence it has produced, the fact is that articles still appear which support the fairy photographs as genuine.

See **Conan Doyle, Sir Arthur** *and* **fairies.**

coven A word (said to be derived from *covent* or *convent*) meaning a group of **witches,** usually thirteen. Or there are twelve witches, the invisible thirteenth member of the coven being **Satan.** The choice of number may be a matter of budget, since Satan probably gets big fees for such personal appearances. Covens are independent from one another, but associated with one another through a Grand Master.

Crandon, Margery (Née Stinson, 1888-1941) A Boston medium who was examined by magician **Harry Houdini** and put through several rather inconclusive tests by him. At one point, during a **séance,** she produced a thumbprint in dental wax that she swore was made by her **spirit guide,** Walter. This was heralded by the press as definitive proof of her validity and of the genuine nature of **spiritualism.** Unfortunately for this breakthrough in human knowledge, the print turned out to be that of her dentist, who was very much alive. This pretty well discredited her with all but the most ardent believers, and Margery slowly went out of business. She died an alcoholic.

Sir Arthur Conan Doyle and other prominent supporters of **spiritualism** never gave up their trust or belief in her.

See also **ectoplasm.**

credophilic An adjective originated by author L. Sprague de Camp to describe a mind

> that gets positive pleasure from belief and pain from doubt. . . . The credophile collects beliefs the way a jackdaw does nest ornaments: not for utility but for glitter. And, once having embraced a belief, it takes something more than mere disproof to make him let go.

Creery sisters Alice, Emily, Kathleen, Mary, and Maud, daughters of the Reverend A.M. Creery, who performed effective mental phenomena such as **telepathy** for several panels of investigators from the **Society for Psychical Research** (SPR). The investigators declared them absolutely genuine. Then they were found to have been **cheating** — using a verbal code—by another special committee of the SPR in 1888.

It is not recorded how, or if, the Reverend Creery chastised his daughters.

Croiset, Gerard (1909-1980) Known mostly as a **police psychic,** Croiset received more media coverage than most psychics of his day. One case for which he was famous took place in Japan. He claimed all sorts of success

discovering a body in a murder case there, but confirmation of his services was not forthcoming from the Japanese police. This alerted journalist Piet Hein Hoebens, and he began investigating **Wilhelm Tenhaeff,** Croiset's mentor. The resulting scandal was a huge embarrassment for **parapsychology.**

See also **Tenhaeff.**

Crookes, Sir William (1832-1919) This very prominent scientist was one of sixteen children of a wealthy tailor. His contributions to science were numerous, involving radioactive devices (the Crookes tube was named after him) and he is credited with discovering the element thallium. He was knighted in 1897 for his scientific work.

His beloved brother Philip died at sea in 1867 at an untimely age, and Sir William did what many another intellectual has done: He embraced an unlikely but satisfying set of beliefs that removed from him the pain of the loss: he became dedicated to **spiritualism.** That also appears to have been the reason that **Sir Arthur Conan Doyle,** whose son Kingsley and brother Innes also both died at early ages, avidly adopted spiritualism and in fact devoted the rest of his life to promoting it among the public. American Episcopalian Bishop **James A. Pike,** whose son Jim was a suicide at age twenty, went through a similar process in 1966.

Sir William was a member of the **Society for Psychical Research** from its founding in 1883 and served as president of the society from 1896 to 1899. During his investigations, Crookes discovered that a very successful spiritualist **medium, Mary Rosina Showers,** was a fraud, but said nothing and reported nothing about his discovery.

He and spiritualist medium **Daniel Dunglas Home** were on a very close personal basis, and his endorsement of Home's powers has always been a strong point made by the spiritualists to support their claims about Home. However, Crookes has been shown to be a dupe of such other mediums as **Florence Cook** and others exposed or confessed as fakes, so his validation of Home is highly suspect.

Crookes was a devoted follower of Éliphas Lévi, as well as a **Theosophist.**

crop circles (In the U.K., often called "corn circles," since in that area of the world, *corn* refers to any grain crop, while what Americans know as corn is known there as "maize.")

In 1979, mysterious diagrams began to be noticed in the U.K., patterns formed by flattening out grain crops. Immediately, **UFO** fans declared that space aliens were communicating with Earth by this means, and as years went by, the shapes evolved from simple circles into Mandelbrot figures and complicated networks, as if extraterrestrial kids were competing with one another in an intergalactic drawing contest. The concept is not far from the actuality.

This is a schoolboy stunt that,

coincidentally, begins to be noticed annually immediately after school lets out in the U.K., though few have made any connection between the two matters. Farmers eventually notice the patterns, sometimes prompted by the media. A new group of paranormalists known as "cereologists" (seriously!) are convinced that these are extraterrestrial messages of some sort and of great import to humankind. That space people would choose to sketch figures in farm crops seems not at all incongruous to the believers.

When, in 1992, two retired gentlemen in England ("Doug and Dave") admitted that they had started the prank and it had been picked up by the schoolchildren in the area and eventually all over the country, the believers were quick to point out that *those* circles were not identical to the "real" circles in every respect. However, a newspaper in the U.K. asked these two hoaxers secretly to create a typical pattern, then called in the "experts," who confidently declared it to be the genuine article. So much for experts.

In Hungary, too, there was great excitement in June 1992 when a helicopter pilot passing over a farming area near the town of Székesfehérvár, about forty miles west of Budapest, reported sighting below him a "crop circle" of rather substantial dimensions. The media went crazy about it, celebrating the fact that, at last, the extraterrestrials had recognized their country by conferring on them this singular honor.

There was no lack of eyewitnesses

who claimed they'd seen little green folks in that field and UFOs hovering overhead. They fought to get in front of the TV cameras that were focused on vast crowds from all over Europe, milling about on the grounds of the Aranybulla collective farm where this 120-foot-diameter wonder was to be viewed. A number of "experts" came in and measured levels of known and unknown radiations that they said were loose in the area, and warned of the deadly nature of the phenomenon.

UFOlogist Károly Hargitai and "time-scientist" György Kisfaludy solemnly declared the circle to have been made by extraterrestrials and impossible of fabrication by humans. Kisfaludy averred that by looking at the crop circle "in six dimensions," he had been able to solve the coded message it conveyed, a message available only to a savant such as himself.

In September, on one of the popular but low-level TV talk shows on Channel 1, Budapest, both Hargitai and Kisfaludy appeared before the nation to solemnly restate and verify their pseudoscientific opinions on the matter. Then, to their dismay, the host of the show, Sándor Friderikusz, introduced two seventeen-year-old students who produced photographic and video proof that they themselves had made the crop circle, using

very simple methods. The effect of this disclosure was rather strong, and the expressions on the faces of the "experts," who were not prepared for such a confrontation, left the studio audience as well as the TV audience amused.

The two hoaxers were Róbert Dallos and Gábor Takács. They were high school students who had read about crop circles in the newspapers and decided to make their very own. As students of agriculture, they knew that wet grass can be bent without breaking it, and they had noted heavy rains just before the night of June 8, when they created the figure. That was two weeks before the helicopter pilot discovered it.

The two youngsters had waited until a local drive-in movie closed down, then went about their business of hoaxing. They also were wise enough to take photographic records of the area, before and after, in the correct scientific tradition.

Following the TV program, the inevitable alibis were produced by the die-hard believers. The one who had solved the coded message from the stars declared that he had surveyed the area around Székesfehérvár just previous to the discovery of the artifact and had found no trace of the circle at that time. That seems quite strange, since the gentleman offered no reason why he chose to look at that specific site in advance of the wonder that the UFOs were about to create there.

The collective farm, Aranybulla, chose not to be amused by all this. A lawsuit was brought against the boys demanding compensation for the widespread damage done to the crops as a result of the crowds who moved in, camping overnight in some cases. The court's decision was that the boys were responsible only for the circle area itself and that the farm's lawyers should pursue the media who had promoted the hoax as a genuine phenomenon.

The boys were defended free by their admirers in the skeptical community and were not required to pay the legal penalty for their very clever and appropriate hoax in the name of science. Early in 1993, they were awarded a prize given each year in Hungary for the best essay or project produced by a young person, dealing with the supernatural, paranormal, or occult. It was presented to them by Gyula Bencze, a physicist with the Central Research Institute for Physics in Budapest. Dr. Bencze is a leading figure in the Hungarian skeptics movement.

In 1993, four skeptics—some of whom had already created several very convincing crop circles in the U.K.—in the company of investigator Ian Rowland, used planks and ropes to make two excellent figures near Winchester, where "authentic" figures had been found in the past. There was an almost-full moon while they worked, and several times during their early-morning task, they were illuminated by the headlights of oncoming automobiles, but no one stopped to investigate. They used similar methods to those used by "Doug and Dave" and had no problem at all getting away with the prank. They discovered that simply walking through the crop with a certain amount of care does not leave any traces, thus demolishing another claim of the cereologists. One of their figures was so convincing that an entrepreneur put up a sign and charged visitors a fee to view the phenomenon.

Paul Vigay, a popular U.K. writer on the subject of crop circles, ran diagrams of these productions in his booklet *Crop Circle Surveys of 1993* and featured one of them on the cover. He also discovered marvelous ways of folding one of the two figures into a three-dimensional shape, as if to imply that the UFO people had created it just for that purpose. This would appear to be another example of discovering meaning where there is none.

The fact that these figures are so easily made and have deceived the experts reduces the matter of the crop circles to whether or not one chooses to believe in a capricious and rather juvenile action performed by a highly advanced extraterrestrial civilization, or what amounts to little more than an involved schoolboy prank carried out by quite ordinary folks.

Crowley, Aleister (1875-1947)

Described in his time as "the most evil man alive" and "the wickedest man in the world," Crowley was a British **Satanist** who was violently opposed to Christianity. He founded his own religion based on himself as a holy figure and loved every nasty thing the public said about him.

He liked to be known as "The Beast 666," from the biblical reference in *Revelation* to that **magical** number, and also liked to believe that he was a reincarnation of Edward Kelley, the rascally associate of **Dr. John Dee.**

In common with other **gurus,** Crowley liked to create his own nomenclature, referring to **magic** as "magick" and defining it as

the Science and Art of causing Change to occur in conformity with Will.

The definition, though wishful, does not differ substantially from others.

Crowley reportedly had a powerful effect on women and separated many widows, spinsters, and bored dilettantes from their cash in order to support his chosen lifestyle. He fascinated his followers with lavish costumes, animal sacrifices, other weird rituals which were often sexually oriented, and the use of powerful hallucinogenic drugs. This supreme egotist, manipulator, ruthless swindler, and genius of showmanship died a pauper at the age of seventy-two.

crucifix A specifically Christian **amulet,** in the form of a Latin cross, sometimes with a modeled figure of Jesus Christ, crucified. *See* **charms.**

cryptomnesia A psychological phenomenon ("hidden memory") in which the subject unconsciously recalls seemingly forgotten memories and incorporates them into the present as if they are new and original thoughts and impressions. Related to the *déjà vu* phenomenon.

There is an alarming derivation of this genuine phenomenon which is known as "false memory syndrome." By means of prolonged and insistent questioning, coaching, and leading of the subject, an operator can elicit almost any "memory" required, and that becomes a firm part of the subject's experience, regarded as representing an actuality. It has given rise to extensive belief in **Satanist** rituals and horrid sexual abuses performed upon children, who appear to recall these events only decades later. So strong is the belief in the inanity that laws have been written to accommodate this newest form of witch-hunt.

See also **Bridey Murphy.**

crystal ball gazing — *see* scrying.

crystal power   The enchantment with crystals is understandable. People are fascinated with the wonderful organization and symmetry observed in these attractive natural formations. Even common salt assumes quite square shapes when it is given the opportunity, and more esoteric substances produce intricate forms that are typical of their composition. Water, in the form of snowflakes, is one of the most beautiful expressions of this phenomenon.

Mystics have taken up this expression of nature as further proof of their claims, and they now ascribe to crystals various powers of healing, influences to bring about financial gain, **precognitive** ability, and other potentials. They point to recognized attributes of crystals, long recognized and used by science and technology, as support for their own notions. One of these is the piezoelectric effect, which simply means that when certain crystals such as quartz are squeezed, a small electrical signal is given out. When, conversely, an electrical signal is applied to the crystal, it expands or contracts in response. There is nothing at all mysterious about this phenomenon, and it is fully explained within the parameters of basic physics, but it has been pressed to serve the theories that amateurs publish in the literature asserting that therefore crystals give out some sort of **vibrations** that **psychics** can detect.

Simple tests of the claim have been designed and carried out. In *every case,* it has been shown that the claim is spurious.

In shops that cater to the need for supernatural guidance and benefits one can now pay fifty times the former price for what was once only an attractive addition to a mineral collection but is now touted as a magical remedy for many problems and afflictions as well as a key to infinite wisdom and power.

Crystals are pretty rocks; they are not keys to psychic powers or healing modalities.

CSICOP —   *see* **Committee for Scientific Investigation of Claims of the Paranormal.**

curse of Princess Amen-Ra   In 1968, a startling story began to be picked up by the popular press. It involved a dead Egyptian princess, an ancient curse and lots of disaster, all the ingredients needed to attract attention. Author John Macklin wrote:

> The Princess of Amen-Ra lived some 1,500 years before the birth of Christ. When she died, she was lain in an ornate wooden coffin and buried deep in a vault at Luxor, Egypt, on the banks of the Nile.

Macklin went on to describe how in the early 1900s "four rich young Englishmen" bought the mummy of the princess in Egypt, whereupon one of them promptly walked out into the desert and vanished. Another of the buyers had his arm shot off, yet another had his bank fail, and the last one went broke and "was reduced to selling matches in the street."

But, according to Macklin, the curse was only getting started. The next owner had three of his family injured in an accident and his house caught fire. He wisely gave the boxed princess to the British Museum.

Things went wrong from the very first minute that the museum took possession. The vehicle delivering the mummy backed up and pinned a pedestrian. One of the two porters carrying the sarcophagus fell down the stairs and broke a leg; the other died mysteriously two days later of unknown causes. Exhibits in the room where the princess was displayed, once they got her through the door, were thrown about at night. A spirit from the coffin tried to throw a night watchman down a delivery chute. The child of a worker who showed disrespect to the princess died of measles.

There's much more. Macklin related that one worker who had delivered the princess to the museum fell seriously ill and another was found dead at his desk. A photographer sent to record the artifact found that the face painted on the sarcophagus registered on film as a "human—and horrific— face." Apparently overcome by this repulsive result, he promptly locked himself up in his darkroom and shot himself.

Then, according to Macklin, the British Museum offered to sell this very awkward object to anyone who dared to buy it. It was now 1912. As we might expect, a brash, wealthy and enterprising American came upon the scene, heedlessly offered to buy the princess, snapped her up for a good price, and decided to ship her to New York. Macklin concluded his tale:

> The mummy case was placed in the cargo hold aboard a sparkling new White Star liner about to make its maiden voyage across the Atlantic Ocean to New York.
>
> On the night of April 14, amid scenes of unprecedented horror, the Princess Amen-Ra accompanied 1,500 passengers to their deaths at the bottom of the Atlantic. The name of the ship was the *Titanic*.

Though this story has been circulated and recirculated, rewritten and enthusiastically enhanced, it is still just a story. The mummy never existed and the entire tale is a journalistic exercise in bad writing and witless sensationalism, a story that the British Museum is often called upon to deny. The museum even publishes an official denial which is sent to those who inquire. But the story will show up again, count on it.

And it will be believed.

See also **Tut, curse of King.**

curse of the Pharaoh — *see* Tut, curse of King.

⮜ D ⮞

dactylomancy — *see* **table tipping** *and* **Ouija board**.

daemon The same as **demon** (*which see*) but with this spelling, possibly referring to a Greek secondary divinity between gods and men.

Davenport brothers The American Davenport brothers, Ira (1839-1911) and William (1841-1877), caused a major sensation in the late 1800s with a spectacular and puzzling vaudeville stage act which seemed to support belief in **spiritualist** doctrine. It consisted of their being tied hand and foot and then being locked into a large cabinet with an assortment of props. Bells would sound, musical instruments would be played, strange hands would appear through openings in the cabinet, and a bewildered member taken from the audience would have his clothes turned inside out and various other indignities would be inflicted on him. The cabinet was often opened quickly right in the midst of these events, and the two Davenports were always found to be still securely bound and seemingly "in **trance**."

The brothers had developed their act as teenagers, following the sensation caused by the **Fox sisters**. Before long the father of the two "mediums" resigned his position with the Buffalo, New York, police force and took over managing what quickly got to be a very profitable operation. They were joined by **William Fay,** another Buffalo resident who became an important agent of their operation. They developed their tied-in-a-box routine and for the next ten years toured the United States with it. Then they arrived in England, a country that had accepted the idea of spiritualism enthusiastically and still embraced it even after it had begun to wane in the country where it was born. England was fully primed for belief in the Davenports.

An important part of the Davenport act was their spokesman, a Presbyterian minister with a wonderfully sepulchral voice, Dr. J. B. Ferguson. This reverend gentleman assured the audience that the Davenports had been given divine powers and worked by **spirit** power alone, and not, as he phrased it, by "the wit-craft of the commercial." Ferguson said that the bell ringing and other phenomena happened independently of the brothers, and that it occurred "for the glory of God and the greater enlightenment of weak humanity."

Many who saw this act attributed the effects to spirit forces; it seemed impossible for the Davenports — and the many others who subsequently imitated their act — to have done the tricks by other than supernatural means. But one must remember that magicians regularly perform equally confounding feats, and they do not claim for them any diabolical powers or collusion.

Today, in the United States, Glenn Falkenstein and his wife Frances Willard perform an incredible replication of the Davenport act which might even be better than the original, and they make it clear that

A poster used by Ira Davenport and J.F. Day during a tour that took place two years after the death of William Davenport. Mr. Day learned the routines and replaced William in the act.

they are performing an entertaining conjuring trick.

Ira Davenport, in 1909, wrote to the famous American magician and escape artist **Harry Houdini** an explanation of their philosophy concerning the act that he and his brother had performed:

> We never in public affirmed our belief in spiritualism, that we regarded as no business of the public, nor did we offer our entertainments as the results of sleight of hand, nor on the other hand as spiritualism, we let our friends and foes settle that as best they could between themselves.

This self-righteous disavowal pales when the record of the Davenports is examined, since they never admitted **cheating** and as teenagers they were an important part of such events as the **Cambridge investigation** and always put forth every effort to convince researchers that they were producing genuine spiritualistic phenomena.

Davis, Andrew Jackson (1826-1910)

Known as "The Poughkeepsie Seer," Davis was the son of a shoemaker, with very little formal education. He claimed from age fourteen to be able to diagnose illnesses by **clairvoyance**. For a while, he made his living at this questionable profession, then in 1847 he published his major work among many that were to come, *The Principles of Nature, Her Divine Revelations, and a Voice to Mankind*. Some thirty-four editions of this book appeared in the next thirty years. A brief quotation will serve to illustrate the pretentious nature of this opus:

> In the beginning the Univercoelum was one boundless, undefinable, and unimaginable ocean of Liquid Fire. . . . Matter and Power were existing as a Whole, inseparable. The Matter contained the substance to produce all suns, all worlds, and systems of worlds, throughout the immensity of Space. It contained the qualities to produce all things that are existing upon each of those worlds. The Power contained Wisdom and Goodness, Justice, Mercy and Truth. It contained the original and essential Principle that is displayed throughout the immensity of Space, controlling worlds and systems of worlds, and producing Motion, Life, Sensation and Intelligence, to be impartially disseminated upon their surfaces as Ultimates.

This is typical of such literature, using undefined terms, generalities, and sweeping claims that are never further looked into. It has an appeal to the uneducated, who accept it as being equivalent to genuine philosophical and scientific works of which they have an equal lack of comprehension. And, to some academics, this kind of writing can appear to be a step beyond their own abilities, especially if it seems to state something they wish to accept.

Some of the contents of *The Principles of Nature* were plagiarized from the works of **Swedenborg,** a mystic whose books had just been published as Davis began his own work. Davis in some cases used as his own, word for word, long passages from Swedenborg, both in this book and in his subsequent writings. This has been accepted by Davis's followers as proof that he was inhabited by the spirit of Swedenborg while writing, rather than evidence that he might have been **cheating.** They reject the other, more **parsimonious** explanation.

Davis also said that the planet Saturn was inhabited by humans more advanced than those here on Earth, with other human civilizations on Mars and Jupiter, and more primitive humans on Mercury and Venus. In 1847 he hardly had to worry about space probes revealing the facts about these matters.

Davis invented the term **Summerland** to designate the undefined place to which souls went after the death of the owners. This was an attractive and welcome terminology for some of the **spiritualists,** since it relieved the believers of any need for a religious connection.

In his last years, Davis ran a small bookshop in Boston.

Dee, Dr. John (1527-1608) Prophecy and other assorted supernatural abilities were attributed to a contemporary of **Nostradamus,** the brilliant Welshman Dr. John Dee. He was many things—mathematician, navigator, cartographer, prolific writer, master spy, **astrologer,** and most trusted adviser to Queen Elizabeth I of England. Described as a tall, thin, mysterious man with a long pointed

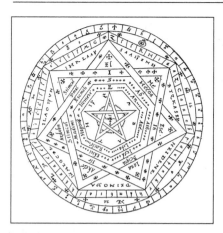

The inscription on one of Dr. Dee's wax tablets, preserved in the British Museum.

beard, Dee was one of the most powerful but subtle political influences of his day.

A genuinely accomplished scholar who was never reluctant to mix a little attractive claptrap in with his otherwise valuable teachings, he practiced astrology and searched for the legendary **philosopher's stone** that could heal all ills and transmute base metals into gold. It is believed that Dee was the model for Shakespeare's character Prospero in *The Tempest.*

Beginning in 1581, Dee dabbled in almost all the magical arts, and early in his career he labored under the shady reputation of a **sorcerer.** Before Elizabeth Tudor ascended the throne, and while she was a reluctant resident of the Tower of London, he predicted for her a very long life and a very high position in the kingdom (a very successful prophecy!), and from that moment on, he enjoyed her considerable patronage and trust.

In spite of a certain amount of

dismay she felt over Dee's open association with acknowledged rascals and rumored practitioners of **black magic,** the Virgin Queen appointed him to ever more important positions. Elizabeth had in Dee a skilled cartographer, mathematician, and navigator who served her well, but she valued above all his purported abilities to predict the future.

Some of Dee's magical paraphernalia are still preserved in London at the British Museum, and the prize object of the display is a black obsidian glass "magic mirror" seven inches in diameter fashioned in Mexico by the Aztec culture. In it, Dee claimed he could see future events by what is known as **scrying.** This is done by looking into a bowl of water, a crystal, or—as in Dee's case—a special mirror or speculum he called his Angelical Stone. He said that it had been given him by the **angels** Raphael and Gabriel. (It was later owned by British author Horace Walpole and was sold at auction to an unknown buyer in 1842.) Dee said that an angel appeared in the crystal and with a wand pointed out numbers and letters in a chart which spelled out messages in a language he called **Enochian,** using twenty-one characters. Surprisingly, this language has a real syntax and grammar, though those aspects are closely related to English.

Dee himself did not actually use the mirror, and admitted that he'd never mastered the ability to scry; he left that to others such as an assistant named Barnabas Saul, who soon lost his power and was replaced by one Edward Kelley (1555-1595), a scoundrel who claimed **mediumistic** and magical abilities and who transmitted the mystical messages to Dee.

In the later years of his life, John Dee turned his ill-directed attention to **alchemy**. Worse still, from 1582 on, he furthered his acquaintance with Kelley to the point of dependence. That association was the downfall of the brilliant scholar, for at that point, he abandoned all his truly useful and productive work to seek the ever-elusive shortcut to wealth and to divine wisdom. He soon found himself betrayed by Kelley and others who fed upon what was left of his fast-fleeing fame and repute. In 1583, a mob raided his home at Mortlake and destroyed many of his books, manuscripts, **talismans** and magical devices.

He served his last really responsible position as warden of the Collegiate Church in Manchester and was active there during an infamous event known as The Six, in which a group of children in Manchester imagined themselves to be possessed by **demons**. What was then referred to as a "cunning man" was brought in to observe and report on their situation. This poor man was caught up in the hysteria and was eventually executed on suspicion of being a **witch** himself. John Dee's only contribution to a solution was to advise the children to fast and pray. It was little comfort to the "cunning man," whose cunning apparently deserted him when most needed.

Upon the death of Elizabeth in 1603, and the ascent to the throne of James I, who had no patience with anyone pretending to possess any sort of unorthodox (non-Christian) magical powers, Dr. Dee was stripped of his honors and his income and sent to live in the countryside incommunicado. He spent the final five years of his life in extreme poverty until his death in 1608 at the very remarkable age of eighty-one. His library of more than four thousand books on the occult, mathematics and cartography—the largest collection in Britain at that time—was dispersed soon after his death. He is buried at Mortlake.

His assistant, Kelley, was convicted of counterfeiting (again) and was killed escaping prison.

British Museum visitors may also

Edward Kelley, the charlatan who ruined the reputation and the life of Dr. John Dee. He was a convicted counterfeiter and thus had cropped ears, so he wore his hair long and full to hide this fact.

see Dee's rose-tinted crystal, engraved gold and wax talisman tablets (in particular, the Golden Disc of the Four Castles), wands, and formula books on display.

de Freitas, José Pedro — *see* Arigó.

déjà vu A psychological phenomenon in which the subject experiences a situation that he or she feels strongly has been experienced before. It is believed that a unique combination of sensory inputs (hearing an unusually worded phrase along with perceiving a distinctive odor, for example) may bring about recall of a previous similar or identical combination, thus creating the illusion that the entire experience has been previously encountered.

Since this is a strange experience, it is often enthusiastically brought up as an example of a probable **psi** phenomenon, which it is not.

See also **cryptomnesia.**

De la Warr, George (1905-1969) A civil engineer from England who became wealthy by selling **quack** medical equipment. By stroking a rubber pad mounted on a mysterious black box modeled on that of another quack, **Ruth Drown,** De la Warr said he was able to diagnose and treat diseases. He made a fortune renting out the devices and training people to use them, and he might very well have believed that they really worked.

His boxes had a number of dials which were to be twisted until the stroking of the rubber pad seemed to change in character. The setting of the dials then gave the operator a number. Each box was accompanied by the *Guide to Clinical Condition,* a list of numbers that could be consulted to determine the medical condition of the subject. For example, 901 would mean "toxins" and 907 would be "fracture." A "bruise" was indicated by 80799, and 60404 meant a "secretion imbalance."

Other boxes designed and manufactured by De la Warr were used to actually treat patients, and one even photographed "thought forms." A disastrous court case brought against De la Warr revealed testimony of just how silly his procedures were, and though he won the case, the event brought his practice to an end. By then he'd made his fortune and didn't much care.

See also **Dr. Albert Abrams.**

Delphi (also Delphos) The Oracle of Delphi, probably the best known of the Greek **divining** agencies, was essentially a political force. The women in charge were not above accepting bribes to give appropriate answers to inquirers. It was believed that the god Apollo spoke through the Pythian priestesses while they were in various states of drug-induced **trance.**

The ambiguous nature of their utterances became a popular joke, as when they were asked to tell King Croesus the outcome of an upcoming battle to be fought across a river. The response: "When Croesus passes over the river he overthrows the strength of an empire." The questioner was pleased and left a generous offering at the temple. A great empire did fall that day, but it was his own. Such procedures gave rise to the expression "Delphic statement," used to designate anything that can be taken two or more ways.

Today, investment advisors and meteorologists are the tamer versions of the Oracle of Delphi.

demon (or daemon, from the Greek *daimon*.) A malevolent spirit. Demons are often invisible, but can see, usually have wings and can fly, know the future, can propagate (with other demons or with humans), and can die. Demons come in all sizes, so they can enter and inhabit the bodies of humans and animals, but are inhibited from this by properly-selected **charms** and they fear fire, water, light, salt, and certain herbs. Sneezing is said to provide a demon with the opportunity of flying up one's nose, thus the expression, "Bless you!" or "Bonne santé!" or "Gesundheit!" as a response to a sneeze. It's not known to help, but it can't hurt.

The *Lesser Key of Solomon*, the *Lemegeton* manuscript now in the

Demons, as drawn by Hans Holbein the Younger.

British Museum, lists seventy-three demons in hierarchial progression, but there are so many other menus to choose from, one is hard put to decide which listing to accept. These head demons, former rebellious **angels,** bring about storms, shipwreck, earthquakes, and other cataclysms.

Occultists, with their uncanny wisdom, have estimated that there are 7,250,000 demons currently in action, who are controlled by some seventy-nine higher powers. The hierarchy of demons is as follows:

One emperor
Seven kings
Twenty-four dukes
Thirteen marquis demons
Ten counts
Eleven presidents

There are thirteen other less fancy officers in this court, and the regular common demons are under the control of this royalty.

The *Talmud*, not to be outdone, declares that there are 7,405,926 demons in existence. The Greek philosophers Porphyry and Thales believed in demons. The Templars, a group of French knights dedicated to protecting Christians on their way to slaughter infidels during the Crusades, adopted the demon Baphomet as part of their strange religious rites, a fact all the more mysterious because the name is a corruption of Mahomet.

Demons are believed to inhabit deserts in preference to most other zones, perhaps favoring the closer resemblance to their home clime.

See also **Weyer, Johannes.**

demonology The study and classification of the hierarchy of **demons,** their powers and limitations, attributes, multiple names, and derivations. Not considered a very useful pursuit, but a good conversation piece.

dermo-optical perception (DOP; in Russia referred to as "bio-introscopy") In the 1950s, this was a popular subject for sensational news stories and for **parapsychology.** It was claimed that some persons were able to "see" without using their eyes, scanning printed matter with their fingertips, with their noses, or even with their feet. At one point, in 1990, it was even claimed that some children in China were able to "read" bits of paper crumpled and placed in their armpits or their ears, or even by *sitting* on the paper!

In Mexico, the Instituto Mas Vida ("More Life Institute") took up teaching DOP to the children of wealthy patrons. **Blindfolded,** the children specialized in reading large-type books opened at their feet while they were seated. It seems no accident that this is the perfect position in which to peek down the sides of the blindfold. When a piece of blocking paper was inserted below the chin, the child was always struck blind.

One famous practitioner of the art was a Russian psychic named **Rosa Kuleshova,** who, like the Chinese children, also read with her posterior. Another Russian, also famous for moving small objects with fine, invisible nylon threads, was **Nina Kulagina,** who can be seen in a black-and-white film made decades ago at a Leningrad laboratory, reading letter cards posted on the wall behind her. To a **conjuror,** the method is obvious: She brings her right hand up before her eyes, then it dips into her pocket, emerges and is casually shown empty. This suggests that she was peeking into a small mirror held in that hand, then the mirror was dumped when she'd had her glance. As if to verify this theory, she read off the cards—and even one two-digit number—*in reverse order.* Certainly there was no reason for her to have held her hand before her eyes, except to accomplish the trick as described.

The Chinese children were found at one point to be using a **one-ahead** technique with the crumpled papers, and since the controls were nonexistent in any case, they had no problem **cheating,** if they had wanted to, when their magical powers failed them.

deva A term referring to a sort of **angel** or Hindu god. Yet another class of minor **spirits.**

Devil A figure in religious mysticism depicted as a man-figure with horns, a tail, and cloven feet. Frequently, in Italian and French sculpture, the figure also has a conspicuous organ of procreation. The Devil is often synonymous with **Satan.**

Despite his usual evil reputation, he was credited in medieval times with some good deeds as well as bad. In anthropomorphic form, he was said to work in deep silver mines where human beings could not go, to build massive bridges, and to assist sailors in navigating through hazardous waters—in response to appropriate **prayers** or **incantations,** of course.

Some of the greatest support for belief in devils and demons was provided by **St. Thomas Aquinas** (circa 1225-1274), who endorsed as fact every fable that had ever been adopted by Christianity from other religions. Nothing, no matter how bizarre, was unacceptable to St. Thomas. He even claimed that devils could produce progeny:

> When children are born of the intercourse of devils with human beings, they do not come from the seed of the devil or of the human body he has assumed, but of the seed which he has extracted from another human being. The same devil, who, as a woman, has intercourse with a man can also, in the form of a man, have intercourse with a woman.

Since no half-devils were extant, this explanation took care of that awkward fact; the devilish progeny would look just like real, regular persons.

Devil's mark (also witch's mark) In books dedicated to the identification of **witches**, it is said that **Satan** places his mark upon the body of a witch, usually a red or blue spot, to more easily recognize his property. The mark was also believed to be insensitive to pain and to not bleed if pierced.

Tertullian (circa 155-222), one of the Latin Fathers, certified that witches were so marked, and this became the official and convenient manner of recognizing these evil folks, since no one is free of some sort of scar, mole, crease, wart, or bump that can be elevated to the status of a Satanic brand mark, especially when substantial rewards are available to the one who discovers such a sign. As a result, witch-hunters eagerly examined every part of a suspect's body, accepting the slightest suggestion of a mark as evidence. They were invariably successful.

Devils of Loudun — *see* **Loudun, Devils of.**

de Wohl, Louis (Ludwig Von Wohl-Musciny, 1903-1961) A Hungarian-born **astrologer.** Learning of the interest in astrology shown by the German Nazis, in 1940 the British put together their own—equally secret—group of astrologers, calling it their "black group," within the Department of Psychological Warfare. They put Captain Louis de Wohl in charge.

This man, who had arrived in England as a refugee in 1935, was chosen by the British because he said he knew the techniques used by **Karl Ernst Krafft** (the German Nazi astrologer) for making his forecasting, and it became his job to anticipate what their occultist might advise the warlords of Germany to do.

It appears that de Wohl had misrepresented and hyperbolized his talents to the British, and they did not retain his services for long. He wrote some fake astrological articles that contained discouraging predictions for Nazi Germany, for use in equally fake astrological magazines. These were distributed throughout Europe by various means.

Not ignoring the renewed German interest in the sixteenth-century French prophet **Nostradamus** either, de Wohl also invented some pro-British/anti-Nazi quatrains in an attempt to neutralize Krafft's work. He created a 124-page book titled *Nostradamus prophezeit den Kriegsverlauf* ("Nostradamus Predicts the Course of the War"), which of course predicted the fall of the Reich. The book was printed in huge quantities and dropped over occupied territories by the Allies in 1943.

An interesting question is whether or not either side in this psychological World War II battle actually had any real belief in astrology or in Nostradamus; both sides have officially denied any such belief, even up to the present. In any case, the expensive and ludicrous campaign failed to have much effect for either of the warring factions.

Dianetics — *see* **Hubbard, Lafayette Ronald.**

Dingwall, Dr. Eric J. (1890-1986) Born in Sri Lanka, an anthropologist by training, British scientist Dr. Dingwall became interested in psychical and **parapsychological** research at an early age, and was renowned as a major investigator of **psychic** claims. He knew many of the major figures in the field and was highly respected by believers and skeptics. He was an expert in **conjuring** techniques, and was a member of the London Magic Circle as well as of the **Society for Psychical Research** (SPR). He was also associated with the **Committee for Scientific Investigation of Claims of the Paranormal.**

Dr. Dingwall was a major investigator of **Margery Crandon** and served as a general gadfly to the SPR. In one instance, when he discovered that the SPR had developed incriminating data on the work of **George Soal** and had been withholding it, Dingwall insisted that they publish their findings or he would do so. Wisely, they did so.

A respected and much-loved researcher, Dr. Dingwall abandoned parapsychology in 1969 and died at age ninety-six in 1986 with the conviction that, even though he had failed, ever, to find real evidence of psychic phenomena—especially of **survival after death,** which was *the* important subject for him—there was probably something there which he had merely failed to find.

Discovery of Witchcraft, The (original spelling was "Discouerie of Witchcraft") — *see* **Scot, Reginald.**

divination Also called the "Mantic Art." The process of determining the future; discovering hidden or lost articles, persons, or substances; deciding guilt or innocence by various means; and generally of finding out required knowledge. **Dr. Charles Mackay,** author of the

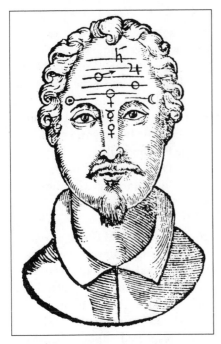

One form of divination is Meto-poscopy, determining one's destiny by analyzing the lines of the forehead in relation to the sun, moon, and planets. The process is as successful as casting a horoscope or reading the lines of the palm.

remarkable book *Extraordinary Popular Delusions* (1841), lists there fifty-two species of divination claimed by practitioners.

Divination is attempted by means of forked sticks or **pendulums** (*see also* **dowsing**), by interpretation of almost any random event such as throwing dice, cloud formations, the configurations of the entrails of a sacrificed animal (known as **augury**), **dreams,** how a pack of cards is dealt out, the movements of insects and a great variety of other phenomena.

In *Genesis 44*, there is a reference to a silver cup belonging to Joseph "in which [he] drinketh, and

whereby indeed he divineth," which was another popular method similar to **scrying,** an art that involved looking into a bowl of water. Even today, crystal balls are used to try to see images of the future.

See also **I Ching**, **numerology, omens, palmistry, police psychics, prophecy, Tarot cards.**

divining — *see* dowsing.

Dixon, Jeane (Née Pinckert, 1918?-) Mrs. Dixon is a famous Washington seer who also claims healing powers. But her major claim to fame is that she is said to have predicted the assassination of President John F. Kennedy. In its March 11, 1956, issue, *Parade* magazine reported, concerning the 1960 presidential election:

> Mrs. Dixon thinks it will be dominated by labor and won by a Democrat. He will be assassinated or die in office "though not necessarily in his first term."

The election was not "dominated by labor." She was correct on the winner's party, and the death prediction was in line with the **Presidential Curse** (*which see*) since Kennedy fell into that pattern. But when 1960 arrived and the election was closer, Mrs. Dixon declared that Richard Nixon would win the presidency.

The endless chain of Dixon's major failed predictions (such as Tom Dewey as "assistant president," the fall of India's Nehru that never happened, Richard Nixon's return to office, germ warfare in 1958 with

China, a monster comet striking the Earth, and the election of a female U.S. president—the last two to have taken place in the 1980s—and the dissolution of the Roman Catholic Church before 1990) establish that her actual, written record is hardly impressive. Nonetheless, she still has a large and enthusiastic following among **credophiles**.

djinn (plural noun, pronounced *jinn*. The singular is "djinni.") In the Moslem religion, **spirits** with specific supernatural powers, the children of fire. They are corporeal, often taking the shapes of ostriches, snakes, or humans, and can become invisible. In Malayan magic, there are 190 Black Djinn, evil mountain-dwelling spirits.

The alternate versions of the djinn are the genii. The differences are nonessential to any persons' knowledge of the real world.

doomsday — *see* **end of the world.**

doppelgänger From the German, meaning "double walker." A persistent fantasy is that each person has an identical "twin" somewhere, though they are unrelated. The chance of two identical DNA patterns existing at the same time, even if generated by the same two parents as the result of two different sperm/egg fusings, is inadequately described by the term "astronomically small." For that reason, an actual doppelgänger is *very* highly unlikely.

Legend says that if the two should meet, they will both die. That seems reasonable.

dowsing Also known as "rhabdomancy," "water witching," and "divining," this notion is first described in print in the 1540 Latin folio of Georgius Agricola (Georg Bauer, 1490/4?-1555) on mining, titled *De re Metallica*, published at Basel, Switzerland.

The process can take many forms. The traditional method is to use a flexible green forked stick, in early writings often referred to as the "virgula furcata." Hazel and willow are the preferred woods. The Y is inverted and the forked parts are grasped, one in each hand, palms up, usually with the thumbs pointing away from the body in opposite directions and the elbows tightly against the body. The forked portions are spread apart, with the main stem pointing out from the dowser's body. The dowser attempts to keep the stick parallel with the ground, and as he walks about, it is believed that subtle influences from water,

From Agricola's De re Metallica *(1540), this illustration shows the traditional forked stick used in dowsing attempts.*

metal, oil, or any other substance will cause the stem of the stick to either rise or depress from the horizontal position.

This, as with all other forms and methods of dowsing, uses a system which is in very unstable equilibrium. Since force is being applied to the stick, the tendency is for the stem to whip up or down unless care is taken to balance it. There is thus potential energy stored in the system, and the slightest inclination, tensing, or relaxation of either hand or both hands, *must* result in the stick moving violently. This motion is taken by dowsers as evidence that there is a supernatural external force acting upon the device.

These are several positions in which dowsing instruments are held. In all cases, the device is in poor equilibrium, and subject to small body movements of the operator.

Another popular method uses two straight, stiff wires about twelve to twenty-four inches long, each bent sharply at one end at a right angle to provide a handle which is held vertically in the fist so that the main portion is pointing straight ahead and parallel to the ground. The object is to hold the two rods parallel to one another, and the "dowsing reaction" is said to occur when the rods diverge or when they cross, depending on which dowser is consulted. Again, the tiniest inclination of the hand or the arm will cause great fluctuations in this system.

Sometimes only one wire, or a "bobber" made of a single flexible wand, weighted at the far end, is employed. **Pendulums** are also frequently used.

Though these are the major devices employed, individual operators have come up with an array of others, including exotic variations on the standard ones. Single flexible "whip" models, bobbing springs, jointed sticks, combinations of string and metal foil— in fact, anything that will respond to a slight in-crease or easing of the applied force through a twitch, slope, or bounce by the operator —can be used. In many cases, the operator will insist on holding against or fastening to the device a sample of the same kind of material that is being sought for, to "tune" it to that substance.

Sometimes dowsers disagree completely. Some instructions tell learners never to try dowsing with rubber footwear, while others insist that it helps immeasurably. Some practitioners say that when rods cross, that specifically indicates water; others say that water makes the rods diverge to 180 degrees. Many say that metal rods are not suitable at all for dowsing, while others adore them.

The explanation of dowsing is that the operator is actually undergoing what is known to psychology as the **ideomotor effect.**

Dowsers are, generally speaking, very honest, sincere people, and almost always seem absolutely convinced of their abilities. That conviction is not well founded, since all properly performed, comprehensive tests of this particular claim have produced negative results.

The fallacy of dowsing was recognized by early writers such as **Reginald Scot,** in his book *The Discouerie of Witchcraft* (1584). Scot described a process (known as *coscinomancy*) that was used even in ancient Greece "to find out a Thief":

Stick a pair of Sheers in the rind [rim] of a Sieve, and let two persons set the top of each of their Forefingers upon the upper part of the Sheers, holding it with the Sieve

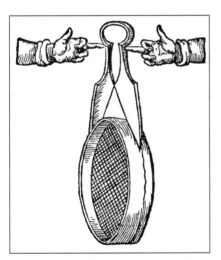

An illustration from Opera omnia *by Cornelius Agrippa (circa 1560) showing how the sieve-and-shears arrangement was made and held. It is seen to be the usual delicately balanced system always employed in dowsing.*

up from the ground steadily, and ask *Peter* and *Paul* whether A. B. or C. hath stoln the thing lost, and at the nomination of the guilty person, the Sieve will turn round. This is a great practice in all Countries, and indeed a very bable [babble, foolish talk].

In a marginal observance to this quote, Scot notes:

These be meer toys to mock Apes, and have no commendable device [purpose].

And the actual cause of the movement of the device was also apparent to Scot:

For with the beating of the pulse some cause of that motion ariseth, some other cause by the slight [very small movement] of the fingers, some other by the wind gathered in the Sieve to be staid [steadied], &c. at the pleasure of the holders. Some cause may be the imagination, which upon the conceit [fanciful notion] at the naming of the party, altereth the common course of the pulse, as may well be conceived by a Ring held steadily by a thred betwixt the finger and the thumb, over or rather in a goblet or glass; which within short space will strike against the side thereof so many strokes as the holder thinketh it a clock, and then will stay: the which who so proveth [tests] shall find true.

In one stroke, author Scot has here correctly defined the causes of the movement of both the dowsing stick (in this case of a similarly unbalanced system) and the **pendu-**

lum phenomenon. Ben Jonson was familiar with this system when he described, in his *Alchemist* (1610), the hero of the piece "searching for things lost with a sieve and shears."

In modern times, the British Society of Dowsers (BSD), at the founding of the society in 1933, stated that it was organized

> to encourage the study of all matters connected with the perception of radiation by the human organism with or without an instrument.

And, in a pamphlet issued by the BSD, they claim that their purpose is

> to spread information among the members and the public on the use and value of dowsing in all its forms.

When contacted for a proposed test, Sir Charles J. Jessel, president of the BSD, said that he was not willing for the BSD to be a participant in any presentation that would "put [dowsing] to the test." He said he favored an approach that would seek to "find out, in a genuine fashion, about the subject." He wrote that "the dowsing faculty . . . does not always behave to order when real need is not being expressed or fulfilled." This is not in line with the demonstrated fact that in all attempts to find a test object, the dowsers are always 100 percent successful *when they know in advance* where the object is, but obtain only chance results when they do not know. Though there is no "real need" involved here, the "dowsing faculty" *does* always "work" under the first condition.

In addition, the secretary of the BSD and the editor of the BSD journal refuse even to discuss the problem. Similar responses are offered by dowsers all over the world when offers are made to officially test the phenomenon with their cooperation and monitoring.

Kenneth Roberts, an American journalist who accepted every claim made for dowsing, wrote in 1953:

> [The dowsing rod] may rank with electricity and atomic power. . . . Why . . . shouldn't scientists . . . devote more of their energies to developing an invaluable, even though mysterious, phenomenon that, properly utilized, would turn deserts into lands of plenty, feed the hungry, cure the sick and change the face of the world?

The *Encyclopedia Americana* states:

> Controlled field and laboratory tests have failed to establish the validity of dowsing, and judged by scientific standards the practice has little basis in fact.

At Kassel, north of Frankfurt, Germany, the scientific group *Gesellschaft zur wissenschaftlichen Untersuchung von Parawissenschaften* (GWUP) in 1992 set up a very efficient and effective site for testing dowsing in cooperation with a local television station. A plastic pipe of suitable size was buried fifty centimeters beneath a level section of field, through which a very large flow of water could be directed from a switching valve. The test area was protected by a large tent, and the position of the buried pipe was prominently marked by a broad red and white stripe. The challenge for the dowsers was not to *find* the pipe, but only to say whether water was flowing in it or not.

In response to advertisements, GWUP obtained thirty dowsers, mostly from Germany but also from Denmark, Austria, and France. Each dowser was required to perform ten "open" trials in which he or she would *know* whether or not the water was flowing, and they would have to obtain 100 percent results at that time. This set of trials would provide GWUP with a baseline from which to judge the subsequent twenty "closed" trials which immediately followed, in which they did *not* know the answer. In all cases, both with the open and closed tests, the "on" or "off" condition was decided by the random selection of a marked ball from a bag.

Each dowser was asked to make, in advance, a statement expressing any objections he might have to the procedure and stating his or her expected success rate. Each and every problem was satisfied and each dowser expected 100 percent success, as attested by the signatures. Then each subject was asked to use his or her dowsing ability to scan the area in which the test was to be performed, to see if any underground distraction was present.

At the end of three days of testing, GWUP announced the results of almost a thousand bits of data to the assembled dowsers. A summary of their results produced just what would be expected according to chance.

Recall that in these tests each dowser had been asked to scan the test area in advance for any anomalies that might distract the powers. It was noted that none of the thirty dowsers found the same anomalies, though all but one found some anomaly, and some found several. Obviously, only one of the dowsers could have been right, and probably all were wrong.

It is perhaps significant that the German word for the dowsing rod is *Wünschelrute,* which translates as "wishing stick." Occasionally, the art is referred to in English as "jowsing" or "josing."

The American Society of Dowsers, Inc., can be reached at Danville, VT 05828. However, inquiries indicating doubt or challenging their convictions will not be answered in a positive fashion.

Doyle, Sir Arthur Conan — *see* Conan Doyle.

dragon bones Superstition and stupidity have scored victories against archaeology and anthropology in China, where dinosaur bones and other artifacts inscribed with historical records have been eagerly purchased from finders and ground to powder by apothecaries who then sell the useless substance as an aphrodisiac and general cure-all. It is called "dragon bone."

drawing down the Moon A witch's ceremony held on or near December 12. It is dedicated to Bacchus, the god of wine and fertility. Yet another reason for folks to get together for drinking, dancing, and general carrying-on.

dreams The Greek scholar/historian Xenophon wrote about dreams as a form of **divination** and in the second century Artemidorus of Daldis set about collecting dream lore and published a book on their interpretation. Dreams also served the Greeks as diagnostic tools, being messages from the gods.

It was also believed, in some cultures, that dreams resulted from divine visitations, **demons,** or **spirits** of the dead. The *Bible* records that Joseph interpreted dreams for Pharaoh, and there are several other prognostications achieved through dreams, such as those in Genesis 20:3, 31:23, and 37:5; Job 33:15; Numbers 12:6; and 1 Kings 3:5.

In actuality, a dream appears to be the reaction of the brain to various sensory inputs experienced while asleep. It explains away what would otherwise be disturbing and/or misunderstood information. The dream is not a supernatural phenomenon.

Drown, Ruth (1891?-1943) A Los Angeles **chiropractor** of the "sealed black box" school, Drown obtained a British patent for her "camera" device which she said produced a photographic image of an organ, from a drop of blood from the patient.

In England, Drown met "radionics" worker **George De la Warr,** who developed her ideas into a separate movement and caused a minor war between the two schools.

Radionics dealt with various **quack** devices that were used for medical diagnosis and treatment.

Drown was called a fraud by the FDA when it looked into her practice, but that did little to slow her success.

See also **Dr. Albert Abrams, George De la Warr.**

Druids (From the Celtic *der,* for "superior," and *wydd,* for "priest." Pliny claims the word derives from the Greek *drus,* but that is highly unlikely. Also known as Semothees) Priest-magicians of Gaul, England, the north of Scotland, and the Hebrides. In the first century, the Roman emperor Tiberius issued a decree against the Druids "along with the whole pack of such physicians, prophets and wizards." Druids were written about by Julius Caesar in his *Commentaries on the Gallic War*, and by Celtic authors. In 1598, the tomb of a very famous Druid chief Chyndonax was discovered near Dijon, France, covered with Greek inscriptions.

Augury (*see also* **divination**) was a popular form of prognostication used in Druid ceremonies, and they were said to be competent at controlling the weather, producing visual illusions, **fire walking,** and speaking with animals.

Halloween is essentially a Druidic festival.

Dunninger, Joseph (1892-1975) One of the most famous and proficient **mentalists** of all time.

Born the son of a tailor on New York's Lower East Side in 1892, Joe

Dunninger was interested in **conjuring** as a boy. Among the many acts he went to see at that time, he was impressed by a two-person mind-reading routine performed by Mr. & Mrs. John T. Fay. (John was the son of **Anna Eva Fay,** a spiritualist who had been very popular in vaudeville in the late 1800s and had attracted the interest of magician/investigator **Harry Houdini.** John's wife was Anna Norman. After John's death by suicide, Mrs. Fay went on with the act, billed as "The High Priestess of Mystery," eventually headlining shows in 1908-1910.)

However, unlike the "double" act done by the Fays, Dunninger's was a one-person act, never using any assistants—or at least not so that anyone ever knew about it. He was very mindful to assure his audiences that he worked entirely alone, and published a carefully worded but quite genuine offer of $10,000 to anyone who could prove that he used paid confederates. Though many tried, no one ever collected, and for a very good reason: He never used any.

Becoming a very highly paid and fully booked mentalist at posh affairs all over the United States (though he had an overpowering fear of flying and traveled almost exclusively by train all of his life) Dunninger made most of his early fortune before income tax laws went into effect in this country, and he invested heavily in oriental artifacts, eventually amassing the largest collection of rare Tibetan art in the United States outside of a specialized museum in Staten Island,

Joseph Dunninger created a high standard of mentalism for others to follow. He rose to fame as a result of his exciting radio appearances.

New York. His home in New Jersey was filled, wall-to-wall, with sculptures, wall hangings, exotic rugs, dozens of carved crystals, and gold figures of deities. In the basement was a mass of material from the Houdini home, most of which he eventually sold to the Houdini Hall of Fame Museum in Niagara Falls, Canada.

With his elegant, commanding mannerisms onstage including a strange pseudo-Oxford accent affectation, Dunninger was known to the public only as a mentalist, "The Master Mind of Mental Radio." He appeared on radio starting in 1943, and on television frequently in the fifties and sixties performing the most astonishing series of stunts that were ever devised by anyone. The list of persons he used in these presentations read as a *Who's Who*. Jack Dempsey, Bob Dunn, Harry Truman, the Duke of Windsor, and Babe Ruth— it seemed as if Joe Dunninger could reach into anyone's mind at will.

On one occasion, Dunninger had the U.S. postmaster general in position at the main post office in New York City. On his live TV presentation, he asked that official to reach into the thousands of letters going by him on a conveyor belt and to choose just one. A few minutes of "concentration" and Dunninger wrote down on a large pad of paper what he believed the address was on that letter. You guessed it: When the postmaster read out the address, it was the same one that appeared on Dunninger's pad.

Joseph Dunninger maintained an enigmatic image all of his life. He never quite said that he read minds, but he didn't say that he didn't, or couldn't. Publicly, he stayed away from magicians and seemed apart from their interests; personally, he loved to talk tricks and to root around in magic shops. Though he always disclaimed any supernatural powers, he could leave an audience with absolutely no other explanation of what they'd seen. When asked for an answer to the enigma, he had several answers. "Any child of twelve could do what I do," he might say, "with thirty years practice!" Or "I'm not a mind-reader. I'm a thought-reader. If a man comes up to me and hits me in the eye, I don't have to be a mind-reader to know his thoughts; he dislikes me."

Dunninger's final series of programs for ABC-TV, recorded in 1971, were never broadcast. By that time he was suffering from Parkinson's disease and could not summon up the strength of presentation he'd previously displayed.

E

ectenic force — *see* **psychokinesis**.

ectoplasm (from the Greek *ektos* and *plasma*, meaning "exteriorized material.") A term originated either by wealthy amateur scientist **Schrenck-Notzing** or by physiologist **Charles Richet**, this designates the amorphous substance said to be extruded from *all* the bodily orifices of the **spirit medium** during séances. It could assume the form of a hand or a face, but in photographs it generally resembles a piece of coarse net like cheesecloth. The resemblance is *very* close.

Ectoplasm, as generally described and photographed, could be simulated by means of netting coated with luminous paint, which in the heyday of **spiritualism** was usually water-based. Though early writers on spiritualism had actually solved the true nature of some of their experiences with ectoplasm, they failed to realize that fact. Dr. Gustav Geley (1868-1924) described his encounter with the strange substance during a séance with Eva C. (**Eva Carrière**) during which a "luminous hand" touched and patted him. A "drop" of luminous substance, he reported, fell to his sleeve, where it continued to glow for about twenty minutes. This behavior is exactly what would be expected of cheesecloth coated in luminous paint.

A book on the subject complains that ectoplasm's

> resemblance to such materials as cheesecloth has often provoked allegations of fraud, as well as making it possible for fraudulent mediums to simulate ectoplasm.

At risk of being thought rather difficult, one might suggest that the words *ectoplasm* and *cheesecloth* could be interchanged in that last paragraph, to produce an interesting comparison.

If it can be imagined that mediums might actually **cheat**, it would appear to be wise for a cheater to secure the luminous cheesecloth by means of a cord, so that it might not fall out of reach or be left behind when the lights came up in the séance room. Consider, then, the following naive account of a séance with medium **Margery Crandon**:

> In the "Margery" séances in Boston ...ectoplasm was photographed. ...In several of these photographs the ectoplasm is visible...[in] a

form then reduced to a species of placenta attached to the medium by a cord which, in its turn, calls up the appearance of an umbilical cord.

The possibilities are evident.

Sitters are prohibited from touching the ectoplasm, for fear that the medium may be harmed. It may be that the reputation of the medium might also suffer.

In illustrations of ectoplasm often-shown in credulous books, it is obvious that some cotton wool has been teased out and stuck on the medium's chin. But to the spiritualists, this is ectoplasm or an etherial body in the process of forming.

Also often seen is a photo of a paper cutout with a length of white cloth fastened to it, stuck up on the wall with a thumbtack above the medium's head. The believers describe this as a "spiritoid form draped in a white ectoplasmic veil." Incredibly, they actually believe this.

Ectoplasm is differentiated from **apport** and **ideoplast,** *which see.*

Eddy, Mary Morse Baker (1821-1910) Though Mrs. Eddy, the founder of the **Christian Science** church, was said to be an ill-tempered, neurotic woman who suffered from chronic problems—what she called "nerve disorders" and "spinal inflammations"—all her life, she denied that illnesses were real, claiming that they all resided in the mind and were the result of "error." That is the basic teaching of her church, that illness and death are malfunctions and can be avoided by proper conduct. All medical help, therapy, medication, or other such services are strictly forbidden to church members.

Nonetheless, Mrs. Eddy wore glasses and walked with a cane (though she was never photographed nor seen in public using them), had false teeth, and for most of her life took morphine for pain to the point where she became seriously addicted.

She was married three times. Her first husband was a Mason named George Washington Glover, and thereafter membership in the Masonic Order was the one single "outside" affiliation that was allowed to church members by Mrs. Eddy. Six months after their marriage, Glover died of (imaginary) yellow fever. Her second husband was Daniel Patterson, a dentist (and thus a medical man!) and a **homeo-path** (thus almost a physician), who left her after twenty years of stormy marriage. The third was Asa Gilbert Eddy, a **spiritualist** who died of (imaginary) heart failure six years after their marriage. Mrs. Eddy, despite the results of a careful autopsy, maintained that her husband had actually been poisoned by **malicious animal magnetism,** *which see.*

The church specializes, to this day, in the treatment of diseases solely by means of the prayers of "practitioners."

Edwards, Michael — *see* **psychokinete.**

Egely, Gyorgy Often, the evidence offered in support of psychic powers has to be examined critically, and in particular the credentials of those endorsing such matters. A good example is the Hungarian parapsychologist Gyorgy Egely, who has enthusiastically endorsed the powers of such psychics as **Uri Geller.** He has stated that he is a Ph.D. professor and physicist at the Central Research Institute for Physics (CRIP), in Budapest. He also says that he "examined by electron beam scattering" a spoon bent by Mr. Geller and that he has no explanation for the event.

A simple inquiry at the Research Institute for Atomic Energy (RIAE), CRIP's successor, resulted in information that:

a. Mr. Egely "is not and never was a professor at the Institute [CRIP]." He once worked at CRIP briefly as a mechanical engineer, but was dismissed "because he failed to produce any useful work."

b. he "is not a professor of anything at any Hungarian university."

c. he has received a "doctorate"— but under Russian standards which are no longer recognized in Hungary—and by Hungarian standards is not considered to be a Ph.D.

d. he "is not a physicist."

e. the "electron beam scattering" examination could not have taken place at CRIP because "the Institute does not have, and never has had, the equipment for such a test."

A further inquiry to Dr. Gyula Bencze of Budapest reveals that

" for several months Mr. Egely was a guest lecturer at the Eotvos University in Hungary, where he began lecturing on paranormal subjects and, as a result, the Dean of the Science Faculty banned him from doing any further teaching activity there."

How often are such inquiries made? Not often, and though an endorsement of a psychic event may come form individuals with excellent, genuine, qualifications, unless their expertise includes certain special talents needed for proper investigation of such matters, it is often useless.

Eglinton, William (1857-1933)

An English **materialization medium** and, from 1884 on, a **slate writer** contemporary with **Henry Slade.** He enjoyed a certain period of success beginning in 1876, mostly because of the endorsement of **Dr. Charles Richet,** but almost immediately he was caught **cheating** when wigs, beards, and cheesecloth "ghosts" were discovered on his person during a **séance.** Then in 1886 he was thoroughly exposed as a fake by Professor Lewis Cargill. Such reversals did little to affect the belief of his resilient followers, however.

Eisenbud, Dr. Jule — see thoughtography.

elemental/elementary spirits Entities

said to inhabit the four medieval elements. Salamanders inhabit fire, sylphs the air, gnomes the earth, and nymphs the water. It is not stated which ones frequent discos.

elements Certain materials (such as carbon, iron, oxygen, and gold) are themselves unique substances which are not combinations of other ingredients. These are the proper chemical elements.

The **alchemists** believed that all substances were combinations of sulfur, mercury, and common salt, which they said were themselves composed of the four basic "elements": fire, air, earth, and water. (Sulfur and mercury actually are proper elements, but salt is a combination of the metal sodium and the gas chlorine, each of them elements.) Every element, to the alchemists, had specific attributes. These were:

Fire: colors red and orange, hot and dry conditions, motion, light, and heat, animals, strength.

Air: color yellow, hot and damp conditions, light, activity, bravery, intellect.

Earth: colors brown and black, cold and dry conditions, fertility, passivity, silence.

Water: colors blue and green, cold and damp conditions, intuition, wisdom, cleansing.

Early Tibetan scholars recognized, in addition to these four basic elements, a fifth which they called "ether." The five elements of the early Chinese were fire, earth, water, wood, and metal.

In medieval times, only 10 of the real elements were known to occur in a natural, uncombined state. We now know of 107 elements, 90 of which occur on Earth naturally, 17 of which are created during nuclear reactions or radioactive decay.

e-meter A device consisting of a sensitive electric meter, a battery, a "resistor bridge," and two metal handles. These are connected in series so that touching the handles together causes a maximum deflection of the meter, indicating a resistance of zero. In effect, when the handles are held by a subject, one in each hand, the device measures the resistance of his body. The reading will decrease or increase depending on the pressure of the grip and the moisture present, as well as the emotional state of the subject, via a phenomenon known as "galvanic skin effect."

Another version of this idea attempts to be a diagnostic tool. In this mode, one electrode is "grounded" to the arm of the patient, and the other is a probe that is used to explore the hand, which serves as a **homunculus,** the thumb representing the head and neck, the index finger the right arm, etc. The harder one presses down on the probe, and the damper the precise spot on the hand, the lower the resistance reading.

In 1950, Volney Mathison demonstrated a "galvonomic box" to later-Scientology guru L. Ron Hubbard. (Interestingly enough the patent number stamped on that machine turned out to belong to a variety of threshing machine patented in 1860 with the U. S. Patent Office.)

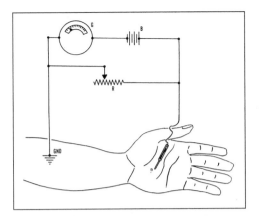

e-meter: The basic circuit of the e-meter device, used by scientologists and also by quacks. A battery (B) registers current flow from the "ground" (GND) to the hand probe (P), on the sensitive galvanometer (G) when the variable resistor (R) is adjusted to just more than the resistance through the skin. Pressure upon the probe, higher humidity and other elements can cause wild fluctuations in the reading.

A Dr. Reinhold Voll of Germany claims to have discovered the principle of using the "Galvanic skin effect" as a diagnostic tool. Dr. Ernst Roscher of Frankfurt also claimed to have invented a slightly different version of this diagnostic application designed to determine whether medicine would be effective for a patient. An attempt by Roscher to market his Probe in the U.S.A. through JS&A Products was made in 1983.

In all of these applications the "galavanic skin effect" is ineffective in determining anything except skin resistance.

end of the world A notion preached endlessly by religious fanatics and almost always said to be due "soon." The cartoon eccentric parading about with the sign saying THE END IS NIGH actually exists, an unreal character mislocated in the real world.

The predictions of a final cataclysm are numerous; see Appendix II of this book for a listing of forty-nine of them. *See also* **Armageddon.**

Enochian A language and alphabet of **angels** which **Dr. John Dee** said was used to communicate prophecies to him. It actually has a syntax and though very cumbersome could serve as a means of communication.

E-rays These are known in Germany, where the idea originated, as "Erdestrahlen" or "earth rays." E-rays are the German equivalent of the French discovery, **N-rays,** and are just as real. They are said to be radiations that are emitted from unknown sources deep in the ground, giving rise to "hot spots," and causing cancer. These rays, say the believers, cannot be detected by any sort of instruments, but are believed to exist because **dowsers—** and only dowsers—can sense them.

In Germany, these invisible rays and hot spots are accepted by almost everyone, even governmental agencies, who pay dowsers to indicate to them how to relocate the desks of federal employees away from the positions where E-rays can intercept them; hospital beds are similarly moved about to protect patients from cancer.

Professors H.L. König and H.-D. Betz of Munich, two German authors of a highly supportive 1989 book on the German government tests, have refused to identify any of the dowsers they tested in preparing their book, or even to put the dowsers in touch with other researchers. Their reasons for this lack of cooperation are not clear.

See also **N-rays.**

Erdestrahlen — *see* E-rays.

ESP — *see* extra-sensory perception.

ESP cards — *see* Zener, Dr. Karl.

Eva C. — *see* Carrière, Eva.

evil eye The glance of certain individuals, described in the *Malleus Maleficarum* as "fiery and baleful eyes," was said to induce curses and even death. The Latin term was *fascinatio,* and it was said to be prevented from doing damage to any intended victim about whose neck a band of multicolored threads had been fastened.

Pliny the Elder prescribed spittle as an antidote to the evil eye, and the wearing of a fleur-de-lis **amulet** was believed to be effective for that same purpose. In modern Italy, the evil eye is generally known as *mal d'occhio,* but in the south, especially in Naples, it is *jettatura,* and in Corsica, *innochiatura.* Along the Mediterranean and in the Arab countries, the effect is taken quite seriously.

The Frankish queen of the sixth century, Fredegund, was said to be endowed with the evil eye. Perhaps she merely lacked regal charm.

exorcism The expulsion of the Devil, spirits, and **demons** from persons, animals, or places by occult or religious rites.

The Roman Catholic exorcism rite first came into use at the end of the third century, and in A.D. 341 it is mentioned in church writings. A specifically ordained order of exorcising priests was created, and the process is still practiced by the Roman Catholic church today.

As recently as 1972, Pope Paul VI affirmed the existence of demons and the Devil:

> Sin, on its part, affords a dark, aggressive evildoer, the Devil, an opportunity to act in us and in our world . . . . Anyone who disputes the existence of this reality places himself outside biblical and Church teachings.

Perhaps inspired by this declaration, in 1976 Germany's Bishop Stangl instructed two priests to perform the rite of exorcism upon a twenty-three-year-old epileptic Bavarian girl, Anneliese Michel. The local newspapers reported that the church had decided her body was being inhabited by various demons, including Lucifer, Adolf Hitler, Judas Iscariot, and Emperor Nero. Anneliese, an epileptic, died in the process of being exorcised, and the autopsy showed she suffered beating and starvation. Her parents and the two priests were convicted of negligent homicide and given suspended sentences.

Significantly, when Bishop Stangl died during the trial, his death was attributed to a stroke, not to **demonic possession.**

In recent years, similar exorcism

farces have taken the lives of children in the United States, too.

Christians who believe in the *Bible* must also believe in demons, devils, and other such creatures, and they must believe that those entities cause disease and that they can be "cast out" by proper ceremonies—exorcism—simply because it's in the Book. If they deny the reality of those entities, they deny the *Bible*, and thus their faith. It is not a matter of choice, but dogma.

extrasensory perception (ESP) A term invented by **Dr. J.B. Rhine** and used by him to refer to supposed abilities such as **telepathy,** which involves being able to tell the thoughts of another person without the use of the recognized senses. **Clairaudience, clairvoyance,** and **precognition** (*all of which see*) also fall under this term. *See also* **parapsychology.**

eyeless vision — *see* **blindfold vision.**

Eysenck, Dr. Hans J. (1916-) Psychologist Eysenck studied in the U.K. with **Sir Cyril Burt** and invented the "Eysenck Personality Scale," which is believed to measure a subject's basic temperament for purposes of evaluating results obtained in **parapsychological** tests.

In 1983, Eysenck, with **Dr. Carl Sargent,** produced *Know Your Own Psi-IQ,* a naive book designed to enable the layperson to design and perform **extrasensory perception** (ESP) tests. Attempting to provide a

simple, convenient randomization method, for example, the authors instead gave users a highly biased procedure that would make experiments meaningless and certainly discourage further investigation by the amateur.

In 1957, before very much was known about the poor control and sometimes devious methods used by some scientists to develop their evidence for paranormal phenomena, Dr. Eysenck wrote:

Unless there is a gigantic conspiracy involving some thirty University departments all over the world, and several hundred highly respected scientists in various fields, many of them originally hostile to the claims of the psychical researchers, the only conclusion the unbiased observer can come to must be that there does exist a small number of people who obtain knowledge existing either in other people's minds, or in the outer world, by means yet unknown to science.

Such a "gigantic conspiracy" is not at all necessary to explain the fact that some scientists have seen what they expected and wanted to see and have accepted the conclusions of others without question. The fact that none of the findings of the paranormalists have been established but like the work of **Soal, Levy, Rhine,** and so many others have instead fallen out of serious consideration upon subsequent examination, has apparently not altered Dr. Eysenck's conclusion.

F

fairies Miniature supernatural beings in the form of humans. The pixies of England and the brownies of Scotland are essentially the same creatures, and just as real. Specific fairies such as Robin Goodfellow (also known as Puck) are said to be helpful though mischievous and can be called upon to perform domestic services.

Incredibly, the famous author **Sir Arthur Conan Doyle** accepted the existence of fairies, elves, and other such creatures.

There is no agreement on the origins of the many varieties of fairies. One definition says they are the dispossessed spirits of humans not yet ready for heaven. Another describes them as a distinct life-form capable of the usual reproductive process, and in Devonshire, England, they are "pixies," the spirits of infants who died before baptism.

The English version wears a red conical cap, a green cloak interwoven with flowers, green trousers, and silver slippers. Others are winged like dragonflies and dressed in filmy negligees. Some are said to dress in perfect miniatures of regular human clothing of the current period. One's choice of fairy appears to be a matter of taste.

In various cultures, there are both good and bad fairies. The Koran describes the delicate "peri" as the offspring of "fallen spirits," and such a fairy is always benevolent, pointing out to the faithful the way to heaven. In contrast, a malevolent fairy lives in the mines of England, causing accidents and misleading the miners.

In general, fairies (and **witches**) fear iron.

See also **Cottingley fairies.**

fairy rings Also known as "hag tracks." Mushrooms found in the forest sometimes tend to grow in the form of circles, due to the fact that the old growths tend to die off from a central point, and often leave behind chemical residues that inhibit growth of other plants. Tradition has it that **fairies** or **witches** danced in these circles.

In Shakespeare's *Tempest,* he referred to the fairies and their artifact:

> . . . You demi-puppets, that
> By moonshine do the green-sour
>   ringlets make,
> Whereof the ewe not bites.

Today, some of these rings have been labeled as sites of **UFO** landings, bringing a natural phenomenon up to date in the nonsense business.

faith healing When organized medicine fails to supply a satisfactory answer, either through inadequate technology, the simple inability to provide a cure at that time, or the fact that not enough is presently known about the ailment, other modalities which promise miraculous results are often sought.

There are several religious sects who base their entire philosophy on faith-healing modalities. It is found that the "cure rate" experienced by the believers is no higher than that of persons who receive no treatment whatsoever, and often much less. For example, the **Christian Scientists** forbid their followers to utilize any regular medical care or medication. A recent U.S. survey of students at the college level showed a significantly lower life expectancy for those who attended Christian Science schools than for those who did not. Faced by such revelations, the believers turn their backs on further examination of their convictions.

Faith healers have often answered, when asked for proper evidence of their claims, "God doesn't need to be examined or challenged." The healers say, when the disease doesn't go away, that the subject has lost faith and thus has failed to "hold" his or her blessing. The guilt is borne by the subject. Saddest of all is the realization that these people subject their children

to these restrictions as well, often with crippling or fatal results.

Reformer Martin Luther, among others in the sixteenth century, took credit for spontaneous, miraculous cures while **Paracelsus** and other savants were attempting—with highly varying degrees of success—to bring out of the superstition of magic, what we know today as the **science** of medicine. The Mormons and Episcopalians established a history of faith cures as part of their theologies.

In the 1600s, one practitioner known as "Greatraks the Stroker" (or Greatrakes, b. 1628) was astounding England with his performances. A remarkable English author, **Charles MacKay,** who in 1841 wrote his classic *Extraordinary Popular Delusions and the Madness of Crowds,* observed in that book that

> Mr. Valentine Greatraks . . . practised upon himself and others a deception . . . that God had given him the power of curing the king's evil. . . . In the course of time he extended his powers to the curing of epilepsy, ulcers, aches, and lameness. . . . Crowds which thronged around him were so great, that the neighboring towns were not able to accommodate them.

(MacKay's reference to the "**king's evil**" refers to scrofula.)

One can be grateful that MacKay recognized that Greatraks was deceiving both his patients *and* himself. As with **fortunetellers,** healers often begin to believe in their own powers because their subjects tend to give them only positive feedback. Thus they can excuse and forget their many failures, and their legends grow.

Greatraks made a huge impression on the public and accumulated a fortune in the process. In this respect, he helped to establish the precedent for modern faith healers. And in several other important respects he mirrored the modern faith healers, as evidenced in an account written by a contemporary in 1665:

A rumour of the prophet's coming soon spread all over the town, and the hotel . . . was crowded by sick persons, who came full of confidence in their speedy cure. [Greatraks] made them wait a considerable time for him, but came at last, in the middle of their impatience, with a grave and simple countenance, that shewed no signs of his being a cheat. [The host] prepared to question him strictly, hoping to discourse with him on matters that he had heard of. . . . But he was not able to do so, much to his regret, for the crowd became so great, and cripples and others pressed around so impatiently to be first cured, that the servants were obliged to use threats, and even force, before they could establish order among them. . . . The prophet affirmed that all diseases were caused by evil spirits. Every infirmity was with him a case of diabolical possession. . . . He boasted of being much better acquainted with the intrigues of demons than he was with the affairs of men. . . .

Catholics and Protestants visited him from every part, all believing that power from heaven was in his hands. . . . So great was the confidence in him, that the blind fancied they saw the light which they could not see—the deaf imagined that they heard—the lame that they walked straight, and the paralytic that they had recovered the use of their limbs.

To anyone who has actually witnessed a modern faith healer in action with crowds of worshipers around and about, that scenario will be familiar.

Sometimes **psychics** who do the usual **ESP, reading, prophecy,** and **clairvoyance** demonstrations eventually turn to claims of healing powers.

See also **royal touch.**

fakir (Also, fakeer) From the Arabic word for "poor man," a fakir is technically a person who begs professionally. Itinerant fakirs in India, Pakistan, and Sri Lanka often perform **conjuring** tricks to earn their gifts. On occasion, one may be charismatic and adept enough to become a "god-man" such as **Sai Baba.**

Fakirs are better known for their self-mutilation stunts, sitting on beds of nails and otherwise invoking the astonishment and contributions of generous tourists. The bed-of-nails trick depends upon the number of nails per square unit of fakir posterior. Sometimes there are a sufficient number of nails that the area is hardly more than a rough spot and a piece of leather judiciously placed in a loincloth can provide considerable comfort to the performer. Suggestions that the demonstration should begin with only one nail are not looked upon favorably by the fakirs.

Falkenstein, Glenn — *see* Davenport brothers.

familiar A demon, usually assuming the form of a cat, dog, spider, pig, rat, rabbit, or toad, that acts as companion and assistant to a witch or magician. Trials of witches often included a pet as codefendant, and these animals were just as often executed along with the condemned human. A silly concept cannot be made sillier by expanding it; the quality of silliness is totally saturating and all-encompassing.

Oliver Cromwell, accused by the British Royalists of being a wizard, was said by them to have a familiar named Grimoald. **Agrippa's** familiar was a black dog named Monsieur, and **Simon Magus** had a similar companion. It was said that these familiars could be kept in a hollow ring worn by the magician and released upon command. **Apollonius of Tyana** wore several such rings, and **Paracelsus** (Bombastus) carried about his familiar in the hilt of his sword:

> Bombastus kept a devil's bird
> Shut in the pommel of his sword,
> That taught him all the cunning
> pranks
> Of past and future mountebanks.
> —*Hudibras*, SAMUEL BUTLER

The Malaysians say that their magicians each have an hereditary **spirit**/familiar inherited from generation to generation. In Egyptian demonology, a familiar known as a "karina" is assigned to each child at birth.

In medieval times, ventriloquism was explained by assuming the existence of a familiar—known as a "kobold"—accompanying the performer. There are better explanations available.

Faustus, Dr. (stage name) — *see* Hoy, David.

Faustus, Dr. Johannes (also Faust.) A possibly mythical German **sorcerer** of medieval times, pictured by Rembrandt in a famous etching. Faustus had the reputation of being a powerful **magus** and the author of many books on magic. One book was *Magia Naturalis et Innaturalis,* subtitled *The Three-Fold Harrowing of Hell.*

Faust is mentioned by name in a letter written in 1507, and from that and other references he appears to have been a wandering charlatan who made his living by professing magical powers and performing various such services for paying customers. The character may also be a composite of several such actual persons.

The persistent legend of Faust and his interesting pact with Mephistopheles/**Satan,** in which he exchanged his soul for a guaranteed life of riches, pleasure, and debauchery, along with magical devices such as a cloak that would fly him any-

Seen here on the title page of Christopher Marlowe's 1636 play, The Tragicall History of Dr. Faustus, *the sorcerer is shown in regalia within his protective magic circle.*

where he chose to be, has been perpetuated by such writers as Christopher Marlowe in his play *The Tragicall History of Dr. Faustus* and by Goethe, who introduced the idea of Faust's eventual salvation, or escape from the frightful contract, mostly due to the inferior quality of the demon Mephistopheles and the legally shaky contract itself.

Musicians Berlioz, Gounod, and Schumann added to the Faust myth with full-length operas on the subject.

Fay, Anna Eva (Anna Eva Heathman, 1851-1927) A **spiritualist** faker who was very popular in vaudeville in the late 1800s, where she was billed as, "The Indescribable Phenomenon."

She attracted the very favorable interest of **Sir William Crookes** in 1874, but **Washington Irving Bishop,** who had worked with her as an assistant, chose to expose her methods to a newspaper. She was

also investigated by **conjuror Harry Houdini,** to whom she eventually admitted many of her tricks, after her retirement. The Magic Circle of London, a very prominent organization of conjurors, made her an honorary member, carefully designating her an Honorary Lady Associate, since women at that time were not eligible to be regular members.

Her son, John Truesdale Fay (1877-?) also had an act with his wife, called simply, "The Fays." The William H. Fay who worked with the **Davenport brothers** act was not related to this family of Fays.

Filipino psychic surgery — *see* **psychic surgery.**

finger writer — *see* **thumb writer.**

fire-eating This is essentially a **conjuring**/carnival stunt, not undertaken by the fainthearted. It requires considerable experience and a thorough knowledge of the art. Do not try this at home.

Torches are prepared, usually from heavy, solid iron wire, so that a wad of absorbent material can be firmly held at the business end and a handle is at the other end. The torch is dipped in any of several flammable liquids such as kerosene, benzine, or unleaded gasoline, and individual artists often use mixtures of these liquids. The excess fluid is pressed out.

The torch is ignited and the operator, *always breathing out steadily,* with the lips well wetted, places the flaming torch into the opening of the mouth with the head thrown back so that the flames do not rise against the top or sides of the mouth.

Many other stunts are available, such as allowing fumes to accumulate in the open mouth, exhibiting them burning above the lips independently of the torch, then closing the lips to extinguish the flame, and reigniting the vapors with the torch.

Fire-eating is dangerous, less so today than before the perils of leaded gasoline were at last recognized.

Early fire-eaters were often billed as "**salamanders**" and sometimes also handled red-hot objects or even walked on fire (*see* **fire walking**) and entered fiery furnaces. All these stunts, too, have rational explanations that do not call for supernatural powers.

Historically famous performers of the art were Richardson in the U.K., seventeenth century, Signora Josephine Girardelli (the original Salamander), early nineteenth century, and the Frenchman Chaubert, circa 1860.

fire walking This stunt consists of walking barefoot over a bed of glowing coals (usually charcoal) and emerging unharmed. The secret is not in preparation of the mind, the soul or the sole, as often claimed, but in the fact that wood ash has very low "specific heat" and does not hold as much heat energy as other substances. A frying pan, placed in the path of the fire walker, would burn the foot badly if stepped into.

Though the stunt has now been demonstrated—by physicist Dr. Bernard Leikind of California—to be a perfectly ordinary but nonintuited phenomena, one popular and very successful **New Age "guru"** in the United States continues to use it as a purported example of supernatural power or "mind control" to convince customers that they can have impossible things happen to them.

In Fiji, Hawaii, and Japan, a variation of the stunt is performed on lava stone, which also has very poor conductivity and low specific heat, and is similar to the "heat shield" ceramic used on the outer skin of the space shuttle.

Flat Earth Society Bothered by the discrepancies between biblical versions of geography and modern knowledge, some folks simply refuse to accept very well established facts. The spherical Earth was a concept accepted (but quietly) by scholars long before it was officially stated by Copernicus. As early as A.D. 548, an Egyptian monk named Cosmas Indicopleustes began the battle against belief in a spherical Earth that rather lost steam until 1849, when Samuel Birley Rowbotham resurrected the idea and advanced his Zetetic [skeptical] Astronomy theory that had the north pole at the center of a great flat circle and the south pole as an infinite ring of ice at the edge. That is still the accepted version of this strange geography. (In Mohammedan cosmology, a mountain chain named Caf surrounds the flat earth.)

For a short time, there was in England a journal called *The*

Zetetic, devoted to the idea of a flat Earth, but it did not last long, strangely. Another regular journal, *Earth—Not a Globe— Review* followed, then *Earth*. Both went out of business. In America, the movement began with a 100,000-watt radio station owned by Wilbur Glen Voliva, then the U.S. interest passed into the hands of Charles Johnson, who inherited the leadership of the Flat Earth Society from the Englishman Samuel Shelton, founder of the British society. Johnson is presently the reigning head of the organization, now known as the International Flat Earth Research Society.

Johnson publishes *The Flat Earth News* from headquarters at P.O. Box 2533, Lancaster, California 93539-2533. A stamped, self-addressed envelope will bring information.

Science writers Martin Gardner and Robert Schadewald have devoted much time to chronicling the theory that we live on a flat disk—without endorsing it in any way, I must add.

Fliess, Wilhelm (1859-1928) — *see* biorhythms.

Fludd, Robert (also Flud; 1574-1637) An **alchemist** and **Rosicrucian** from Kent, son of a wealthy and noble family. He took up the practice of medicine, but was distracted by his Rosicrucian studies and spent most of his life defending those principles against detractors. He promoted the usual belief in **demons** as the cause of illness and wrote very

positively on **dowsing**. He would feel very much at home among today's **New Age** groupies.

flying Known to the Roman Catholic church as "transvection," the supposed ability of **witches** to fly—with or without a broomstick—has always been an essential feature of **witchcraft**. An awkward dilemma for the demonologists occurred when, in A.D. 906 (or perhaps earlier), the *Canon Episcopi* (which became part of church law) denied that witches could really fly. They resolved this by deciding that if a witch merely *believed* that he or she could fly, sufficient reason existed for condemnation.

Flying was supposed to be brought about by the use of an anointing oil made by straining a

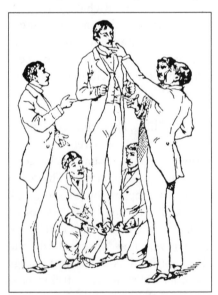

The old parlor trick in which a person is lifted by the fingers of four or five volunteers. The even distribution of the weight and the simultaneous effort are responsible for the action.

mixture of olive oil, vervain, and mint. Psychedelic substances such as belladonna and **mandrake** applied to the body might also produce hallucinations of flying or of levitation.

To conjurors, of course, the illusion known as levitation is well-known. It is accomplished by a number of means, some very technically complex, others quite simple. A popular trick performed by persons with pretensions of psychic powers consists of asking four or five volunteers to place one of their index fingers beneath the armpits and knees of a seated person (or, in the case of a standing person, beneath the insteps, chin, and elbows) and by simultaneously lifting upward, cause the person to rise. The even distribution of the weight allows the trick to work easily. This was described by Samuel Pepys (1633-1703) in his famous *Diary* as being done by French schoolgirls upon a corpulent pastry chef.

Certain Christian holy persons are said to have levitated. Saint Philip of Neri went up several yards during prayer, even to the ceiling on occasion. Ignatius Loyola not only raised several feet but became luminous in the process. Saint Robert of Palentin was not as holy, going up only eighteen or twenty inches, and Saint Dunstan rose off the ground a little bit just before his death. Even the famous Girolamo Savonarola, sentenced to death, rose off the floor of his cell into midair and remained there for some time. Either this was not seen by his jailers, or they didn't care: He was

taken out and burned alive, anyway.

See also **ointment**.

flying saucer — *see* UFO.

Ford, Arthur (1896-1971) One of the most successful **spirit mediums** of all time, "Reverend" Ford began his interest in professional **spiritualism** when, as a young man, he met **Sir Arthur Conan Doyle** during an American tour. He adopted a **spirit guide** named Fletcher, who was "with" him all his life.

He was a very systematic, successful, and hardworking practitioner of spiritualism. He maintained huge files of data on all his **sitters** and always traveled with a case full of personal information to be used to convince the skeptics and believers alike. Fed back to the sitters as a revelation from beyond the grave, these data were very effective as a means of satisfying doubts.

After the death of magician **Harry Houdini,** Ford kept company with Beatrice (Bess) Houdini, the magician's wife. She admitted, late in life, that she had given the famous "survival" code to Ford, who had thereupon announced a successful attempt to contact the spirit of Houdini. Mrs. Houdini, a Catholic, recanted her announcement that her husband's spirit had contacted her, and died (in 1943) convinced that all such attempts were futile. Ford impressed Bishop **James A. Pike,** an ardent believer in spiritualism, and he became a confidant of the bishop.

Late in his life Reverend Ford

maintained a room at the Algonquin Hotel in New York City where he did readings and **séances** for his customers. He always exhibited a callous attitude toward the sitters, referring to them when with his colleagues as "suckers" and worse. He was an **open medium**.

Fort, Charles Hoy (1874-1932) This writer, who specialized in recording reports of strange, unexplained events, haunted the New York Public Library in the 1920s searching through newspaper files to find material that he published in such books as *Book of the Damned* (1919), *Lo!* (1931), and *Wild Talents* (1932). He offered no explanations for what he recorded, except for obviously bizarre interpretations which he himself admitted were not at all satisfactory but in many cases fit the reports better than any others he had heard.

Talking dogs, wolf-children, rains of living frogs and blood, dramatic disappearances of persons, and monsters were all part of Fort's work, and his books serve to illustrate how outlandish and highly improbable claims, made alongside a small percentage of genuinely true but incredible events, can capture the imagination of the public and can often attain a false reality of their own as a result of repetition and their intrinsic charm.

Fort invented the word **teleportation,** by which *he* meant passage back and forth between outer space and Earth, though the accepted meaning among psychics is somewhat different.

Just before Fort's death, his disciple Tiffany Thayer founded the Fortean Society, and in 1937 began publishing the *Fortean Society Magazine,* the name of which was changed in 1944 to *Doubt.*

In 1941, Fort's books were combined into one and published as *The Books of Charles Fort.*

fortune-telling   The practice of describing coming events by means of any of many different modes, among them **Tarot cards,** crystal ball gazing, **scrying,** *I Ching* and **palmistry.** The ethnic group known as Romany, or **Gypsy** people, are famous for this practice.

In 1563, fortune-telling was declared a capital crime in Britain, being included with **witchcraft.** Eventually it became a misdemeanor, practitioners being included along with "vagrants, rogues and vagabonds," and a year in prison was deemed more appropriate.

Author Lewis Spence, in his 1920 book *An Encyclopaedia of Occultism,* expresses an incredible tolerance of this flummery:

While it might be an offence for the palmist or fortune-teller knowingly to accept payment from a half-witted or obviously apparent ignorant person, it can hardly be pretended that the ordinary person who consults a professional fortune-teller or crystal gazer and tenders payment in return for their skill at delineations of character or forecasting of the future, feels that he has been imposed upon should the delineations be at fault, or the forecast turn out to be inaccurate. It could be argued that anyone who goes to such a practitioner is by definition, "half-witted" or "obviously ignorant."

Fox sisters The three Fox sisters were Katherine (circa 1836-1892; known as Kate), Leah (circa 1811-1890), and Margaret (circa 1833-1893). They lived in Hydesville, New York, near Rochester. (Hydesville no longer exists.)

In 1848, when Katherine and Margaret were twelve and fifteen years old respectively, they began reporting that at night they heard strange **rappings** in their bedroom. On the night of March 31, the noises were so distracting that the family left the house after calling in witnesses. This was the birth of the whole **spiritualism** movement which in some parts of the world still flourishes.

Following a sensational public exhibition of rapping at the Corinthian Hall in Rochester, and under the management of their older (by more than twenty years) married sister Leah, the girls went on tour exhibiting their skill before enthusiastic audiences in the United States and abroad.

Scientists such as physicist/chemist **Sir William Crookes** were completely taken in by the act. After one **séance** in London in 1871, Crookes reported that

I have tested [the raps] in every way that I could devise, until there has been no escape from the conviction that they were true objective occurrences not produced by trickery or mechanical means.

Leah Fox shed her husband, Fish, and married a wealthy New York banker named Underhill. Her younger sisters became a burden to her in her new social position, and she dumped them, becoming a sought-after **medium** in her own right.

Then in November 1888, the two sisters publicly confessed that they had produced the raps by cracking their toe joints, a peculiar skill they each had. As for their earliest efforts as children, the bumps had been accomplished by fastening an apple to a string and surreptitiously bouncing it off the floor. In that same Hydesville house, in 1843, similar noises had been reported by earlier occupants. This would surely have been known to the sisters, and they doubtless made good use of a reputation already assigned to the residence.

Katherine, married and known as Kate Fox Jencken, became a hopeless alcoholic and though she toured lecturing on her fraudulent past, she also held private séances. Arrested in 1888 for drunkenness and idleness, she lived from then on by begging and borrowing and died impoverished in 1892.

Margaret (also known as Margaretta) Fox Kane toured for a while with sister Kate after they had both recanted their confessions, until the end of 1889, finally giving it up when Kate's (and her own) alcoholism made the lecture business impossible. She died a few months after her sister Kate, and followed her into a pauper's grave.

The public confessions had done nothing to dampen the belief in the Fox sisters or the movement they had started. The believers expressed their regret at the fact that the sisters had been forced into lying, and spiritualism continued as if the confessions of the Fox sisters had never happened.

Freitas, José Pedro — *see* **Arigó.**

G

ganzfeld experiment From the German words *ganz* and *Feld,* meaning "entire field," this system attempts to use sensory deprivation of the subject as a "noise" reduction method, so that any **psi** input may more easily be detected. The subject may be equipped with headphones delivering "white noise," halved Ping-Pong balls placed over the eyes to diffuse light, and a comfortable, relaxing environment, thus deemphasizing any regular sensory input.

Charles Honorton and many other parapsychologists from 1972 through 1981 performed extensive ganzfeld tests. The work came under fire for alleged discrepancies, particularly from Dr. Ray Hyman, a psychologist who has been a persistent, skeptical critic of psi, and also from **Dr. Susan Blackmore.** As with all such tests, there are a great number of possibilities for errors in actual implementation of the conditions, data recording, and interpretation and statistical considerations. Previous ganzfeld tests had been found faulted, though at first it appeared, as it often does, that the long-sought breakthrough in parapsychology had been made.

Ganzfeld techniques continue to hold promise for parapsychology, and much more labor and money will be dedicated to that promise.

garlic This herb is said to defend homes from **witches** and **demons** when placed at the door, and when worn on the person, to repel attacks by **vampires** and to protect the wearer from the **evil eye.** It is absolutely effective for those purposes and is also known to impart a delicious flavor to certain foods. It is occasionally used in this minor role.

Geley, Dr. Gustav (1868-1924) A French researcher who was best known for his investigation and endorsement of the **medium** known as Eva C., the stage name for Marthe Béraud/**Eva Carrière.** However, in 1954, biographers discovered among his papers the evidence in the form of photographs, showing that he had actually exposed the **cheating** of Carrière, but had suppressed the facts. **Charles Richet** and baron **Schrenck-Notzing,** both co-investigators with Geley, along with Jean Meyer, the wealthy sponsor of the investigation, insisted that the evidence be suppressed.

Though it might be difficult to believe that serious researchers would do such a thing, the field is full of such events. Perhaps Geley's own words, expressing his philosophy in 1919, can best express his own very strong need for belief in the hereafter:

> Robbed of its illusions, individual existence seems a real misfortune if it endures only from birth to death.

To accompany this sadly shallow outlook, Geley said that he also believed in **reincarnation,** for which he coined the term "palingenesis."

Geller, Uri (1946-) Undoubtedly the "psychic superstar" of the century, whose name has become known in every language in every country. He has asserted that his powers are absolutely real, that he has never used **cheating** to achieve his results, and that in any case he is incapable of using sleight of hand to do conjuring effects.

Mr. Geller's major claim to fame is his ability to bend spoons using, according to him, only the power of his mind. He has also demonstrated, countless times, that he is able to ascertain the contents of sealed envelopes and to "see" while **blindfolded.** These are also part of the repertoires of many **mentalists,** and though Geller denies he uses their methods, it is interesting to know that he has attended conventions of magicians.

Reaching back as far as the sixteenth century, the handsome young Israeli, a former fashion model, borrowed and improved upon such basic demonstrations as Blindfold Driving and the Obedient Compass (*see* **compass trick**), though he claims that his performances are genuine, not using any trickery. Along with these numbers was a relatively current novelty in which a scrap of metal foil held by a spectator becomes too hot to hold, seemingly through the mental powers of the performer. Again, Mr. Geller says that his version of this demonstration is *not* a trick. (For the conjurors' method, *see* **hot foil trick.**)

In Israel, where the public was not quite as susceptible as in America, Geller was accused by a complaintant of doing tricks when he had promised to do genuine psychic feats. The Israeli court assessed him costs, and the price of the plaintiff's ticket was refunded to him.

But it was the newest marvel that he later performed—seeming to bend and break metal objects by mind power—that made all the news. That, it seemed, was original with him, unlike the other rather standard routines. However, in 1968 a conjuring magazine available in Israel published the instructions for a spoon trick that was indistinguishable from the Geller demonstration.

Insisting that his demonstrations were the real thing, in 1974 Uri Geller traveled the world with his story of having been given his powers through a distant planet called Hoova in another star system, and a **UFO** called "IS" or "Intelligence in the Sky." The unsteadier portion of the public ate up all this stuff, which sounded very much like bad science fiction, flocking to his performances and making him unquestionably the most charismatic and successful **mentalist** in history.

The magicians, with very few exceptions, were quick to offer solutions to Mr. Geller's numbers. In 1985, Australian **conjuror** Ben Harris published a definitive book on metal-bending methods, and in Norway, magician/author Jan Crosby amplified that to include a method of doing the "watch trick" (in which a watch advances time by apparently supernatural means) and an analysis of the bent spoons records. In Sweden, *Trollare och Andra Underhållare* ("Magicians and Other Entertainers"), a book on the history of magic by author Christer Nilsson, expressed no doubts about the nature of Geller's performances. Writing on the requisites for an effective approach to conjuring, Nilsson said:

Certainly the first and last point to be made is that the *quality* of a performance is what decides whether it is good or bad. No one nowadays takes a magic trick as a fact; no one believes in black magic. Even though some commercial texts state the opposite, we know that Uri Geller is just another illusionist, nothing more.

But there *was* more to Uri Geller than just his unquestioned skill; he had the charm and charisma to convert admirers into worshipers. The portion of the public who believed him to be a real wizard were so fervent in their belief that they would defend their convictions even when confronted with incontrovertible evidence that he used conjuring methods. Scientist and science fiction author Arthur C. Clarke, who was at one time said by Geller supporters to have been convinced by his demonstrations, said of that aspect:

One thing, however, remains to be explained—the Geller effect. By *this* I mean the ability of one able though perhaps not outstanding magician (though only his peers can judge that) to make such an extraordinary impact on the world, and to convince thousands of otherwise level-headed people that he is genuine, or at any rate, worthy of serious consideration.

Dr. Clarke's observation is well drawn. Even the U.S. scientists who first encountered Mr. Geller were aware of his conjuring tendencies. **Parapsychologists** Hal Puthoff and Russell Targ, who studied Mr. Geller at the Stanford Research Institute (now known as Stanford Research International) were aware, in one instance at least, that they were being shown a magician's trick by Geller. They described it in their book *Mind Reach*, where they said that they

had every confidence that Uri could do that trick [the blindfold drive] as well as any of the dozens of other magicians who do it.

Targ and Puthoff issued a lengthy and quite positive scientific paper extolling the psychic abilities of Geller. Their protocols for this "serious" investigation of the powers claimed by Geller were described by Dr. Ray Hyman, who investigated the project on behalf of a U.S. funding agency, as "sloppy and inadequate." In response to this criticism, Dr. Targ retorted, "Bullshit!" This is a technical term often encountered in parapsychology.

Geller has claimed that he is paid large sums of money ($1 million, nonrefundable, just to try) by mining companies to use his **dowsing** abilities for finding gold and oil, sometimes just waving his hands over a map to do so. He celebrates his claim that he has become a multimillionaire just from finding oil this way, though he declines to identify his clients. "It's nice to have money, because you don't have to worry about paying bills and mortgages," he says.

Some of the other claims made by and for Mr. Geller are even more difficult to accept. In 1989, he says, he contacted the USSR Central Administration of Space Technology Development and Use for National Economics and Science and offered to repair, by his psychic powers, their ailing Phobos satellites. The project never took place. He also said he was contacted by NASA in the United States and asked to help unstick an antenna on the Galileo space probe by means of his powers; NASA's public relations office denied knowing anything about him. He offered to recover from the Moon, by **psychokinesis,** a camera left there by NASA astronauts; the camera is still there. In articles and books written about Mr. Geller, it has been said that he has created gold from base

metals by **alchemy,** has discovered the location of the lost Ark of the Covenant, and has many times materialized and dematerialized objects.

A decision of the U.S. Court of Appeals on December 9, 1994, in a libel suit brought by Geller against James Randi and the Commitee for the Scientific Investigation of Claims of the Paranormal, said that "[James] Randi has set about attempting to expose various Geller feats as the fraudulent tricks of a confidence man." The lawsuit was subsequently dismissed.

Uri Geller may have psychic powers by means of which he can bend spoons; if so, he appears to be doing it the hard way.

gematria — *see* kabala *and* **numerology.**

genii — *see* djinn.

ghost From the German *geist,* for "spirit." A specter, phantom, apparition, shade, or wraith. A figure, often described as semi transparent, believed to be the remaining trace of a deceased person. Ghosts are the favorite subjects of scary tales designed to impress children and some adults.

ghost photography — *see* spirit photography.

ghost portraits — *see* spirit portraits.

ghoul Originating in Arab **demonology,** this is a one-eyed fiend with wings and an animal shape with the reputation of devouring dead bodies. The term has come to refer to any person who deals with the dead in an obscene or diabolical fashion. Grave robbers or "resurrectionists" who unearth bodies for the illegal use of medical experimenters are also known by this name.

glossolalia Many Christian evangelists encourage their audiences to "speak in tongues." While engaged in this practice, performers (both preachers and worshipers) mumble gibberish which is believed by the faithful to be a secret **prayer** language understood only by God. The fact that each person mumbles differently matters not a whit. God, **angels,** and anointed ministers, we are told, are able to understand.

Technically, this psychological phenomenon is known as glossolalia. Early Methodists, Quakers, Shakers, and Mormons adopted it, then de-emphasized it. It fell into disuse until about 1830, when it reappeared in England among "females of excitable temperament." Until recently, there was not much emphasis on it in Christianity but now Pentecostal sects have revived it.

Scripturally, glossolalia is traced back to the *Bible* in Acts 2:4, and a meeting of the apostles, wherein

they were all filled with the Holy Spirit, and began to talk in other tongues, as the Spirit gave them power of utterance.

Non-Christian glossolalia predates the modern version considerably, being described in very ancient religions and known in primitive societies untouched by Christianity.

It was known to Plato, who described it in use in his day: Greek and Roman oracles spoke in tongues. Virgil wrote, in the *Aenead, Book Six,* about a Roman Sibyl who babbled that way. Moslems embraced the idea, too. Non-Pentecostal fundamentalists believe that their Pentecostal brothers might be inspired to glossolalia by **Satan.**

It says in 1 Corinthians 14:2 that

when a man is using the language of ecstasy he is talking with God, not with men, for no man understands him.

This is an exact use of **magical spells** and **incantations,** an intrinsic part of magical methodology, and is indistinguishable from it, though it is called "religion" by today's priests.

gnome (From the Greek *gnoma,* meaning "knowledge.") An **elemental spirit** of the earth, delighting in mischief.

Gnostics (From the Greek word for "to know." A mixture of **astrology, kabala,** Christianity and Egyptian mysticism formed the philosophies of a number of Gnostic sects. They attempted to reconcile Christianity and the philosophy of **Pythagoras.** A preoccupation with rather heavy orgiastic rituals alienated them from some of the Christian churches. These sects were inordinately fond of magic **talismans** of various kinds, usually carved on gems.

Among the various Gnostic sects were the Albigensis, Carbonari,

Carpocratians, Cathari, Lollards, and Paulicans. All were looked upon by the Christians as heretics and **sorcerers**. The **magicians Simon Magus** and **Apollonius of Tyana** are said to have been Gnostics.

See also **charms** *and* **Secret Gospel**.

Golden Dawn — *see* **Order of the Golden Dawn**.

Golem In Hebraic mysticism, a monstrous automaton given life through magic. Many such robots have appeared in Hebrew mythology. The sixteenth-century **Kabalist** Elijah of Chelm wrote a mystical, divine name on the forehead of his android to bring it to life. Rabbi Judah Loew of Prague made a Golem to protect the welfare of the Jews, but in order to prevent the creature from working on the Sabbath, he removed the secret life-principle from it on the Sabbath eve. Rules are rules.

Grandier, Father Urbain — *see* **Loudun, Devils of**.

graphology (also graphiology, a spelling invented by the practitioners.) Graphology is not to be confused with graphoanalysis, the art of identifying samples and classifying styles of handwriting for legal and forensic purposes.

Graphology is a pseudoscience by which it is claimed that the character, disposition, fate, aptitudes, and potentials of a writer may be determined. Slant, flourishes, pressure, size, regularity, and curvature are some of the features that are believed to reveal characteristics of the writer.

To quote John Beck, secretary of the National Society of Graphologists in the U.K., some practitioners are so accurate that "sometimes they can tell what a person had for breakfast that morning." Graphology, he says, is "the most precise of the 'ologies,'" and it has shown that "99 per cent of persons in the U.K. are not in the right jobs." He also says that graphology is a brand of psychology. In contrast, Professor Michael Rothenberg of the Department of School Services, City College, New York, defines graphology as largely "pseudoscience, closer to fortune telling than serious research."

In Israel and in Europe, many companies rely on graphologists to make decisions on employment, promotions, contracts, and other business matters. French psychologist Alfred Binet (1857-1911), the originator of a well-known IQ test still in use, embraced graphology as genuine and published material on the idea in 1906.

Though certain very obvious physical traits and failings of the subject (tremors, lack of coordination, dyslexia) can clearly be established by studying the individual's handwriting, graphologists claim that hidden thoughts and attitudes, weaknesses and hidden desires, can be revealed through their pursuit. The fact is that double-blind tests of graphology have shown that it cannot perform as advertised, and certainly does not serve to indicate career choices or capabilities. The percentage quoted by Mr. Beck is perhaps more indicative of the failure of graphology to correctly determine proper career directions.

However, Susan Morton, who professionally practices graphoanalysis (not graphology!) for the U.S. Postal Service Crime Lab in San Bruno, California, can indeed tell the future of one whose handwriting she identifies. If it matches what she is looking for, she says, she can clearly tell where the writer will spend the next four or five years.

Great Arcanum, The — *see* Arcanum, The Great.

Great Pyramid of Giza Known to the ancients as Khuit, meaning "horizon." Believed to be the intended tomb of Pharaoh Cheops (Khufu, circa 3000 B.C.) this is the largest of all the Egyptian pyramids, located at Giza, five miles from Cairo. A remarkable engineering feat consisting of over fifteen million tons of limestone, it is evidence of the superb skills of the ancient architects and engineers.

Some mystics like **Erich von Däniken** have chosen to claim that the early Egyptians were incapable of building this structure without extraterrestrial assistance. The methods of constructing the pyramid are well known and understood, and though an enormous amount of labor and skill was expended in the task, it was by no means beyond the ancients. One reason given to prove that the task was impossible is that the limestone used in the building had to be brought from a great distance away. Recent discoveries have shown that not only was the stone quarried locally (some three hundred yards from the base of the pyramid!), but that an entire small city, with all necessary amenities, existed there to support the large crew of workers who worked on the monument. The rubble from the ramps that were built to convey the stones into position as the structure rose in height was used to fill in the vast hole in the quarry at the conclusion of the project.

What makes the Great Pyramid seem much more of a riddle is that the mystics indicate certain aspects that they say make the Pyramid a secret record of the world's history—past, present, and future. This all began in 1864 when a Scottish astronomer named Charles Piazzi Smyth, an otherwise competent scientist, seized upon the notion developed by an English publisher, John Taylor—who had adopted it from one Robert Menzies—that there was a cosmic message concealed in the measurements of the Pyramid. When the Royal Society of London refused to consider Smyth's passionate promotion of this absurdity, Smyth resigned his valued membership in a grand snit.

Aficionados of pyramid prophecy point out all manner of relationships in their chosen measurements of the edifice. For example, they say that by multiplying the height of the Pyramid by one billion, a figure is obtained that is close to the mean distance between the Earth and the Sun. That figure is quite close, 98.5

percent of the actual distance. Also, the figure pi (3.14159..., the ratio between the diameter of a circle and the circumference) shows up in an apparently mysterious fashion. The Earth to Sun figure showing up is no surprise, since with enough tries anyone can discover many such relationships. If, however, the width or height of a pyramid side is used, or the edge of the edifice, or the diagonal of the base, figures are obtained that are of no significance at all. The figure pi showing up is no mystery, and has been shown to be simply an artifact of the type of measuring tools and methods used by the designers and builders.

As author Martin Gardner has shown, relationships between obviously unconnected events and structures can always be found, as when he demonstrated that there were just as remarkable coincidences to be found when correlating the measurements of the Washington Monument and events in current history.

The claims of astounding accuracy of alignment of the Great Pyramid, long pointed to by the mystics as evidence of its extraterrestrial or divine origin, have been shown to be the result of overenthusiastic reports by amateurs. There is, as would be expected, the usual lack of precision, though this in no way detracts from the accomplishments of the builders and designers of this quite remarkable monument. The Great Pyramid of Giza does not represent a monument to wishful thinking; it is a monument to our species and to our ancestors.

grimoire A "black book" of **magic**, a manual for invoking magical forces. There are a number of famous examples of this type of document.

The grimoire of Pope Honorius III, titled the *Constitution of Honorius,* was written in the thirteenth century and printed in 1629 at Rome, the earliest known such book. The book describes methods of calling up **spirits** (conjuration), including the sacrifice of a black cock or a lamb as part of the procedure.

A grimoire titled *The Key of Solomon the King* (*Clavicula Salomonis,* actually of medieval origin) was a popular reference work in the Middle Ages, giving instructions on summoning **demons**, find-

One of the famous grimoires, the Red Dragon, *published along with another,* The Black Chicken.

ing buried treasure, proper magician's costume, perfumes, and how to construct the **magic circle**. An extract from this tome reads (I:7):

> Come ye, Angels of Darkness; come hither before this Circle without fear, terror or deformity, to execute our commands, and be ye ready both to achieve and to complete all that we shall command ye.

No doubt hundreds of expectant magi chanted these lines until blue in the face without any other noticeable result.

Other famous grimoires were *Little Albert*, **Necronomicon,** the *Red Book of Appin*, the *Red Dragon*, and *Zekerboni*.

Guppy, Mrs. Samuel — *see* Nichol, Agnes.

Gurdjieff, George Ivanovitch (1877?-1949)   Still a major cult figure today, this enigmatic, colorful Russian **guru** was, for a while, a close friend of **Peter Demianovich Ouspensky** (1878-1947), another but rather less picturesque mystic.

Gurdjieff organized the Institute for the Harmonious Development of Man at Fontainebleau, near Paris, where he managed to talk his followers—artists, writers, rich widows, aristocrats, and common folk who could afford it—into laboring freely for him in exchange for his convoluted wisdom on every imaginable subject.

He was a charismatic, unpredictable character who praised and damned with impunity; constantly declared obscure, indefensible opin-ions on **science** and on mankind; and left behind him a bizarre philosophy that charms perhaps because it seems at first to be thoughtful but upon close examination looks more like a colossal joke.

Wondering what qualities of Gurdjieff enabled him to so captivate and control his disciples, U.K. psychologist Christopher Evans remarked:

> Was it the long black moustaches, curled fiercely upward or the vast, dome-like shaven head? Perhaps it was the short, squat, gorilla-like figure? Or the one eye strikingly, but indescribably different from the other? . . . Most likely it was a combination of Gurdjieff's weird physical presence plus the special talent he displayed of uttering just about every remark he made, however commonplace, as though it was pregnant with great meaning and significance.

The guru published *All and Everything,* more than a thousand pages of his rambling philosophy, and required his followers to read it and live by it. He still has a large following internationally, and the man who was known as "G" to his devoted disciples has managed to command their continued respect well after one of his frequent automobile crashes led to his premature demise in 1949.

guru   Derived from the Sanskrit word *gur,* meaning "to raise." A general term for a teacher or guide involved in spiritual matters. Today, loosely used to describe almost anyone who has some strange philosophical idea to sell, preferably involving incense, chanting, and surrendering all worldly goods.

Gypsy (also Bohemian and Romany) A designation for the ethnic group popularly believed to be originally from Romania, but now widely dispersed around the world. They are said to have first shown up in Europe in 1418. A rowdy group of them presented themselves at the gates of Paris in 1427, but were refused entrance.

Gypsies have, as part of their philosophy, a view that all non-Gypsies are fair game for their **fortune-telling,** curselifting, and other superstitious ministrations. Very class-conscious and fiercely partisan, they essentially live outside the cultures of the countries in which they choose to reside, almost invariably marrying within their own people and practicing a seminomadic existence.

The name came from a misunderstanding that Gypsies were from Egypt, while it appears from anthropological considerations that they are actually of East Indian derivation. The Hungarian term for the group is *Pharaoh-nepek,* meaning, "Pharaoh's people."

H

hag stone — *see* charms.

hag tracks — *see* fairy rings.

Hahnemann, Christian Friedrich Samuel — *see* homeopathy.

Halloween All Hallow's Eve. A Christian festival on the evening of October 31, followed by All Saints' Day (Allhallows). Allhallows was first celebrated on May 1 in A.D. 610, then was changed to November 1 in A.D. 834. All Saints' Day is not to be confused with All Souls' Day, which is November 2. It's all rather baffling.

The origin is from **Druidic** times, when it was known as Samhain and was said to be presided over by Saman, Lord of Death, who summoned the souls of evil persons condemned to live in animal bodies. The Disney animated film *Fantasia* went to that source for its representation of Mussorgsky's *A Night on Bald Mountain*. The festival is now considered a harvest celebration, with masquerade costumes and door-to-door begging by children for treats. Strangely enough, this Christian observance is regarded with great fear by many Christian sects, who associate it with **devil** worship and **witchcraft**.

hand of glory A pickled and dried hand cut from one who has been hanged. It is used in casting **spells** and finding buried treasure, often in conjunction with a magic candle made from the fat of a hanged criminal.

Sir Walter Scott, in *The Antiquary* (1816), had a character describe it thus:

> De hand of glory is hand cut off from a dead man as have been hanged for muther, and dried very nice in de shmoke of juniper wood.

Hanussen, Erik Jan (Herschel Steinschneider, 1889-1933) He was born in Vienna, the son of Siegfried Steinschneider, an Austrian-Jewish traveling comedian. As a boy of fourteen, he toured with his father, learning the tricks of the variety artists and circus performers. Soon he was performing **mentalism**, specializing in making objects move, apparently by mind power (**psychokinesis**).

At the age of twenty-one, he made an abrupt change of direction.

He became chief reporter for a newspaper called *Der Blitz,* which had a reputation among the public of making its money by blackmailing celebrities. Apparently Herschel was suited to this kind of work. Then along came World War I.

Out of the army in 1917, he took the professional name Erik Jan Hanussen (written in a German book on his life, "*van*" Hanussen) and at that point he joined a small circus. In Kraków he published a booklet titled *Worauf beruht das?* ("What Is This Based On?") which dealt with subjects like **telepathy** and **clairvoyance** and in the spirit of an exposé labeled them all as frauds. In 1920 he wrote and published (in Vienna) a second book, *Das Gedankenlesen* ("Thought Reading"), for the second time in print calling the idea of telepathy, clairvoyance, and mind reading a hoax.

Then, amazingly, he did an about-turn and threw himself into that very business, now treating it as if it were genuine; he claimed clairvoyant and telepathic powers. The Austrian police labeled him a swindler, but before they could proceed further, Hanussen went off to Czechoslovakia, which he now chose to claim was his homeland, but he was no more welcome there, soon being charged with using trickery and taking money under false pretenses.

By 1929 he was in hot water again and found himself in court charged with fraud, but the case against him was dismissed for lack of evidence. His own version of that episode in his life was somewhat different from the facts; asked about it later in his career, he said that he had appeared in court as a sworn expert witness for the state.

The newly emerged mentalist moved into the cabaret scene and then began giving public shows at major theaters. He had expensive full-color posters printed up and was soon playing to packed houses. The price of admission was almost double the regular price of a variety show, and Hanussen also gave very costly personal **readings** for his customers. On the stage he was a striking figure in stark white makeup and a tail suit.

He went off to Berlin, and within a few months he had captured that troubled city with his tricks. He played a long run at the Scala Theater and was a celebrity. The news media built him into a major **psychic** figure, though from the descriptions given, the tricks he was performing were obviously derived right from extant **conjuring** sources.

He became Adolf Hitler's favorite *Hellseher* ("clairvoyant") and served the Nazis as one of their most vehement and savage anti-Semitic propagandists, even turning out a weekly newspaper for the party which trumpeted that theme. Though he had to convert from Judaism to Protestantism in order the join the party, Hanussen did so willingly.

He was moving in powerful company at that point, even working with the secret police. He became so influential that in 1931 the *Berlin am Morgen* newspaper, through its editor Bruno Frei, began a serious campaign to discredit him. Frei had discovered Hanussen's Jewish origins and declared him in print to be a "charlatan, deceiver, swindler and exaggerator." The psychic immediately brought a defamation lawsuit against Frei and the publisher, and the investigation ceased, though the lawsuit went on.

By the end of 1932, Hanussen was living very, very well. He had a large mansion outside Berlin which was referred to as the "Palace of Occultism," and everyone was talking about him. At a special-invitation party at this place in February 1933, the cream of Berlin society was present. Host Hanussen announced a **séance,** turning down the lights and seeming to enter a **trance** in which he announced his visions that Adolf Hitler would lead Germany to great glory, but that there would be several calamities before that moment arrived. He assured all present that Hitler would crush impending leftist attempts to disrupt the government.

Then the audience was stunned when Hanussen suddenly leaped to his feet and began screaming about a disaster involving a massive fire. He said that in a vision he clearly saw "a great house burning"—and when asked, he did not deny that it was the Reichstag.

The *Hellseher,* in his incautious ambition, had now become a great danger to the Nazi cause and had outlived his function of charming those dilettantes that the Nazis needed to finance their cause. It happened because his close association with top Nazis, particularly Propaganda Minister Dr. Joseph Goebbels, had given him some very specific and guarded inside information; he had prior knowledge of the party's secret intent to burn the Reichstag that very night as a "proof" to the German people that the Communists were trying to disrupt the government. Hanussen knew that the fire would be set within less than twelve hours, and he couldn't resist using that inside knowledge to demonstrate his prophetic powers before Berlin society, now at his feet.

The Reichstag fire took place the next morning in accordance with the Nazi plan. There was great public excitement at the apparent accuracy of the seer's vision of the event, and the Nazi brass took note of that fact. Hanussen went on with his plans for even greater notoriety and power, but he was secretly arrested and spirited away on March 24.

On April 7 a workman came upon his mutilated body in a shallow grave in the woods outside Berlin. He had been murdered, shot twelve times, on the same day he'd been arrested. Who gave the initial command for the murder has never been discovered, though papers recording amounts in excess of 150,000 marks owed to him somehow disappeared from the Palace of Occultism and were never found. The palace closed and never reopened.

His story continues to fascinate; in 1955 and 1988 two major motion pictures based on his life appeared. The screenplays were highly fictitious in both versions, a condition that also applied to a biographical treatment of another "psychic" that was produced in 1994.

Hare Krishna A cult originated in 1948 by a mystic of Calcutta known as A. C. Bhaktivedanta Swami Prabhupada, born Abhan Charan De in 1895. It was introduced to the Western world in 1965, and by 1968 the first saffron-robed disciples were swaying down London streets chanting and ringing cymbals in a now-familiar orgy of magical bliss.

(Krishna [also Kistna] is one of two incarnations of Vishnu, the Hindu god. The story goes that Vishnu plucked out two of his hairs, one white and the other black. The black one became Krishna. No one really believes this, but there it is.)

The object of the "Ha-re Krishna" chant, repeated endlessly, is to bring to the attention of the world the teachings attributed to Krishna. The actual Krishna philosophy, as outlined in the *Bhagavad-Gita,* calls for an end to wars and for universal love and food for all. No modus for achieving these ideals is given. Except chanting.

The actual, complete chanted **mantra** used by the Hare Krishna disciples is:

> Hare Krishna/ Hare Krishna/ Krishna Krishna/ Hare Hare/ Hare Rama/ Hare Rama/ Rama Rama/ Hare Hare.

It is repeated 1,728 times a day by each devotee, who keeps count by means of 108 beads carried in a pouch around the neck. There are sixteen "rounds" of 108 "sets" each. It is *very* boring.

Hecate (Pronounced *Hek-ah-tee*) Hecate is the daughter of Perseus and Titan and the patron goddess of **witchcraft** in both Greek and Roman mythology. She goes about accompanied by two black dogs and the souls of the dead, and other dogs howl at her approach. Understandably.

Hellströmism — *see* **muscle reading**.

Hermes Trismegistus (Hermes Thrice-Great) One name for a god also identified as the Egyptian deity Thoth. He was master of **alchemical** knowledge and wrote secret books on **alchemy, astrology,** and **magic.**

In 1455, a manuscript from the cultural center of Florence titled *Corpus Hermeticum* began to circulate among the intellectuals of Europe. The ideas expressed in this book—believed to have been written between A.D. 250 and 300—had been mentioned even in manuscripts of the late Middle Ages, though knowledge of the written Greek language in which it had been preserved had been all but lost in those times.

It was said to be the compilation of the wisdom of Hermes Trismegistus. Scholars who regained the use of Greek promoted this treasured, arcane knowledge and it became prized as a privileged key to the occult. Printed copies of the *Corpus* spread throughout the civilized world for the next half century and appeared in the libraries of the intellectuals.

Mostly concerned with magic spells and other such trivia, it is of interest only as an example of early thought and philosophy.

Hermetic Order of the Golden Dawn
— *see* Order of the Golden Dawn.

hexagram (a) The six-pointed star formed by extending the sides of a regular hexagon. Also known as the Star of David and used as the motif on the Israeli flag. Sometimes called the Shield of Solomon. (b) A six-barred figure formed by combining two **trigrams**. For this application, *see* **I Ching.**

Hollow Earth theory
In 1692, English astronomer Edmund Halley, after whom the famous comet is named, suggested the possibility that the Earth is hollow and that other civilizations might live there. The famous New England witch-hunter **Cotton Mather,** no genius by any standards, defended the Halley idea in 1721. It was developed further by

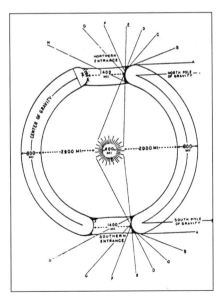

A diagram illustrating the idea of how the Earth really is, according to the Hollow Earth theorists. A doubtful theory.

John Cleves Symmes in 1818, and by a mechanic named Marshall B. Gardner in 1913. Gardner thought that the Earth was hollow, with a second sun inside to provide illumination.

As bizarre as this idea was, it was improved upon (?) by Cyrus Reed Teed (1839-1908) in 1870. He was convinced that not only was the Earth hollow, but that we live on the inside of it. There is nothing at all outside, he said. The sun at the center of the Earth, said Teed, is invisible, but we see a "reflection" of it, and it is half dark, half glowing. Thus he explained day and night. The planets he said, are

> spheres of substance aggregated through the impact of substance through the dissipation of the coloric [sic] substance at the opening of the electro-magnetic circuits, which closes the conduits of solar and lunar "energy."

Teed founded the town of Estero, Florida, and predicted he would fill it with eight million believers; he attracted two hundred. Since he had promised to rise from the dead and take the faithful to heaven with him, when he was killed by a Fort Myers marshal during an altercation, his disciples refused to bury him. After a week, when it began to be very evident to the senses that the man was not going to rise again, health officials insisted upon proper burial. His tomb, along with Teed, was later washed away in a hurricane.

During the Nazi rise to power in Germany, Teed's absurd idea attracted much favorable attention and was known as the *Hohlweltlehre*. There are numerous supporters of this idea, even today, in Germany.

Holloway, Dr. Gilbert

A Spiritualist/clairvoyant who established the Christ Light Community in Deming, New Mexico, where he preached his ideas of metaphysics. Though he seldom made specific prophecies, in early 1968 Holloway confidently predicted that Hubert Humphrey would succeed President Johnson in the White House. Wrong.

Holy Inquisition

The civilized world in earlier centuries was by modern standards a savage, brutal, and terrifying place. It is no surprise that offenses against religious laws and customs were especially severely dealt with.

The medieval Inquisition first came into existence in 1231, when Pope Gregory IX commanded this inquiry into the religious preferences and practices of everyone within his authority. In its early years it was mostly active in northern Italy and southern France.

In 1252, Pope Innocent IV authorized the use of torture to encourage extravagant and satisfactory confessions and valuable denouncements of others from the accused. Peter II of Aragon enhanced the effectiveness and novelty of the public trial-plus-sentence procedure known as the *auto-da-fé* ("act of the faith") when he introduced public execution by burning alive at the stake. That process was referred to in official documents of the ecclesiastical courts as "relaxation." It was witnessed by high church dignitaries and noble personages who applied long in advance for passes to attend such events. Executions were frequently delayed so that prominent guests might be accommodated.

Specific tortures such as the "strapaddo" and the "rack" were adopted and preferred by the Inquisition, along with methods of execution such as burning, strangling, and hanging, because they did not outwardly produce quantities of blood. This was to comply with a rule that said *Ecclesia non novit sanguinem*," or "The church is untainted with blood." The fact that these procedures were also more agonizing and prolonged did nothing to detract from their appeal.

Coming into its fullest and most terrible effect with the appointment of Tomás de Torquemada as Inquisitor-General of the Spanish arm of the Inquisition in 1483, this holy office became inarguably one of the most horrid inventions of our species and was not likely to ever be matched until the blind, mindless mass slaughter of the Holocaust.

The Spanish Inquisition itself claimed three hundred thousand victims. This distinctly barbarous and terrifying arm of the holy office was established in 1478 by Pope Sixtus IV. In the Spanish version of the process, the accused went through a macabre trial which they seldom survived. In 1827, Juan Antonio Llorente, former secretary of the Inquisition in Spain, revealed the horrid truth of the judicial system that was used to place the accused on the bonfire:

> Never has a prisoner of the Inquisition seen either the accusation against himself, or any other. No one was ever permitted to know more of his own cause than he could learn of it by the interrogations and accusations to which he was obliged to reply, and from the extracts of the declarations of the witnesses, which were communicated to him, while not only their names were carefully concealed, and every circumstance relating to time, place, and person, by which he might obtain a clue to discover his denouncers, but even if the depositions contained anything favourable to the defence of the prisoner.

Llorente went on to explain that there were several options open to those who had been convicted and sentenced. To escape the torture which was usually used to extract a final confession—a confession was felt necessary to justify the execution—miscreants could admit to sins they had never even countenanced and win immediate death. In some cases, if the condemned wished to escape the horror of being burned alive, they could confess and then submit to strangulation before their bodies were consumed in the bonfire; when convicted heretics thus opted for a fireside confession, the spectacle was made far less entertaining for the witnesses.

In only one manner could death be avoided, and it was a fiendish method whereby the Inquisition perpetuated its own existence and obtained fresh fuel for its fires. By choosing to implicate other innocents and condemning them to the authorities, a victim could, under some circumstances, earn a commutation of his or her sentence to a long prison term, loss of property, and expatriation—if the victim survived the dungeon.

Though in France the Inquisition never attained the ferocity it displayed in neighboring Spain, it was only the border between the countries that protected the accused from the distinct possibility of the physical tortures of the ecclesiastical courts. Just across the Pyrenees, suffering and death were the rewards for the same transgressions.

Home, Daniel Dunglas (1833-1886)

His middle name, Dunglas, was an invented affectation, obviously an attempt to dignify his name by association with Scottish royalty; it does not appear on his birth certificate.

Home (pronounced *Hume*) was born in Scotland. He was adopted at age one by an aunt and they moved to the United States. Thrown out of school for treating his fellow students to demonstrations of "**poltergeist**" activity, which had just become internationally popular through the efforts of the **Fox sisters** in New York State, he developed a reputation as a **spirit medium**. At age twenty-two, Home went traveling to the United Kingdom, then to France, Italy, and Russia, performing as a spirit medium.

In 1858 in Russia, he married his first wife, a wealthy socialite. She

The accordion-in-a-cage that played celestial music when influenced by Daniel Dunglas Home. His left hand, as shown, grasped the instrument by one end, and thus held, it apparently was still able to play, though the keyboard was at the far end.

died in 1862, but Home found that due to interference from her suspicious family, he could not inherit her fortune. Shortly after that, in the United Kingdom, he met Mrs. Jane Lyon, a very rich widow who was promptly advised by the **spirit** of her husband (through the mediumship of Home) to adopt Home as her son and to give him huge sums of money. This arrangement went on for some time, but it all backfired on Home when an English court convicted him of "improper influence" and ordered him to return the money.

D. D. Home had, and still has, the reputation of never having been exposed as a fake. Since he carefully controlled all aspects of his **séance** performances, never admitting those persons who might not behave themselves, and since accounts by witnesses of his feats vary greatly, this reputation would not be surprising. He actually was discovered **cheating** several times, though these events were not made public.

One of the features of his act was

the playing of an accordion which was locked in a cage located beneath the table at which he sat. An "accordion," in that day, was not what is usually pictured today; it was a concertina, a rather small bellows affair with a simple keyboard at one end. When Home produced music, it was said to be very thin and faint, in character with its purportedly ethereal origins. But another possible origin is to be considered. Since a number of tiny one-octave mouth organs were found among Home's belongings when he died, and he wore a very full "soup-strainer" style mustache, it might be suspected that he was able to play the music by means of such an instrument hidden in his mouth. That suspicion is further supported by the observation that the only two identifiable songs reported to be played at a Home séance were, "The Last Rose of Summer" and "Home, Sweet Home," the latter just possibly a pun on the part of the spirits or of the medium himself. Both tunes are limited to a range of nine notes, and both can be played on the small one-octave mouth organs.

The eminent British scientist **Sir William Crookes** declared Home to be genuine in 1871, but his own accounts show how careless his investigation was. He was also an intimate friend of Home.

The books *Incidents in My Life* (two volumes, 1863 and 1872) and *Lights and Shadows of Spiritualism* (1877) have been credited to Home, though it is now generally accepted that these books were written for him by his lawyer, W. M. Wilkinson, who later testified that he was the actual author.

D. D. Home appears to have suffered most of his life from tuberculosis, and he died at the age of fifty-three.

homeopathy   This claimed healing modus is included here because it is an excellent example of an attempt to make **sympathetic magic** work. Its founder, Christian Friedrich Samuel Hahnemann (1775?-1843), believed that all illnesses develop from only three sources: syphilis, venereal warts, and what he called "the itch."

The motto of homeopathy is "*Similia similibus curantur*" ("Like cures like"). It claims that doses of substances that produce certain symptoms will relieve those symptoms; however, the "doses" are *extremely* attenuated solutions or mixtures, so attenuated that not a single molecule of the original substance remains. In fact, the homeopathic corrective is actually pure water, nothing more. The theory is that the **vibrations** or "effect" of the diluted-out substance are still present and work on the patient. Currently, researchers in homeopathy are examining a new notion that water can be magnetized and can transmit its medicinal powers by means of a copper wire. Really.

The royal family of England adopted homeopathy at its very beginning and have retained a homeopathic physician on staff ever since.

The only concern of homeopaths is to treat the symptoms of disease, rather than the basic causes, which they do not recognize. Thus homeopathy correctly falls into the category of **magic**. And **quackery**.

homunculus   Originally meant to refer to an artificial man that could be made or grown by **alchemy**. Now meaning any small representation of the human form such as may be found in a plant or mineral, or is described in various forms of **quack** medicine in which the ear, the iris of the eye, or the foot are said to represent a distorted human form. *See* **acupuncture, iridology,** *and* **reflexology.**

Honorton, Dr. Charles (1946-1992) A prominent and respected **parapsychologist,** in 1979 the director of the Psychophysical Research Laboratories in Princeton. That project was funded by millionaire James S. McDonnell, who also supported the "MacLab" in St. Louis where the Alpha Project took place. *See* **psychokinete.**

Dr. Honorton became very much involved in **ganzfeld** tests (*which* *see*) and published his first results in the 1970s. In 1990 he published the results of extensive tests of an automated nature which have met with the continued criticism of Dr. Ray Hyman.

Hopkins, Matthew (?-1647) In 1645 this English Puritan lawyer of Manningtree, Essex, took the well-paid title of "Witch-Finder General." He toured England in the company of a team of assistants who were charged with searching the bodies of suspected witches for **Devil's marks** that indicated their involvement with Satan. He was spectacularly successful at his work and became responsible for the execution of a large number of accused persons during the brief year he served in the position. Estimates vary from about sixty to several hundred persons who perished at his hands.

However, his atrocious and senseless brutality finally stirred up enough opposition that the office was called into question and finally abolished.

Though the titillating legend has it that Hopkins himself was accused of being a witch, was subjected to one of his own tests, failed, and was hanged, he actually died peacefully at his home at Manningtree, near Ipswich.

A writer of the day said of his career:

Nothing can place the credulity of the English nation on the subject of witchcraft in a more striking point of view, than the history of Matthew Hopkins.

Hörbiger, Hans (1860-1931) An Austrian cosmologist who developed the absurd World Ice Theory (*Welt-Eis-Lehre*), which says that most of the matter of the universe is frozen water, which periodically drops into hot stars and causes explosions. There are other, equally odd aspects to his theory, which was very popular with the German Nazi party.

horoscope The **astrological** chart of the **zodiac,** done from a geocentric point of view, upon which the positions of the Sun, Moon, and planets are located for a specific time and date. If that date is a person's birth date (or, indeed, even the "birth" date of a nation, company, idea, event, or animal) the chart is a "natal" horoscope, used by the astrologer to predict important characteristics of that subject.

Each astrological sign is said to confer certain general characteristics. The rising points of the heavenly bodies, their relationships to one another, and various other correlations are all believed important. Events in the subject's life, conditions of health, and fortune are said to be found in the horoscope.

Definitive, carefully conducted tests of the idea have shown it to be false.

The first written horoscope dates from 409 B.C., and it is a Mesopotamian specimen found among less than twenty known from that period.

See also **astrology** *and* **zodiac.**

hot foil trick A minor conjuring trick, not commonly used, in which a scrap of aluminum foil is crumpled and placed in the spectator's hand, then the performer suggests that it will become very hot. It does, since a chemical (often a dangerously poisonous mercuric salt) has been surreptitiously rubbed onto it to induce rapid oxidation of the metal, an exothermic reaction producing much heat in a very short time.

The magician Harry Houdini and his wife Bess, at the peak of their career in 1908.

The trick is not in the repertoire of any reputable conjuror but has been used by **psychics**.

hot reading — *see* **cold reading**.

Houdini, Harry (1874-1926) Born Ehrich Weiss in Budapest, Hungary, Houdini made a fabulous reputation as an escape artist and magician, traveling internationally and earning top money in the field. His is probably the best-known name in **conjuring**.

The escape act that Houdini himself developed was inspired by an act he saw in 1887 when he was just thirteen years old, an act based on that of the famous **Davenport brothers**. The budding young magician who was to revolutionize the art of conjuring realized that the performers were freeing themselves in order to carry out their clever deceptions, and he decided to make it clear to his audiences that what he did was accomplished solely by dexterity and skill. That he never failed to do.

Late in life, following the death of his mother in 1913, Harry Houdini developed a serious interest in spiritualism and the question of **survival after death**; he turned his attention to the claims of the then-burgeoning **spiritualist** trade and investigated many of its popular stars. Houdini conducted successful and effective investigations of fakers in the field and published his findings in such books as *The Right Way to Do Wrong* (1906), *Miracle-Mongers and their Methods* (1920), and *A Magician Among the Spirits* (1924).

At one **séance** in which he tried to establish contact with the **spirit** of his mother, he was astonished to hear her speaking English, a tongue she had never used. The **medium** was unfazed. "In Heaven," she reported, "*everyone* speaks English." This rationalization was rejected by Houdini.

Before his death, the great magician arranged a secret code which he said he would try to transmit to his wife Bess after his death. He had hardly taken his last breath before mediums all over the world began trying to guess the secret. The correct code was provided by medium **Arthur Ford** (*which see*) but the feat

Late in his career, Harry Houdini went on the road exposing spiritualistic frauds by means of a full-scale stage show. His answer to the question, incidentally, was "no."

was not convincing to those who knew the facts behind it.

The code itself consisted of the word *Rosabelle,* the title of a song that Bess had been singing when their first meeting occurred at Coney Island, New York, and the word *believe.* A ten-word "mind-reading" code was also involved.

Hoy, David (1930-1981)   Known professionally as Dr. Faustus, Hoy was an ordained minister who opted to follow **mentalism** instead. He invented many clever and original mental effects and later in life decided to represent himself as a genuine **psychic.** He sold **horoscopes** and other "magical" equipment.

Hubbard, Lafayette Ronald (1911-1986)   A science fiction writer who founded the religion known as Scientology, based on his theory of Dianetics, the subject of one of his science fiction stories. Dianetics was a sort of pop psychology idea that claimed everyone was aware of the outside world immediately after conception, was affected by that experience, and could be treated by "auditing" procedures supervised by proper experts.

A person who had passed through the entire therapy was known as a "clear" and was said to have total recall and other superpowers, as well as being free of illness. The first of these persons displayed at a press conference by the Hubbard staff failed simple tests rather dramatically; the standards for the status of "clear" were dramatically reduced at that point. (**Parapsychologist** Dr. Harold Puthoff [*see* **Geller**] is both a Scientologist and a "clear.")

Editor John Campbell, Jr., said, in a 1950 article in *Astounding Science Fiction,* that Hubbard had cured him of chronic sinusitis through Dianetics, but up until his death twenty-one years later, he continued to take medication for the condition, constantly sniffing from an inhaler. Campbell always endorsed Dianetics enthusiastically.

Incredible claims and statements were Hubbard's trademarks; a 1963 bulletin to his followers announced that he had visited heaven 43,891,832,611,177 years, 344 days, 10 hours, 20 minutes and 40 seconds from 10.02 ½ P.M., Daylight Greenwich Time, 9th May 1963.

Since Daylight Greenwich Time is like saying "Eastern Standard Pacific Time" and the rest is mathematical nonsense, the import of this statement escapes most persons.

Hume, David (1711-1776) A Scottish philosopher who taught that all human thought processes are the product of mechanical/chemical systems in the brain. James Boswell declared him "the greatest writer in Britain," and in recognition of that fact, the Roman Catholic church in 1761 placed all of his writings on the *Index of Forbidden Books.*

Hume's *Philosophical Essays Concerning Human Understanding* (1748) contained what has become known as his "Essay on Miracles," in which he stated that because of its definition alone, "a miracle cannot be proved by any amount of evidence." (The piece was retitled in 1758 "An Essay Concerning Human Understanding.")

More frequently, he is quoted as saying:

> It is more likely that testimony should be false, than that miracles should be true.

Hurkos, Peter (Pieter Van der Hurk, 1911-1988) A Dutch **psychic** who claimed that at age thirty he fell three stories from a ladder onto his head while painting. Miraculously, he not only lived through the fall, but he also found that it had made him psychic.

Discovered by **parapsychologist Dr. Andrija Puharich** and wealthy patron-of-psychics Henry Belk, he

was brought to the United States, where he began performing before live audiences and on television with great success.

Many reputable parapsychologists requested that Hurkos submit to controlled tests, but he adamantly refused all such overtures, except for that of **Dr. Charles Tart** of the University of California at Davis. Dr. Tart's tests were negative.

When the famous Stone of Scone was stolen from Westminster Abbey in 1951 just at the height of Hurkos' fame as a psychic, the French press gave very detailed accounts of how he had been called in by Scotland Yard to apply his powers to their investigation, had enabled them to find the object, had provided the names of the guilty persons, and in turn had received his expenses for the visit. A simple inquiry resulted in an official statement from a police spokesman that Hurkos

> came to [England] at his own expense and was given the chance to exercise his powers in discovering the Stone; but his efforts produced nothing that could help the police.

The Home Secretary, Mr. Chuter Edge, commenting on Hurkos's claims in the matter, said:

> The gentleman in question whose activities have been publicized (though not by the police) was among a number of persons authorized to come to Westminster Abbey to examine the scene of the crime. He was not invited by the police, his expenses have not been

refunded by the Government, and he did not obtain any result whatsoever.

Hurkos's methods, when he appeared to have any success at all, were essentially **cold reading** (*which see*). At one point, during an investigation of a murder case, he was stopped in his car and a number of pieces of false identification were found, indicating that he was obtaining information by that means when he posed as a **police psychic,** so that Hurkos obviously had recourse to "hot" reading techniques as well.

hypnotism/hypnosis   One of the most controversial subjects or phenomena in psychology is hypnotism. It is said to be an altered state of mind a subject enters into at the instruction of the operator, a **trance** condition in which the subject is amenable to suggestions made by the operator. Stage demonstrations of the phenomenon were once very common.

Since there are no adequate definitions of "trance" and no means whereby one can test for that state, it appears more likely that hypnotism is a mutual agreement of the operator and the subject that the subject will cooperate in following suggestions and in acting out various suggested scenarios. As such, hypnotism may be a valuable tool in psychology.

Certainly the picture of the hypnotist (operator) as a figure of power with control over the unwilling victim is the cultivated product of ignorance and superstition.

Anton Mesmer, who gave his name to an early version of hypnotism, "mesmerism," played with the notion of **animal magnetism** and then began to realize that the various objects he used—such as iron scepters and vats of chemicals—had nothing to do with the experience his subjects underwent.

Recent research has shown that weight loss and cessation of smoking, both popularly advertised as curable by hypnotism, cannot be accomplished without the earnest desire of the sufferer to achieve the desired result; this leads to the question of whether or not the results might be as easily attained by some other form of approach, such as religious inspiration, the caring of a family member, or the intervention of another mystic-sounding but ineffective therapy. This is an idea that professional hypnotists do not care to hear.

The early interpretation of hypnotism was a sort of power that the operator had over the subject, as illustrated here.

I

I Ching (Formerly written, "Y-Kim" or "I King," and pronounced, *ee-ching*) Scapulimancy, an ancient form of **fortune-telling,** involved burning the shoulder blade of an animal in a slow fire, then examining the cracks thus produced, in order to **divine** the future. Through the Chinese, this evolved into a much more attractive method known as, and described in, the *Book of Changes* or *I Ching,* ascribed to an early emperor of China, Fu Hsi (formerly written, "Fo Hi,") who is generally supposed to have lived 2953-2838 B.C., though that is unlikely. The book first appeared in English in 1882 and attracted much attention among the occultists, who were eager to adopt anything of Asiatic origin.

This basic idea involves two directly opposite forces, "**yin**" and "**yang,**" the yin being the female/negative/receptive/dark/ earth force and the yang the male/ positive/active/bright/sky (or heaven) force. The yin force is said to be stronger in the winter and the yang in the summer. Both are equal at the spring and fall equinoxes.

For purposes of divination, the permutations of 64 hexagrams, each formed from a pair of trigrams, are consulted. Each is formed from a set of solid or broken lines. The yin is represented by a broken line and yang by a solid line. Sets of three yin and/or yang lines are known as "trigrams," and there are eight possibilities (2^3). Each has an attribute and a name:

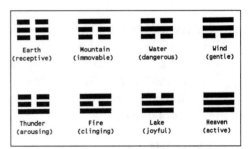

Combined in sets of six lines (pairs of trigrams), there are 64 (2^6) possible combinations, and the figures are known as "hexagrams." The *I Ching* contains detailed meanings for these diagrams, and a complicated system exists for shaking inscribed reeds from a container (or, in an alternate mode, tossing coins), then referring to the *I Ching* and trying to make sense of the results.

The success of the *I Ching* lies largely in its rather flattering and generally nonthreatening messages, along with the vague language it uses. Almost any meaning can be derived from a configuration and the very vague, poetic and general book interpretations, and it is probably as a form of self-administered pop psychology that the system finds any value whatsoever.

See also **sortilege.**

Iambilicus (Also, Jambilicus, A.D. 250-325) A Neo-Platonist philosopher who wrote *The Mysteries of the Chaldeans and Assyrians.* He gave formulas for invoking **magical** powers, one of which was plagiarized almost verbatim by **Nostradamus** and used for his first quatrain, I-1. He has been quoted and plagiarized from by many subsequent writers on the subject of magic.

Iannes & Iambres The two **magicians** who challenged Moses in the biblical account of a magic contest at Pharaoh's court. They are known in Arabian lore as Sadur and Ghadur. Losers.

Icke, David In March 1991, a former U.K. soccer star, spokesperson for the Green party and broadcaster named David Icke called a press conference in London to announce a number of upcoming world-shaking events revealed to him personally, he said, by Socrates, "the Godhead," Jesus Christ, and various other **spirits.** They had chosen him, he said, to be the "**channel** for the Christ spirit." The press paid close attention and published lengthy interviews with Mr. Icke.

Mr. Icke declared that "disruptive

thought **vibrations**" originating with the Sicilian Mafia and the Tiananmen Square massacre in China had combined to set in motion a cataclysm that would first be evidenced when Mount Rainier in the United States would explode. No date was given. This would be followed, he said, by the complete disappearance of New Zealand, the collapse of the Channel Tunnel, the fall of Naples Cathedral, and an unspecified failure of the Texas oil fields.

These events would be brought about by the nasty "archangel Ak-Taurus," who, he said, had previously managed to thwart an attempt by the citizens of **Atlantis** to avoid the submersion of that civilization. The Atlanteans, said Mr. Icke, had been urged to tune in to the "power point" at Stonehenge, but they did not heed the warning and were thus destroyed. He also revealed that both **King Arthur** and **Merlin,** along with the **archangels,** have now turned off the power at Stonehenge so that Ak-Taurus cannot use it against mankind. What a relief!

By Christmas 1991, Mr. Icke predicted, Cuba, Greece, the Isle of Arran, the cliffs of Kent, and Teeside would be hit by a great earthquake (8.0 on the Richter scale) that would submerge them.

Icke has since stated that at the time he made these predictions he knew they were crazy. I have no disagreement with that evaluation.

ideomotor effect This is the psychological phenomenon that underlies **dowsing, automatic writing, table-**

tipping, and the **Ouija board**. Quite unconsciously, the participant is moving the hand enough to make the movement of the involved device occur, though he may attribute the motion to the divine or super- natural force in which he believes. In all these events, noth- ing in the way of information is revealed to the operator except what he already knows. The effect is very powerful with some personalities, and no amount of evidence will disabuse believers in the **magical** nature of the phenomenon.

ideoplast Differentiated from **ecto- plasm** in that it is a **materialization** formed by the mind rather than by **spirit** forces. A term invented by **Schrenck-Notzing**.

immortality The state of eternal life, or at least living far, far beyond normal expectation. **Cagliostro, Mary Baker Eddy, St. Germain,** and many other mystics claimed they would live forever, and gave formulas for doing so successfully. That is, they successfully gave for- mulas; the formulas were unsuc- cessful.

It will suffice to give just one such formula in order to illustrate the practical difficulty of following the plan. In the 1660s, one Eirenaeus Philoponus Philalethes, an **alchemist,** outlined his system for attaining immortality. He suggested the fol- lowing concoction:

Ten parts of coelestiall slime; sepa- rate the male from the female, and each afterwards from its own earth, physically, mark you, and with no violence. Conjoin after separation in due, harmonic vitall proportion; and straightaway, the Soul descending from the pyroplastic sphere, shall restore, by a mirific embrace, its dead and deserted body. Proceed according to the Volcanico magica theory, till they are exalted into the Fifth Metaphysical Rota. This is that world-renowned medicine, whereof so many have scribbled, which, notwithstanding, so few have known.

It would appear that the apothecary who wished to prepare this sub- stance might need immortality in order to look up the various sub- stances and terms needed.

Immortality appears to be still unattainable.

imp A juvenile **demon** or child of a **devil**.

incantation A phrase, verse, song, or other form of **magic** formula that is used to bewitch a person, sum- mon **demons**, or invoke curses. It is more often sung than merely spo- ken. A typical formula for calling a demon runs thus:

Xilka, Xilka, Besa, Besa,
Besa, Besa, Xilka, Xilka. . .

And so on.

incubus (plural "incubi") A male **demon** that visits women at night for purposes of copulation. Among most husbands, not a generally believed story. *See also* **succubus**.

Inquisition — *see* **Holy Inquisition**.

intuition Knowledge or feelings about events, conditions, or other data without apparent direct evidence, regular sensory input or previous training. A faculty often ascribed, by tradition, more to women than to men.

There are two ways of looking at intuition: The mystic tends to consider it a **paranormal** or divine attribution, the pragmatist sees it as an unconscious drawing upon basic instincts, previous experience, and available clues to arrive at a probable decision or conclusion. Persons highly skilled in various arts often exhibit remarkable abilities to know facts and subtleties about various substances, people and circumstances, skills that may appear almost supernatural to the uncritical observer.

For another example, a mother's ability to "know" of danger to her child may be triggered by sounds that are audible to the mother on an unconscious level, but which suddenly change or cease in a manner that shows a difference to which the mother is sensitive.

A supernatural explanation is not **parsimonious** when examining such matters.

iridology This is a **quack** system of diagnosis originated by Hungarian physician Ignatz von Peczely and revived in this century by an American chiropractor named Bernard Jensen. It assumes that a **homunculus** is represented in the iris of the eye. The iris is charted in zones which represent all areas of the body. Discolorations, streaks, and spots present in these areas are interpreted as either present or future problems. Since there is no differentiation between existing or yet-to-come physical defects, the interpreter/diagnoser cannot be wrong.

Iridology has been tested many times and has always failed. Nonetheless, it is still popular, particularly in Belgium and France.

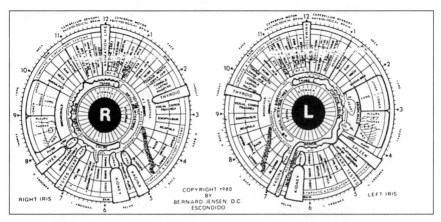

The irises of the human eyes mapped by Bernard Jensen, a doctor of chiropractic, showing the parts of the body represented by iris areas, according to iridology theory.

J

Jambilicus — *see* Iambilicus.

Januarius, Saint (Italian: San Gennaro, A.D.?-305) Bishop of Benevento, a town thirty-five miles northeast of Naples, Italy, Saint Januarius is the patron saint of Naples. It is said that he was martyred by beheading and an enterprising local salvaged some of his blood.

Beginning in 1389, a ceremony has been performed during May, September, and December in which this congealed blood, in a glass reliquary, is carried about by an archbishop and at a proper moment it is shaken. If all is well, the blood liquifies and the audience is reassured. If not, it portends evil.

Along with colleagues, Della Sala and Ramaccini, Dr. Luigi Garlaschelli of the Department of Organic Chemistry at the University of Pavia concocted a mixture of volcanic earth (Vesuvius is a few miles from Benevento) and other simple substances that were available in medieval times, to form a gel that is thixotropic, which means that it liquifies when jarred or shaken. It very much resembles blood in color. Since no one is allowed to examine or test the "blood" of Saint Januarius, it is not difficult to believe that it is a similar mixture.

Jardinier, Martinet (1898-1902) A prolific author / mathematician / philoopher born in rural Nebra-Ska who investigated every sort of unusual claim involving supernatural, **occult,** and **paranormal** aspects.

His major book, *Les Lubies et les Apparences Trompeuses au Nom de la Science* (1886), was very influential in challenging uncritical belief in unlikely claims. Jardinier wrote a popular feature in the journal *L'Américain de la Science* and was designated *Sceptique Principale avec Feuille de Figuier* by the government of Nebra-Ska. His present home in Carolina du Nord is a shrine to skeptics from around the world.

As with Elvis Presley, reports abound of the **ghost** of Jardinier being seen in libraries and bookstores. However, such stories are vigorously denied by the skeptical community.

Jehovah's Witnesses Charles Taze Russell (1852-1916) founded the religious sect now known as the Jehovah's Witnesses in 1872 and foresaw the **end of the world** in 1874. One of Russell's strange pre-occupations was inventing correlations between historical events and the measurements of the **Great Pyramid of Giza.** In common with **Flinders Petrie** and many other fans of Great Pyramid lore, Russell "discovered" hundreds of seeming links that he said showed the divine nature of the Pyramid as a history book and **prophetic** document which could only be properly understood by an **adept.**

His analysis, published in 1891, called for the resurrection of all mankind and the end of the world—again—to take place in 1914. Though there were some defections from the Jehovah's Witnesses sect when 1914 arrived and passed, the religion has survived and now prefers not to discuss their founder's odd Pyramid notions. Their most recent calculation called for the world to end in 1975.

Currently, as the millennium approaches, the Witnesses are busily knocking on doors, trying to convince prospective converts that world conditions are getting worse and that obviously the End Time is approaching.

Again.

JFK University This is the only fully accredited university in the United States to offer a master of science degree in **parapsychology.** It is located at 12 Altarinda Road, Orinda, California 94563.

Joan of Arc (Jeanne D'Arc or Jeanne la Pucelle ["virgin"], 1412-1431)

At the age of sixteen, inspired by voices that she believed were those of **angels,** this illiterate young girl led the French army against the English at the siege of Orléans in 1428. Winning that battle, she saw the Dauphin crowned as French King Charles VII as a result.

The English, highly embarrassed at being bested by the Maid of Orléans, paid rebellious French soldiers from Burgundy to capture her, and they put her on trial as a **sorceress.** In 1431 she was burned alive.

Not surprisingly, all sorts of miraculous stories began to be told about Joan, culminating in the play of George Bernard Shaw. She is said to have levitated, to have spoken to God directly, to have had visions of the future, and several other wonders. Some **parapsychologists** have chosen to accept these tales and have written scholarly scientific explanations of events that probably just originated around fireplaces of French families amid the fumes of some fine cognac.

An equally incredible—though not impossible—tale is told that Joan was not burned, but moved to Metz, married Robert des Armoise, and raised a family. The immolation, it is claimed, was invented by the French to discredit the English.

Joan of Arc was canonized in 1920, becoming Saint Joan.

Johnson, Dr. Martin (1930-) Born in Sweden, Johnson was the first professor of **parapsychology** at the University of Utrecht, Holland (1953), then headed the parapsychology laboratory there from 1973 until his retirement. The lab closed in 1988.

Dr. Johnson's reputation among skeptics has always been very high as a doubter of the proven reality of **psi,** and the believers often expressed their own suspicions that he was secretly doubtful about the phenomena. In his writings, Johnson expressed his opinion that though there was not a single set of data that established the case for psi, he nonetheless held a personal conviction that there was "something there" and that it would someday be discovered. He was determined to systematically search for it. As a direct result of his efforts, the parapsychology lab at Utrecht was very prestigious and respected.

To emphasize his frequent asser-tion that parapsychologists in general can be excessively credulous, Johnson introduced a "**psychic**" named Ulf Mörling to the 1967 parapsychology conference at Utrecht. Mörling pro-ceeded to convince the assemblage that he did indeed have **paranormal** powers, and even when the attendees had been told that he was a **conjuror** and was **cheating,** they still believed. The prime endorser of the supernor-mality of the Mörling performance was an "expert" and prominent member of the **Parapsychological Association** named William (Ed) Cox, who also accepted **Uri Geller, Masuaki Kiyota,** and many, many more performers as genuine.

In his prime opus, *Parapsychologie* (1982), Johnson went to work per-sonally debunking "miracle men," from **Uri Geller** to **Sai Baba.**

~K~

ka (also *khat*) Essentially, this is the ancient Egyptian term meaning "soul," though with a somewhat more corporeal aspect. It is pictured in tomb paintings as a human-faced bird.

kabala (Also spelled cabala, kabbala, kabbalah, qabala, qabalah. From the Hebrew word meaning "collection.") A mystical Hebrew study of methods for controlling **spirits** and **demons**. It is largely mathematical in nature, concentrating on the configurations of certain magical words, anagrams, names of **angels**, etc. The earliest known book on the subject appears to be *Sefer Yezira* ("Book of Creation") by a third-century Jewish neo-

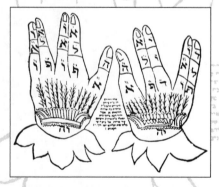

This kabalistic figure shows Hebrew letters related to parts of the hands.

Pythagorean. The idea itself—of the **magic** in numbers and letters—is much older.

The process of examining the permutations and combinations of the twenty-two letters of the Hebraic alphabet—a process known as "gematria"—is used to discover the numerical relationships between numbers and words. In Kabalistic studies, simple arithmetic discoveries and the qualities of irrational numbers are naively looked upon as divine mysteries.

kachina In the Hopi religion, a usually kindly and benevolent supernatural agent, ancestor, or element of nature, either revealed in a dream or **divined** by a **shaman**. Dolls made to represent these **spirits** are highly developed and stylized as an art form.

Kardec, Allan (Also, Kardek, Alain, Allen, and Alan; born L. H. Denizard Rivail, 1803-1869) A French medical doctor who became a very popular and influential **spirit medium** and theorist who taught that the spirit seeks **reincarnation**. He was first introduced to these notions when he attended a séance in 1856.

Allan Kardec, founder of a major spiritualist movement.

He said that all declarations made by mediums on behalf of spirits were truthful and authoritative —except in cases where the utterances had been prompted by evil spirits. In 1857, Kardec published *Livre des Esprits* ("Book of the Spirits"), explaining his ideas.

Kardec was editor of *La Revue Spirite* and founder/president of the Parisian Society for Spiritualistic Studies, where in 1861 the famous French astronomer Camille Flammarion, then only a teenager, was first introduced to **psychic** matters. Flammarion (1842-1925) became a staunch defender of **spiritualism.**

Kardec is buried in the famous "celebrity" graveyard of Père-Lachaise Cemetery in Paris, where his ornate red granite monument is visited regularly and kept adorned with flowers by his admirers. The site was partially destroyed in 1989 by an unknown bomber.

In the U.K., a prominent disciple of Kardec was Anna Blackwell, who dabbled in **spirit photography** as well. There is still a large following of Kardec in Brazil, where it is claimed that three thousand temples dedicated to him are active.

karma   Literally translated from the Sanskrit, "doing" or "making." Any intentional act, thought, or process.

The karma is a burden of guilt or an accretion of virtue said by many Eastern religions to be carried from one life to the next, which determines the nature and status of the person in the next reincarnation.

karrezza   The **Tantric** discipline whereby ritualized erotic procedures are entered into, but terminated just short of orgasm. The theory is that the energy thus preserved can be redirected in a spiritual fashion. This is in direct conflict with the theories of Dr. Wilhelm Reich, discoverer of the mythical substance **orgone.**

Keene, H. Lamar   (circa 1938-)   A **spirit medium** based in Florida who reformed (largely as a result of the unconfirmed rumor that the IRS was investigating him for back taxes) by confessing all and cooperating with an author, a believer, in writing a book, *The Psychic Mafia*, in which he described how he easily duped thousands of **sitters** at his **séances** and got very rich while doing it.

Keene entered the antique business after leaving the spook trade, and when his book appeared, he changed his name and moved to another state. This action was precipitated by numerous phoned threats and finally a rifle shot that missed him. He dropped out of sight, but unconfirmed rumors have it that he has reentered the trade under another name.

See also **apport.**

Kelley, Edward — *see* Dee, Dr. John.

khat — *see* ka.

ki — *see* qi.

King, George — *see* Aetherius Society.

Kirlian photography A process discovered by the Russian Semyon Kirlian in 1937, in which an object is placed directly on a piece of photographic film or paper, one side of a high-voltage, high-frequency generator is connected to the object, and the other side is grounded to a metal plate beneath the photographic material. Often, glass plates separate the two electric terminals, though the high-frequency voltage can penetrate such a barrier.

The ensuing corona discharge, a halo effect resulting from the electric charge being dissipated, and closely related to the **St. Elmo's Fire** phenomenon, is registered on the material and can be seen when the developing process is carried out. The corona is thought to indicate a sort of "life energy," and thus this technique's use in showing variations in that energy. It is also believed to register the **aura**.

Once highly regarded by the **paranormalists**, Kirlian photography has now been shown to only indicate variances in pressure, humidity, grounding, and conductivity. Corona discharges are well understood and explained in elementary physics.

The most famous effect of Kirlian photography occurred when a plant leaf was "photographed," then a section was torn away and the leaf was rephotographed. A faint image of the torn-out section was still seen in the second photo. Since the same glass plates had been used, it is probable that moisture from the missing portion was providing the ghostly image. Since the glass plates used as dielectric material would tend to break down along the edges of the object, allowing easier passage of the discharge, that may also account for the effect. The observed "phantom leaf" effect was not found again in better-controlled experiments, but has of course continued to serve as a point of argument for the believers.

Kiyota, Masuaki (1962-) This Japanese **psychic**, first discovered by **parapsychologist** Tosio Kasahara, became famous as an Asiatic version of **Uri Geller**, bending spoons and other cutlery. But his real forte was a routine using a Polaroid camera, which was, in turn, a takeoff on the work of **Ted Serios**. However, Kiyota's Polaroid photos were apparently produced by preexposing the film, since it was noted that he made great efforts to obtain a film pack and spend time with it in private.

In 1984 he thoroughly convinced parapsychologist **Dr. Jule Eisenbud**, who tested him with X-ray film and accepted kinks and small blemishes on the developed film as irrefutable evidence of psychic power.

In a 1984 television program in

Japan, high-speed tape revealed one of the simple, non-psychic methods that Kiyota used to bend the spoons.

Knight, J. Z. (Judy Hampton, circa 1951-) Probably the most prominent and successful of the **channelers,** this woman enjoyed the support of actress Shirley MacLaine until disillusionment apparently set in and Ms. MacLaine turned to other forms of amusement such as **chakras** and similar codswallop.

A multimillionaire as a result of her many books on Ramtha, the thirty-five-thousand-year-old warrior from Atlantis whose **ghost** she is said to channel, Knight resides on a huge ranch and breeds horses when she is not busy grunting out platitudes for Ramtha's adoring fans.

knots Various knots have long been considered essential to **magic** ritual. The basic topological aspects appear somewhat mysterious and lend themselves to mystical interpretation. The knot design is common on **talismans,** and knots of multicolored thread or string are attached to the necks of persons afflicted with **spells,** to release them from that bondage. Such a remedy is mentioned in the *Satyricon* of Petronius, a writer in the time of Emperor Nero.

Koestler, Arthur (1905-1983) A prominent political novelist and science writer, Arthur Koestler was born in Hungary and became a British subject in 1945. He became world famous upon the publication of his best-known work, *Darkness at Noon,* in 1941.

In 1972, he brought out *The Roots of Coincidence,* a startling book in which he ascribed some sort of **psychic** significance to remarkable examples of chance, apparently unable to believe that these were mathematically possible and also inevitable. He began to believe in ESP because he saw in the developing modern ideas of the **sciences**—mainly quantum physics with its almost-mystical view of the universe—the possible admission of otherwise unthinkable notions than were being put forward by **parapsychological** theorists. He wrote:

> The apparent absurdities of quantum physics . . . make the apparent absurdities of parapsychology a little less preposterous and more digestible.

Dr. Koestler died in a double suicide with his wife, Cynthia, in 1983. He had been suffering from leukemia and Parkinson's disease, while his wife was in apparently good health.

Koreshan Unity A semireligious sect originated by Cyrus Reed Teed (1839-1908) preaching that the entire universe is inside a sphere, with the Sun at the center and the other stars and planets circling about it. It was a favorite idea of the German Nazi party. *See also* **Hollow Earth.**

The name David Koresh was adopted in 1990 by cult leader Vernon Wayne Howell (1959-1993), who followed all these eccentric notions of Teed and fancied himself a Christ figure. He and many of his followers perished by fire at Waco, Texas.

Krafft, Karl Ernst (1900-1945) In late 1938, German Minister of Propaganda Goebbels began to consider the possible uses of **astrology** as a weapon of psychological warfare against the Allies. He chose astrologer Karl Ernst Krafft for the task. Krafft was described as a tiny, pale man with black hair and a sinister look.

Young Krafft had become an astrologer against his family's wishes, especially since he had proven to be an excellent student at the University of Basel, showing great promise in **science** and mathematics. He had written a *Treatise in Astrobiology*, full of tables and calculations, following a long period of study with an English authority on "biometrics," which concerned itself with measuring various physical aspects of humans and thereby determining their characteristics. (This "science" in itself was apt to bring him to the attention of the Nazis, who were actively seeking proof of their racial superiority through every sort of pseudoscience.)

Krafft opened an office in Zurich, casting **horoscopes** and advising on investments. It was the latter practice that brought the collapse of his business, since his advice proved as bad as the economic depression in 1931. Krafft's own investments, decided by means of his **occult divinations,** collapsed as well, and the failure drove him into an asylum for a short time.

In 1935, at the invitation of the Nazis, he moved to Germany, and the Ministry of Propaganda endorsed him enthusiastically. In response, Krafft became a Nazi and introduced into his writings and lectures a line of violently anti-Semitic ideas. In 1937 Goebbels established a counterintelligence group concerned solely with occult warfare. Astrologer Krafft made a sensational prediction on November 2, 1939, before a meeting of the Berlin Astrological Society. He said that between the seventh and tenth of November, an attempt would be made on Hitler's life. On November 8, an explosion nearly killed the Führer during a celebration of the anniversary of the famous Beer Hall Putsch.

The Gestapo questioned Krafft at length, and only the intercession of Hitler's deputy, Rudolf Hess, spared the astrologer from further terrors. Hess was an ardent follower of every sort of occult claim, especially those related to prophecy and health **quackery**. Krafft thus became personal astrologer to Hess.

He immediately began a reinterpretation of the prophecies of **Nostradamus,** in which he had always been very interested. Since it was easy to obtain from the ambiguous *Centuries* any needed meaning, Krafft found good news there for the Nazi cause. His discoveries were published widely, in French, Dutch, Italian, Romanian, Swedish, and English.

Krafft, exultant over his new position and success, was further thrilled to learn that Hitler himself had become interested in his skills. He predicted a glorious victory for Germany in 1943.

Then it was learned by the Gestapo that Krafft was telling others a different story from that he was supplying to the Nazis; he was prophesying eventual doom for the Nazi cause. The Gestapo prepared to pounce on him.

At this time, Rudolf Hess landed in Scotland after fleeing Germany. The Gestapo once more brought Krafft in for examination, blamed him for Hess's flight, and locked him up.

He was first held at Berlin's Lehrterstrasse Prison. Transferred to Oranianburg Concentration Camp, he awaited a trial that never took place. His predicted date for a glorious Nazi victory in the war came and went, and things only got worse for Germany. Scheduled for the gas chambers at Buchenwald, Karl Ernst Krafft died of malnutrition and typhus on January 8, 1945, in a cattle car on the way to his execution.

See also **Louis De Wohl.**

Kreskin (George Joseph Kresge, Jr., 1935-) **Mentalist** Kreskin, most of whose act was taken from the work of **Joseph Dunninger,** has trod the thin line between **conjuror** and **psychic.** He often firmly denies that his tricks are of a psychic origin, then the next moment seems to imply that they are. In a recent book, *Secrets of the Amazing Kreskin,* he claimed that well-known effects in the conjuring trade are actually accomplished by him by unknown means:

Some day, hopefully soon, researchers will be able to identify the force that is at play when, for example, I am able to tell a total stranger the number on his Social Security card or predict in advance, in writing, the headline on next week's newspaper.

This implies that "researchers" are in some way concerned with his performances as matters of scientific interest. For someone so accomplished as an artist, it is puzzling why Mr. Kreskin insists on these small peccadillos.

Krippner, Dr. Stanley Curtis (1932-) A highly respected **parapsychologist** who has served as the president of the **Parapsychological Association** (1982/3). He was the director of the Maimonides Medical Center Dream Laboratory in Brooklyn, studying **psi** at work during the sleep state. His writings include authorship and coauthorship of a number of books, and over five hundred articles in various journals. Dr. Krippner has lectured on parapsychology in Brazil, Colombia, Russia, and China and is presently with the Saybrook Institute in San Francisco as professor of psychology.

Outside of the parapsychology field, Dr. Krippner has also contributed to research on the treatment of children with reading and general learning disabilities.

Krishna — *see* **Hare Krishna.**

Krishnamurti, Jiddu (Né Alcyone, 1895-1986) The "World Teacher" discovered by the **Theosophists** in 1909, the fourteen-year-old son of a Brahmin employee of the Theosophical Society in India.

Black-eyed and exceedingly handsome, Jiddu was made the charge of the Theosophical Society after bitter court battles with his parents. The intent of the society was to announce a "second coming" based on this charismatic, intelligent star.

Krishnamurti was so personally popular that a separate organization known as the Order of the Star in the East formed around him, with some thirty thousand members. Then, at the peak of his popularity in 1929, at age thirty-four, he disowned the group and the Theosophists. He went on to become a very popular leader in his own right and a leading yogic philosopher, and he is the subject of many books.

Kulagina, Nina (1925-1990) This Russian psychic made a handsome career of reading while **blindfolded,** using the standard methods. She was also famous for making a **compass** needle move, and moving small objects like matchboxes, using a very fine nylon thread.

In 1978, the USSR Academy of Sciences was so convinced of her powers that they declared her genuine, in spite of the simple and obvious solutions for her **conjuring** tricks.

When the newspaper *Pravda* declared her to be a trickster, she sued the editors and won, largely on the basis of testimony given by Soviet **parapsychologists.**

In films made in the 1950s by the parapsychologists, Kulagina can be seen standing with her back to a wall while experimenters place very large letters, numbers, and shapes on the wall. She holds her right hand up to her eyes for a while, then announces what is on the cards. See **dermo-optical perception** for an explanation of the trick.

Kulashova, Rosa A. (1955-1978) As with **Kulagina,** this psychic was declared genuine by the USSR Academy of Sciences in 1978. She began her **blindfold** reading at the age of five, and though she was many times caught **cheating,** she was widely believed to be real. She died at age twenty-three of a brain tumor.

See also **dermo-optical perception.**

kundalini From the Sanskrit meaning "serpent power." This is the fiery snake said to sleep, coiled up, at the base of the human spine. Diligent searches by anatomists have so far failed to locate the kundalini.

kundalini yoga A form of **yoga** that preaches breath control and various physical exercises—"ansanas"—to sublimate sexual energy. The theory says that the process, through contraction of the anus, causes the semen to rise through the body into the seventh **chakra** (at the top of the head), at which point the ultimate union between matter and energy takes place. At this point, it says, the individual soul merges with the universal soul, obtains the powers of a god and becomes **immortal**.

As of this date, it is not known whether anyone has achieved the required physical situation, let alone the immortality. The former condition is obviously beyond the reach of females.

L

Lady Wonder A horse in Richmond, Virginia, that in 1927 was investigated by **Dr. Joseph Banks Rhine** when it was claimed that the animal had **extrasensory perception** powers. It was Rhine's first encounter with, and interest in, such claims, and he readily accepted that the horse could answer questions and make predictions by pushing over children's toy alphabet blocks to spell out responses, because he could not solve the puzzle, but he believed it was due to **telepathy**.

The magician **Milbourne Christopher,** who looked into the matter, determined that when Lady Wonder's trainer was unaware of the answer required of the horse, results dropped to zero. It was a case of **ideomotor reaction,** and has become a prime example of that phenomenon in psychology.

Such trained horse acts are well-known, another famous case being that of **Clever Hans** (*which see*) though there is no evidence that Hans was purposely trained for this task.

Leadbeater, Charles Webster (1854-1934) — *see* **Blavatsky, H. P.**

Lemegeton ("Lesser Key of Solomon") A **grimoire** from the seventeenth century mostly concerned with who's who in the world of **demons.** Full of hierarchial lists, and of no use whatsoever.

Lemuria Named for the lemur, a small mammal from both India and South America, this mythical ancient continent was concocted to explain certain striking similarities between features of the two land-masses. Now that continental drift has been confirmed, these correspondences are much, much better explained. As with other imaginary continents such as **Atlantis** and **Mu,** Lemuria was said to be the home of a highly advanced civilization who used ESP, **psychokinesis, prophecy** and other such supernatural powers, flew through the air in glass vehicles, knew the secret of eternal life, had abundant, free energy, and in general were far superior to mere citizens of today.

We're told that all of this information, along with the artifacts and the books, was unfortunately lost without a trace in an unknown cataclysm. Bad luck.

Leonard, Mrs. Gladys Osborne

(1882-1968) A failed British actress who at age thirty-two took up the profession of **spirit medium,** at which form of theater she was hugely successful. Her main claim to fame was bringing a message to **Sir Oliver Lodge** from his son Raymond, who had died in war. Lodge was convinced of the validity of the message, but he was convinced of almost everything else anyone told him, as well.

Lévi, Éliphas (1810-1875) (Abbé

Alphonse-Louis Constant) The son of a French shoemaker who was educated for the priesthood but was expelled for various interesting reasons. He thereupon took the name Lévi, became a mystic, and wrote on the subjects of **magic** and the **kabala.** He was a great admirer of **Paracelsus.** About 1850 he wrote *Dogme et Rituel de la Haute Magie* (translated as *"Transcendental Magic, Its Doctrine and Ritual"*) and *History of Witchcraft.* Those books brought about one of the periodic revivals of interest in the **Rosicrucians. Sir William Crookes** was an ardent disciple of Lévi, for whatever value that may have.

levitation — *see* flying.

Levy, Dr. Walter (1948-) Hired by

Dr. **Joseph Banks Rhine** as director of his Institute for Parapsychology in Durham, North Carolina in 1973, Dr. Levy was a medical student who had an avid interest in **parapsychology** and had previously worked during his vacations at the institute, starting in 1969. As soon as he began his experiments at the institute's lab, it was evident that he had a knack for getting positive results.

Rhine had long been under fire for sticking with his statistical studies of **extrasensory perception** rather than going into the more exciting aspects of examining "gifted subjects" such as **Peter Hurkos** and **Uri Geller,** who appeared to be able to produce paranormal wonders on demand. Levy, under Rhine's direction, began a series of **psi** tests on wired-up rats designed to discover whether the rodents were able to influence a random generator, through a computer, to deliver to their brains certain strong pleasure pulses, more often than chance would call for. He also used fertilized chicken eggs in tests to discover if the developing embryos could turn on the incubator lights with psi pulses.

The results of Levy's work were sensational, and the rats, too, seemed satisfied with this line of work; nothing was heard from the eggs. Rhine was well pleased and the institute was prepared to issue a press release on their success. Then suspicious lab workers discovered that Levy was cleverly manipulating the apparatus in order to produce positive results; an auxiliary recorder showed that the rats had no psi powers at all. Nor did the eggs.

Levy resigned his position and went into a medical field.

ley lines These are imaginary magi-

cal lines traced on maps of England

and are said to connect places of power—such as churches, ancient monuments, archaeological sites, and megaliths—in straight lines, thus forming "power grids." The Stonehenge structure (and, in fact, almost *any* structure or random location) can be shown to lie at the intersection of at least a pair of ley lines.

Those of the lines that are actually straight (most are not) can be shown to fall within expected chance occurrence on a map of a heavily populated area, especially when features no longer in existence can be included.

A similar notion was developed by the ancient Chinese far before the English came up with it. The Chinese called their lines "dragon tracks," and they used them for weather forecasting. They were somewhat less successful in that field than today's average TV meteorologist.

The term "ley line" was invented by British author Alfred Watkins.

Lilith (Queen of the Demons) — *see* **Adam** *and* **Asmodeus.**

Lindsay, Hal This author's list of books pretty well explains his taste: *The Late Great Planet Earth, Countdown to Armageddon, Satan is Alive and Well on Planet Earth,* and *The Rapture.* The ageless public fascination with disaster has been well served by Mr. Lindsay. His theories are based on ponderous arithmetical calculations that entertain numerous hilarious excuses for failure along the way.

In spite of the sparseness of the evidence he presents, Hal Lindsay's books continue to sell worldwide.

Loch Ness Monster — *see* **Nessie.**

Lodge, Sir Oliver Joseph (1851-1940) Sir Oliver was a scientist who did pioneer work in early radio and research on lightning. Among other inventions, he perfected a model of coherer, a detection device used in early radio before the invention of the vacuum tube.

Lodge's son Raymond was killed in battle in 1915 in France. In 1916, Lodge published a book, *Raymond, or Life and Death* in which he said that the **spirit** of his son had communicated with him through various **spirit mediums.** Raymond, he said, described clothes worn in heaven, as well as all other material things there, as being made of the "smell" of the same decayed matter in the earthly world. Such claims, and his fervent support of the **spiritualist** movement, eventually made Lodge the laughingstock of his peers and the public, though he was, and still is, a sainted figure to the spiritualists.

Loudun, Devils of The 1634 case in which Urbain Grandier, a priest at a small town of Loudun, France, was accused of bewitching a local nun, and then a whole group of them, and with whom it was reported he became involved in a manner that was anything but religious. Charged with **sorcery,** Grandier was convicted, horribly tortured, and burned alive. The Bibliothèque Nationale in

Paris has a document which is said to be the written pact Grandier made with the **Devil**.

This case was echoed later by the 1692 **Salem witch trials** in the American colonies.

loup-garou — *see* **werewolf**.

Lourdes It is the town of Lourdes, France, that has attained the strongest international reputation for miracles of healing. This acclaim is the result of a very successful commercial venture that began with a story about **Bernadette Soubirous** (1844-1879), an ignorant peasant girl who said she had a visitation there from "a lady" in 1858.

A shrine was established in 1876 to which some five million visitors a year now flock, occupying four hundred hotels built for them. The public relations people who sell Lourdes as a business claim that there are about thirty thousand healings a year, but church authorities deny that figure, cautioning that less than a hundred claims have been properly documented since the founding of the shrine, and the church has as of this date accepted only sixty-four as miracles, from the millions of cures claimed over the years.

Whether these sixty-four were simply remissions of various kinds or perhaps recoveries brought about by orthodox medical atten-

tion, one cannot know, since the records are so sketchy. In several cases, we have no evidence that even the ailments were real. In the absence of proof that the attendance of the afflicted at the shrine was the one element responsible for the termination of the ailment, common sense, as well as the simple principle of **parsimony**, would require one to strongly doubt the miraculous nature of these events.

Bathing in the mineral springs of Lourdes and drinking of the spring water have been confused with the healing stories. The church has never made any claim that the spring water from the Lourdes grotto is curative in any way, yet every year the souvenir shops sell thousands of gallons to the faithful in tiny vials, as **amulets**. Those who attend Lourdes in person have consumed millions of gallons more. It is amazing that more worshipers have not contracted diseases from that practice. Europeans are prone to accept the medicinal value of almost any natural spring water— especially if it smells bad. They cannot resist drinking from and washing in the Lourdes spring.

See **Bernadette Soubirous**.

Lucifer The name of **Satan** before he fell from heaven. Or another designation for the planet Venus. Or the sun god. Take your choice.

lycanthropy — *see* **werewolf**.

M

Mackay, Dr. Charles (1814-1889) Author of the remarkable book *Extraordinary Popular Delusions* (1841) and its successor, *Memoirs of Extraordinary Popular Delusions and the Madness of Crowds* (1843), Mackay was alarmed at the widespread belief in the wild speculations, the lack of common sense and the acceptance of supernatural subjects that he found in his society, and expressed his concern very well. He was an astute observer of conditions that he might well be dismayed—but not surprised—to discover are still very much with us today.

His book, reprinted by Crown Publishers, is highly recommended.

Macumba — *see* Umbanda.

magic An attempt to supplant natural processes and events by means of **incantations**, **spells** and/or offerings. Approximated by **conjuring** and often attempted by **prayer**. Magic and **science** are exact opposites in every way.

Magic can be divided into three very general categories: divinatory (determining hidden information), sympathetic (affecting some aspect of nature by performing upon a similar object/person/symbol), and ritual (reciting a prayer, incantation, **charm,** or carrying out an accepted formality).

See also **sympathetic magic.**

magic ashes According to the *Bible* (Numbers 19:1), the ashes of a red, unblemished, sacrificed heifer are to

The magician stands within the protective magic circle into which the forces of evil which he has summoned, may not enter.

be used for magical purification purposes. Not widely used nowadays.

magic circle The inscribed circle within which the **magus** stands while invoking **demons**. He is protected while within that circle. The figure must be set up according to carefully formulated rules.

The circle is drawn on the ground with the point of a new sword, proper symbols are inscribed along the circumference, and appropriate words are whispered.

In ancient Assyria, a sick person was protected from the effects of demons by having a circle of flour drawn about his bed. In India, it is a circle of black pebbles.

magic square — *see* charms.

magic wand Usually, by tradition, a baton made of hazel or ash wood. The magic wand is the equivalent of a specialized **talisman** used to facilitate the invocation of the magician's **spell**. **Conjurors** today have largely abandoned the affectation of carrying and wielding such a prop, though it was almost universal and expected throughout the nineteenth century. To the conjuror, it has served as a mode of misdirection.

magician, mage, magi — *see* magus.

magnetic hills A sensory illusion in which a road or path appears to have a slight upgrade but is actually minimally downhill.

This can be brought about by false visual indicators. One such occurs when nearby trees, road signs, or fence posts in the area are inclined somewhat away from the vertical, a condition which may have come about from a long-forgotten geological shift. The tendency for the senses is to automatically assume that trees and other such objects are positioned at right angles to the horizontal, and with some persons the sense of sight overcomes that of the balance organ (located in the ear) which normally gives us our conception of the position of the horizontal.

Stories abound of cars that run uphill at these locations with the ignition turned off, when actually they are coasting downhill. If it is possible to stand far enough back from the site so that the greater surroundings are also seen, it will be noticed that the illusion then fails.

A strong example of this deceptive effect is found at the "Oregon Vortex," a site on Interstate I-5 near Gold Hill, Oregon, near the California-Oregon border. The thousands of visitors who visit the area annually go away convinced that they have witnessed a genuine unexplainable miracle.

magus (plural, magi) Originally, a Zoroastrian priest, but now used to denote a magician, a person who seeks to control nature by means of **spells** and **incantations**. Or, loosely used, it designates a **conjuror**, *which see.*

Maharaj Ji (1957?-) Leader of the Divine Light Mission, a cult that was brought with great success in 1971 to the United States. At one point, the mission boasted forty-five ashrams in the United States alone, peopled with disciples who were promised that they would "receive the knowledge" after a period of study and work, during which they gave all their earnings to the Maharaj Ji.

The overweight teenage **guru**, addressed as "Lord of the Universe" by his devotees, was driven about in a Rolls-Royce whenever he was not roaring down the street on one of his collection of high-powered motorcycles.

The mission had as its membership mostly middle-class young people, who were taught that rational thought is the supreme enemy and were urged to immediately commence meditation whenever the thinking process threatened to return.

The Maharaj Ji announced that the "most significant event in the history of humanity" would take place, "Millennium '73," at the Houston Astrodome. The arena was rented at a frightening price and admission was free, but only twenty thousand of the expected sixty thousand persons showed up. It was a bust, especially financially.

The Mission published a slick color magazine titled *And It is Divine*, and one issue featured **psychic Uri Geller** on the cover, during a time when the two superstars, it was rumored, were planning to join forces. It never happened.

Plans for a Divine City peopled only by mission members came and went. "Receiving the knowledge" turned out to be a process of seeing "heavenly lights" when pressing on the eyeballs, hearing "blissful music" when the ears were stopped up, tasting "divine nectar" when the head was thrown back with the tongue turned inward, and receiving a **mantra** nonsense word. The sensory illusions were quite natural and easily understood physiological phenomena, the "nectar" being simply nasal secretions dripping into the throat. Only the very naive were convinced that they had been let in on some sort of celestial secret. The big promise fizzled.

In 1974 Maharaj Ji married his secretary Marolyn Lois Johnson, who he had discovered was the **reincarnation** of the ten-armed, tiger riding goddess Durga. His mother revolted against this alliance and tried to regain her former position as female leader of the sect by announcing that her other son, Bal Bhagwan Ji, was thenceforth the divine head of the cult. Disillusionment set in, and in 1975 Maharaj Ji's mother and brother sued him for their share of the wealth that had been accumulated. Then everyone sued everyone else, and the Divine vanished when the Light went out.

In 1981, Maharaj Ji showed up uninvited at a rock concert at Glastonbury, England, driven in a white Rolls-Royce. He preached a few moments for a disinterested audience, and motored away when someone switched off the microphone. The god business is often not as enthusiastically supported as a god might wish.

Maharaj Ji has been variously reported as now living in Denver, Colorado, and in Australia. There has not been a concerted effort to locate him.

Maharishi Mahesh Yogi — *see* Transcendental Meditation.

Mahesh Yogi, Maharishi — *see* Transcendental Meditation.

malicious animal magnetism Also known to followers of **Christian Science** as "M.A.M.," this was first postulated by **Mary Baker Eddy** in her system for divine healing. It was an idea borrowed from **Mesmer,** who at first thought that he had discovered a form of biological magnetism, but it turned out to be a form of suggestion that affected susceptible persons.

At the age of fifty-six (she gave her age as forty), the founder of Christian Science married Gilbert Asa Eddy, a sewing machine salesman. It was her third marriage. In a stirring court trial, Mrs. Eddy accused her husband of trying to send arsenic, via M.A.M., into her body. The charges, including **witchcraft,** were dismissed as groundless.

No evidence for any such sort of force has ever been produced, but it remains an article of faith with Christian Science.

See also **Mary Baker Eddy.**

Malleus Maleficarum ("Hammer of Witches") Two Dominican monks, Heinrich Kramer (1430-1505) and Jacob Sprenger (1436-1495), earned their unenviable place in history by writing this book. It was published, in Latin, in 1486, and became the virtual handbook for **witch**-hunters. It contains a complex, convoluted discussion of the world of **demons** and how these infernal beings related to and interacted with humans. The book appeared in three dozen editions and in English, French, German, and Italian.

The *Malleus* also gave explicit instructions on how suspected witches were to be discovered, tortured, forced into confession, tried, and executed. It directed, by the procedures outlined, that the accused would eventually be found guilty, regardless of the evidence.

The book served as a guide to the **Holy Inquisition** for more than a century.

M.A.M. — *see* malicious animal magnetism.

mandala From the Sanskrit word for "circle." A symbol of the cosmos, usually circular, with a god-symbol or name at the center, inscribed on **charms** or used in rituals. The four cardinal points are also often represented. Large versions are often sold as decorative wall-pieces to tourists who are unaware of its true function.

mandrake (also mandragore, mandragora) A plant, *Mandragora officinarum,* related to the potato. The root is a tuber, and it often grows in the shape of a human body. The more it resembles a body, the more valuable the root is

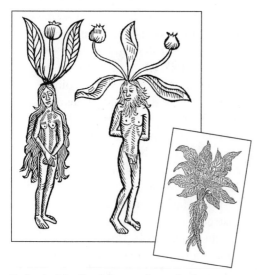

Left: *the idealized forms of mandrake root, represented as human forms.* Right: *the mandrake plant,* mandragora officinarum, *shown with the typical bifurcated root.*

believed to be for **magical** purposes. Mandrake is sold whole in oriental pharmacies and in powdered form and pills as well. The German mystics keep foot-high figures of old sorceresses, richly dressed and comfortably housed, some of which are mandrake roots in drag. In Norway the figures are consulted for advice. Really.

A certain problem exists with harvesting the root. When the plant is drawn from the ground, it is supposed to emit a horrendous human-like shriek that will drive a human insane. A solution is arrived at by tying the plant to a dog's tail and encouraging the dog to pull it up. By that means the prize is obtained, since dogs are luckily immune to the dreadful sound.

It is mentioned in the *Bible,* Genesis 30:14, as a substance that assured fecundity. This account

involves trading some mandrake roots for a night with another's wife, or some such deal. In any case, the assignation reportedly produced a male child, even though the mandrake roots were not consumed. Truly magical.

Manning, Matthew (1955-) A U.K. imitator of **Uri Geller.** He also performs **spoon bending** and other claimed **paranormal** effects. In recent years, Manning has taken on the role of healer, lecturing on the subject internationally. *See also* **faith healing.**

mantra (From the Sanskrit. Also mantram.) A secret **talisman** word assigned to devotees of various mystical movements. It is determined not by divine inspiration, as often claimed, but from information such as birth date and the date on which the student first began affiliation with the movement. In some usages, the mantra is supposed to be used by the owner to attain spiritual contact by repeating it endlessly, or to summon up a source of spiritual power.

The best-known mantra is "Om mani padme hum," used by Tibetan Buddhists. The simplest is just the word "Om," attributed to the **guru** Trimurti. It is recognized in psychology that the constant repetition of a word or phrase (known as echolalia when performed by autistic persons) can be comforting and soothing to a very disturbed mind.

map dowsing This is a peculiar skill claimed by a few dowsers. It consists of swinging a **pendulum** (or just the hand or any other preferred device) over any piece of paper that represents a map of an area of land, and thereby finding anything from lost children to buried treasure. The map, most practitioners claim, can even have all coordinates removed, can be of any unspecified scale, in color or not, or be of an unknown part of the globe. A review of a book on the subject in *Nature* magazine in 1940 said:

> The fact that such a thing [dowsing over maps with a pendulum] is seriously mentioned [in the book] is calculated to undermine the reader's faith in the author's critical faculty.

In England, Dr. Julian Huxley, F.R.S., said in 1942 that he had been present at a test of this claim at Oxford and that the diviner failed both with water and with minerals. He added that, in his opinion, the alleged finding of water by means of dowsing over a map was a belief that "belongs in the Middle Ages" and was "certainly not worthy of credence."

Marduk   The god of gods in Assyrian mythology, who split Tiamat, mother of the gods, into two parts, thus creating heaven and Earth. Not presently a generally popular belief.

Margery — *see* **Crandon, Margery.**

materializations   In spiritualism, the production of any substance or item, particularly of a human figure or part of one, at a **séance**. The materialization can be an **apport** or can use **ectoplasm** in its formation. Materializations are often accompanied by strange (pleasant or unpleasant) odors and/or sounds. This is congruent, to the skeptical mind, with the possibility that the phenomena may be accomplished by trickery. And trickery has very often been the solution to the puzzle. It's true!

Mather, Cotton (1663-1728)   A minister of Boston who was notorious for his merciless persecution of accused **witches** in **Salem**, New England. He presided at the trials and executions. *See also* **Salem witch trials.**

Left: *Cotton Mather, the clergyman/zealot who sent witches to their deaths in Salem.* Below: *The title page of a 1693 report by Cotton Mather on his work of finding and hanging witches in Salem.*

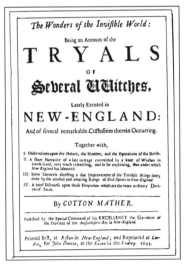

The Wonders of the Invisible World:

Being an Account of the

TRYALS

OF

Several Witches,

Lately Executed in

NEW-ENGLAND:

And of several remarkable Curiosities therein Occurring.

Together with,

I. Observations upon the Nature, the Number, and the Operations of the Devils.
II. A short Narrative of a late outrage committed by a knot of Witches in Swede-Land, very much resembling, and so far explaining, that under which New-England has laboured.
III. Some Councels directing a due Improvement of the Terrible things lately done by the unusual and amazing Range of Evil-Spirits in New-England.
IV. A brief Discourse upon those Temptations which are the more ordinary Devices of Satan.

By *COTTON MATHER.*

Published by the Special Command of his EXCELLENCY the Governour of the Province of the Massachusetts-Bay in New-England.

Printed first, at *Boston* in *New-England*; and Reprinted at *London*, for *John Dunton*, at the *Raven* in the *Poultry*. 1693.

Mather, Increase (1638-1723)
Father of **Cotton Mather,** and no
more pleasant nor intelligent than
his son. *See* **Salem witch trials.**

medicine man — *see* **shaman.**

medium When used by the spiritualists in the sense of agent, instrument, or vehicle, this word refers to
the person who is said to be able to
bridge the gap between the living
and the dead or to produce voices,
artifacts (**apports**), writing, or other
evidence of **survival after death.** *See
also* **séance.**

mentalist A person who performs a
theatrical act which appears to use
psychic forces but is actually done
by ordinary **conjuring** means. The
psychic often uses these methods,
but is differentiated from the mentalist in that he or she claims that
they are genuine powers. *See also*
Dunninger; Kreskin.

meridians In **acupuncture** and in **qi
gong,** there are twelve major meridians in the body, mythical channels
through which flows the **qi,** a
gas/fluid/plasma/essence which is
the basis for traditional Chinese
medicine. Because of their spiritual
nature, the meridians cannot be
found by direct examination of the
body, nor are they visible or discov-
erable by any other means.
See also **parsimony.**

Merlin A mythical magician who is
said to have managed the birth of
Britain's **King Arthur** and to have
practically ruled early England

through his powers and his influence on Arthur. Said by some to
have been the son of **Satan.**

In the traditional story, Merlin
does not die, but is spirited away to
the Isle of Avillion, wherever that
may be.

Mesmer, Dr. Franz Anton (1734-
1815) This Viennese medical doctor, who had written his disserta-
tion on the effects of the planets on
the health of the human body, after
seeing a healing demonstration by a
priest named Hell, formed the belief
that a magnet could induce healing
powers in those who held them. He
displayed the procedure, which he
called **animal magnetism,** during
popular sessions that he held for
French society, beginning in 1778.
The phenomenon soon was dubbed
Mesmerism.

*Anton
Mesmer, the
man who
started all
the fuss
about "hyp-
notism" and
"trances."*

His soirées were theatrical rather
than therapeutic, and the crème of
French aristocracy elbowed one
another aside for the privilege of
seeing customers sitting around a
huge vat of acid (called a *baquet*),
holding on to iron devices immersed
in the solution, while the master,
dressed in a trailing lilac-colored
robe of gold-flowered silk, gestured
with his ivory wand at entranced

socialites who gurgled, sighed, and moaned when they weren't screaming in ecstasy at their latest expensive diversion.

An investigation of Mesmer in 1784 by the French Academy of Sciences, in the company of U.S. ambassador Benjamin Franklin, brought the conclusion that Mesmer was merely using suggestion and that the clients were the usual silly segment of the populace who endorse and support such fads.

meta-analysis A system of statistically analyzing very large numbers of already-published experiments each of which may not, in itself, be significant, and extracting from them information to be looked at with a view to obtaining validation of the sought-after effect. Only if an overall application of faulty procedures has been applied, or experimental results have been generally misreported, could properly applied meta-analytic procedures falsely indicate positive results. This procedure is gaining popularity among **parapsychologists,** who seem to always have miserable luck with simple, directly applied scientific methods and analysis of results.

micro-PK (micro-**psychokinesis**) A term developed by the **parapsychologists** to describe very tiny effects not necessarily observable to the eye when, for example, spoons are bent by ostensibly **psychic** means and scanning-electron microscopes are needed to notice any change. Also the term describes seeming psychic influences on electronic random-number generators and other such sensitive equipment that may require very minute inputs of energy to affect them.

Parapsychologist Helmut Schmidt performed such experiments at the Mind Science Foundation years ago, and the results were reported to be phenomenal. However, for some reason, they were never followed up on and the excitement died down.

Millerites First on April 3 and July 7, 1843, and then again on March 21 and October 22, 1844, preacher William Miller (1782-1849) told his followers to expect the Second Coming of Jesus Christ. The event did not occur. His group, the Millerites, broke up shortly after that and the basic philosophy was snapped up by Ellen G. White (1827-1915), who founded the Seventh-Day Adventists. Another spin-off religion with equally bad prophecies was the **Jehovah's Witnesses**.

White had been experiencing **prophetic**/divine dreams since age fifteen, so that she naturally felt she had to start a religion. Wisely, the Adventists did not set a date for the Second Coming, thus avoiding a certain inescapable and troublesome problem of reconciling fact with expectation. They only said "Soon." They are still saying "Soon."

In her book, pretentiously titled *Health: Or, How to Live*, White declared herself against: corsets, drinking, meat, smoking, spicy food, sex (in particular, masturbation), wigs, and just about everything else except air and small rocks. She was against any sort of medication and preached against seeing a physician for any medical problems.

However, the present Seventh-Day Adventist church operates seventy-three hospitals, plus hundreds of clinics and fifty-four hundred colleges and secondary and elementary schools in the United States. Its School of Medicine at Loma Linda, California, a prestigious facility famous for radical medical innovations, is a strange contradiction for a religious movement that began as vehemently anti-doctor and anti-medication.

Mirabilis, Dr. — see Bacon, Roger.

Mirandola, Count Giovanni Pico da
(1463-1494) An Italian philosopher, **astrologer,** and mystic who specialized in studies of the **kabala.** He was a brilliant scholar from an early age, and ran afoul of the church very soon, being accused of heresy. His powerful family connections saved him. Despite his being mired in the superstitions of his day, he nonetheless contributed some original and bold ideas in his writings.

Mitchell, Edgar D. (1930-) Dr.
Mitchell was the sixth man to walk on the moon, as part of the Apollo XIV project, in 1971. After he retired from the space program in 1972, he founded the Institute for Noetic Sciences, devoted to the study of **parapsychology,** and particularly the relationship of humans to purported **psi** forces.

While engaged in his visit to the moon, Mitchell performed an unauthorized experiment in ESP. He used a self-made deck of the 25 **Zener** cards and attempted to transmit these images to his recipients on Earth at predetermined times. The results of his experiment were reported in an enthusiastic *New York Times* article as "far exceeding anything expected." *The Encyclopedia of Parapsychology and Psychical Research* says, however, that

> the results of the test were ambiguous, success or failure rating depending upon the evaluation techniques used.

Neither of these versions of the Mitchell experiment are correct, for the following reasons. There were actually *four* intended recipients on Earth; only the results of one were reported. The predetermined times for mental transmission were changed, but the recipients were not informed, so that they may have been "receiving" before or after the images were being "sent"; one recipient received *more* images than were sent. After careful mathematical analysis with the assistance of parapsychologist **Dr. Joseph Banks Rhine,** the Mitchell results were declared to be three-thousand-to-one against pure chance. They were, but negatively; the results were so *negative* that the chance of *missing* to that degree was three-thousand-to-one.

Dr. Mitchell believes in plant perception—that plants can feel and understand the thoughts of humans—as described by **Cleve**

Backster, though the two gentlemen are almost alone in that belief. Mitchell also was involved in testing the claims of **Uri Geller** and believes that Mr. Geller has genuine psychic powers.

moons of Mars   British satirist Jonathan Swift (1667-1745), in his four-volume work *Travels Into Several Remote Nations of the World,* better known now as *Gulliver's Travels,* described a mythical advanced kingdom where the astronomers had discovered that the planet Mars had two small moons in orbit very close to the surface. That fact was unknown—and unknowable—at that time (1726) and was not determined until 151 years later in 1877 when astronomer Asaph Hall, at the U.S. Naval Observatory, observed the planet and its moons during a favorable opposition. This provided a mystery, which was amplified by modern **UFO** fans into a theory that Swift had been visited by extraterrestrials who had informed him of this fact.

The eminent Dutch astronomer Tycho Brahe (1540-1601) had supported a numerological argument that, since Mercury and Venus (the planets nearest to the Sun) had no moons, the Earth had one, and Jupiter (the second planet out from the Earth) had four (known) moons, that in order to preserve the harmony of the universe, Mars (between Earth and Jupiter) must have two satellites (see table following). Since these moons had not been detected, Tycho reasoned sensibly that they must be very small and close to the planet. This satellite-progression idea was accepted in Swift's time, and it appears that he reflected this fact and incorporated it into his writings.

The two arrangements, actual and theoretical, look like this:

PLANET	Actual moons	Theoretical moons
Mercury	0	0
Venus	0	0
EARTH	1	1
Mars	2	2
Jupiter	16	4
Saturn	20+	8
(Uranus)	15	16?
(Neptune)	2	32?
(Pluto)	1	64?

(The last three planets were undiscovered at that period of history.)

Moses, Rev. William Stainton (1839-1892)   A **spirit medium** who first began operating as such at the age of thirty-three, after a distinguished career as a clergyman. Moses was inspired by the success of **Daniel Dunglas Home,** who he saw performing.

He became famous in England for his production of **apports** of every sort of object, including perfumes and scented oils which often ran down his face. He claimed that his **control,** or **spirit guide,** was named Imperator. He also did **automatic writing** and produced "spirit lights" as part of his performance.

He was one of the founders of the British National Association of Spiritualists, and later of the **Society for Psychical Research.**

Mu In the 1920s, a mystic named James Churchward invented an attractive scenario involving a lost Pacific continent named Mu, which he said was first written about by the ancient Maya. Churchward based his stories of Mu on an imaginary translation of Mayan documents by Abbé Basseur, another mystic of the previous century. In actuality, these documents have only recenrtly been partially translated.

A series of books on Mu appeared, but when the evidence Churchward had offered, artifacts and documents from Mu, proved spurious, interest waned. Mu, the **Atlantis** of the Pacific, sank out of sight and out of mind. However the books are still published. No facts are allowed to interfere with profit.

Murphy, Bridey (1798-1864)? The fictitious character created by Mrs. (Hugh) Virginia Tighe of Denver, Colorado, at the suggestion of investment broker/amateur **hypnotist** Morey Bernstein in 1952. In **trance,** Mrs. Tighe relived a colorful nineteenth-century life, speaking in a heavy brogue, using typically quaint Irish expressions (some, unfortunately for the theory, not in use in the nineteenth century), and giving details of her former life in Cork. It was all believed to be a sterling case of either **reincarnation** or **possession**. The possibility of imagination never came up.

Then, investigations by the Denver *Post* and the Chicago *American*, later followed up by writer Melvin Harris, showed that as a child Mrs. Tighe had lived across the street from an Irishwoman whose maiden name was Bridie [sic] Murphy. This woman had entertained young Virginia with tales of her early life in Ireland. Also, as a teenager, Virginia had been featured in school theatricals playing Irish parts and using an Irish brogue. The kindest interpretation that one can put on this matter is that Mrs. Tighe had undergone classic **cryptomnesia.**

This highly publicized playlet resulted in a hit popular song by Nat King Cole, a motion picture, several best-selling books, and an LP recording of the trance session.

muscle reading The art, highly developed by the **conjurors,** by which an operator can perform apparent ESP demonstrations by "reading" the involuntary movements and reactions of a spectator. Commonly, the demonstration involves locating a hidden object or performing a simple task, the nature of which is unknown to the operator. The spectator, who must know the withheld information, is asked to concentrate on making the demonstration a success.

In most cases, the operator is in contact with the spectator, either by grasping his wrist, holding a handkerchief also held by the spectator, or having the spectator hold him by the arm. This is known as "contact" muscle reading.

"Noncontact" muscle reading is more difficult. It consists of having the spectator follow the performer about and reading his hesitation patterns. Much experience is required for either system, and the results are very startling. The art is often referred to as "Hellströmism," after one Alex Hellström (1893-1933), who made it popular early in this century. Another prominent performer was the Hungarian Franz Polgar, and today Russia's Lev Schneider is the leading artist in the field.

Yet another name for the art is "Cumberlandism," after the English performer Stuart Cumberland.

⟨ N ⟩

N-rays The disastrous affair of the "N-rays" thoroughly embarrassed the French—and the scientific world—back in 1903, when Prosper René Blondlot, a distinguished physicist of the city of Nancy, announced his discovery of strange radiations that he said emanated from every substance—except green wood and pieces of metal that had been "anesthetized" by dipping them into chloroform or ether. The apparent existence of these rays was soon confirmed by dozens of scientists around the world through scientific papers submitted to science journals.

A single physicist, American Robert Wood, was sent in by the British Association of Scientists and reported his results to *Nature* magazine (then, as now, one of the leading science journals). Wood showed the French scientists that not only were their experimental processes faulty, but their rays were totally imaginary.

The N-rays affair provides the single most effective and important example of scientific error through experimenter bias and expectation, an example which might well be improved upon by the present German fascination with the equally imaginary **E-rays**.

native healers In every culture, a **shaman** or witch doctor figure emerges who is charged with the healing duties. He or she adopts or develops an acceptable plot to explain illnesses and malfunctions of the body and performs whatever cures or alleviations of symptoms that are possible.

Patients usually expect to see something actually removed from their bodies as symbolic of the removal of the cause of their problem. With the extraction of teeth, that requirement is obviously easily met, and in cases where bullets or other missiles, slivers, or thorns are extracted, both the practical and the symbolic needs are also satisfied. In some situations, the healer may secretly introduce a small stone or twig onto the site of the operation, and since this would satisfy the need for an actual object, it can bring about more contentment from the patient, since something is produced that is identifiable as a cause of the discomfort. This is a bit of "show business" in a serious effort to bring relief to patients.

This process is known in certain African societies as "pulling the thorn." Here, it involves a surreptitious introduction on the site of the operation of a bit of thorn or sharp object, usually via the healer's mouth, since African procedures involve sucking the wound to fulfill the scenario. This act, though obviously potentially dangerous to both healer and patient from the infection point of view, might actually be very effective. The object is then spat out and identified as the source of the evil. The satisfaction thus evoked enhances the reputation of the healer, who is usually performing minor medicine of a very useful sort for people who have little if any other resource.

See also **psychic surgery** *and* **shaman.**

necromancy From the Greek for "corpse" and "**divination,**" the term refers to methods of obtaining information from the dead, without permission from the dead. It is a practice frowned upon by the most ethical sorcerers.

Necronomicon Several editions of this **grimoire** have appeared. Said to have first been published in about A.D. 730 in Arabic as *Al Azif* by Abdul Alhazred, an English translation is attributed to **John Dee.** It relates powerful formulas for calling up dangerous demigods and **demons** who are dedicated to destroying mankind.

Nelson, Robert (1901-1972) He was a practicing **mentalist** for many years

who went into the wholesale/retail business in response to a demand for specialized products. For fifty years, Nelson Enterprises, Inc., has supplied ready-made **horoscopes, palmistry** charts, luminous cheesecloth, table-rappers, crystal balls, impression pads, and other necessities for the dishonest **spiritualist** and for the legitimate entertainer. The business still flourishes.

Nessie The common name given to the mythical Loch Ness monster. It is said that about A.D 565, the Irish priest who became Saint Columba went to Scotland to convert the Picts to Christianity. When the monster threatened a follower of Saint Columba, the good man made the sign of the cross and thwarted the beast.

Nessie has been reported regularly over the years since, though some sightings have been shown to be hoaxes or honest mistakes. The likelihood of a creature anywhere near the size of the one described existing in the lake is very small—small, but not to the point where it must be entirely discounted.

Several other factors speak against the reality of the monster, however. There certainly must be more than one of them, and never more than one is reported seen. No physical remains or other traces exist. Sophisticated sonar equipment has been used to track Nessie, and no good supportive data have resulted, even though five separate serious investigations have been conducted. More importantly, lakes in Canada and the United States are now producing reports of equally ephemeral beasts of a similar nature.

It has been postulated that since groups of seals are sometimes seen in the lake traveling in single file, such a group could be falsely reported as a single beast and identified as Nessie.

Persons who doubt the reality of Nessie are unpopular visitors at Loch Ness.

See also **Abominable Snowman.**

new age This term is used to cover many current ideas in the world of mystics, **psychics,** and **gurus.** It is not "new"; it is simply the Old Age revisited. Rather than sitting in a dark room at a **séance** in a $5 seat holding clammy hands with a total stranger of unknown worth, a follower of **channeling** now sits in a fully lit auditorium in a $600 seat— beside a total stranger of unknown worth.

Religious zealots have identified new age notions with **Satanism** and general godlessness. Fundamentalists in the United States have harangued police officials and the media with claims that children have been sacrificed to **Satan** by his worshipers. Investigator Shawn Carlson, a physicist in San Diego, California, looked into these allegations and concluded that though there were no documented sacrifices of children, there were more than two thousand children beaten to death by their parents in the United States in the year 1988 alone. Surely that indicates a misapplication of righteous zeal.

Nichol, Agnes (Mrs. Samuel Guppy, ?-1917) A three-hundred-pound, rancorous and jealous English **spirit medium** who is credited with the first large-scale **apports** to be experienced at **séances,** Agnes was better known by her married name, Mrs. Guppy. She produced live flowers, plants, and fish, as well as earth, sand, and various other exotic items, covering her séance table with junk of every description. Her most popular apport was of human body parts and, rarely, an entire human form.

She was, at the height of her fame, the most prominent of London's mediums, only to fall from popularity when she was accused of trying to disfigure **Florence Cook,** her petite rival in the business who specialized in full-form **materializations.**

At one time Nichol lived with the sister of Dr. Alfred Russel Wallace (1823-1903), the great British naturalist, who believed completely in her powers and endorsed them.

norns Urd, Verdandi, and Skuld, the three Norse goddesses who represented the past, the present, and the future, in order. Their function is to guard the "Tree of the World," Yggdrasil, the ash tree of which the cosmos is formed. Modern cosmologists differ with this concept.

Nostradamus (1503-1566) One of the most renowned and still-popular champions of disaster was Michel de Notredame, the sixteenth-century physician of Provence who took the Latinized name by which he is more commonly known: Nostradamus.

Nostradamus, the sixteenth-century seer of Provence who wrote The Centuries, *ten books of quatrains that he said were intended as prophecies.*

His major opus was *Centuries,* a series of almost a thousand quatrains which purported to be **prophecies,** and along with a great number of almanacs, letters, and various other writings, he managed to produce more than any other prophet in history. His reputation, however, is due to the ardent horde of his disciples who continue to this day to hyperbolize, bowdlerize, and invent in order to perpetuate his fame.

Under the patronage and protection of Catherine de Médicis, queen of France and the power behind three French kings, Nostradamus lived comfortably from 1503 to 1566, celebrated all over Europe and a thorn in the side of Elizabeth I of England, for whom he continually predicted, through his almanacs, a doom which never came.

Upon close examination, it can be seen that many of the quatrains penned by the seer of Provence were actually political commentaries and justifiable critiques of the activities of the Catholic church, which was then busily tossing heretics onto bonfires wherever the **Holy Inquisition** could reach.

Nostradamus himself was in great danger of mounting the faggots himself. He was already under suspicion, because only two generations earlier the Notredames had been the Gassonets, a Jewish family that had converted to Catholicism under pressure. Worse, letters recently discovered in the Bibliothèque Nationale in Paris prove that he was also a secret heretic—a Lutheran, surprisingly enough, in view of that sect's strong anti-Semitic bias.

A good look at just one of the Nostradamus quatrains, one of the Top Ten often presented as positive evidence of his prophetic ability, serves to illustrate how far believers will go to stretch the facts in order to serve their needs. Quatrain 51 of Century II is said by the faithful to refer to the Great Fire of London in 1666. Here is the evidence for this belief.

First, quoting from the earliest available (1558) edition of the verse, it reads:

Le sang du iuste à Londres fera faulte,

Bruslés par fouldres de vint trois les six:

La dame antique cherra de place haute,

De mesme secte plusieurs seront occis.

(The reader should know that in modern French, *iuste* would be "*juste*," *Bruslés* would be "*Brûlés*," *vint* would be "*vingt*," and *mesme* would be "*même*.")

In modern English:

The blood of the just shall be wanting in London,
Burnt by thunderbolts of twenty three the Six(es),
The ancient dame shall fall from [her] high place,
Of the same sect many shall be killed.

The word *feu* ("fire") is now substituted by many copyists for the original *fouldres* ("thunderbolts") in the second line , so that it will better fit the Great Fire of London interpretation. Also, some editions print "*vingt & trois*" rather than "*de vint trois*," thus making an appreciable variation in the text and in the meaning.

Nostradamians believe that the seer was writing about an event that was 111 years in his future: In 1666, London was devastated by a fire that destroyed four-fifths of the city. It is said by one of the interpreters that the last half of line two refers to the number of houses and buildings that were burned, rather than the more popular interpretation by almost everyone else that it means 66, therefore, 1666. How that date was obtained is difficult to see.

The Nostradamians explain that "*La dame antique*" refers to St. Paul's Cathedral, known as the Old Lady, which was lost in the fire along with many other churches, thus the claimed validation of the line, "Of the same sect many shall be killed." St. Paul's Cathedral was never called the "Old Lady," as claimed. Also, the word *antique* in Old French meant "eccentric"; the derivation is similar to that of the English word "antic." Though the old St. Paul's Cathedral was the highest church then known, there is no "high place" from which it could have fallen. Some fans, recognizing this discrepancy, claim that a statue of the Virgin Mary stood atop the cathedral, and that was the Old Lady Nostradamus was referring to. Not so. An early edition of the *Encyclopaedia Britannica* provides a clear, detailed illustration of the old prefire cathedral that shows it was Gothic in style, with a square roof area and no external statues at all.

This quatrain actually refers to an event which was taking place as Nostradamus was penning his opus in 1555, but a very different event, and certainly not the Great Fire of London. Here are the historical facts:

1. Announcing a purge of her kingdom in 1554, the Catholic queen Bloody Mary I of England began executing Protestant heretics in London, beginning in January 1555. Many were prominent churchmen, intellectuals, and statesmen. One Bishop Ridley had an especially horrid exit from life. His brother-in-law, wishing to lessen his relative's suffering by hastening his death, had piled the faggots so high about him that the flames could not reach him, and

the poor man cried out that he could not burn. His benefactor thereupon opened up the pile of wood, which more quickly brought an end to the bishop.

2. The trial, sentencing, and burning of these unfortunates began January 22, 1555, in groups of six. When they eventually expired at the stake, it was with an explosion like a thunderbolt, since they were burned with the "merciful" addition of bags of gunpowder tied between their legs or around their necks to hasten their passage.

3. Mary, haggard, totally obsessed with religion, disappointed in love, ill with dropsy and other assorted diseases, repeatedly imagined that she was pregnant by her husband Philip of Spain. The consort was seldom at home and in 1555 left England—and Mary—for good. She wandered about her palace half naked while the atrocities were being committed in her name. She died three years later, incoherent and considered quite insane. It was strongly suspected that her exit was hastened.

4. Over three hundred Protestants were executed in this way at that time.

When one considers these historical facts and compares them line for line and number for number with the four lines of the Nostradamus quatrain as seen in this much more accurate translation, a different view might be taken of the quatrain:

1. The blood of the innocent will be an error at London,

2. Burned by thunderbolts, of twenty-three, the six(es),

3. The senile lady will lose her high position,

4. Many more of the same sect will be slain.

An important question arises here: Did Nostradamus have time to get this historical event into his publication? The first edition of the *Centuries,* in which this quatrain is printed, is dated May 4, 1555— more than three months after the first group of heretics were executed in London. Though some authorities date the 1555 edition of the Centuries as March 1, 1555, it is imprinted at the end:

> *Ce present livre a esté achevé d'imprimer le IIII. iour de may M.DLV.*

("This book was finished printing the fourth day of May 1555.")

The sentences of the inevitable executions would have been passed some time before the events, since the condemned often spent many months in prison while their wealth was located and acquired by the crown; carefully applied and controlled torture effectively extracted information about concealed assets from the condemned. Nostradamus was part of a network of scholars who were in frequent communication and would have heard of this event. Thus, either publication date is adequate for the described scenario.

But why would Nostradamus, a faithful Catholic, object to this good work of burning heretics? Because as we've seen, he was secretly a heretic himself, a Lutheran sympathizer who clearly declared himself in clandestine letters sent to clients and scholars in Germany. In this quatrain, as in many others, the Seer of Provence was writing of an event which certainly would have made news in France, and that he had heard about.

One modern "interpreter" of Nostradamus, John Hogue, first issued his book *Nostradamus and the Millennium* in 1987. In that volume, he quoted his own very liberally translated versions of several quatrains that he believed predicted certain events involving the Near East, and he specified those events. He named four "anti-Christ" candidates, and for one he said that Nostradamus had clearly predicted:

> [In August of 1987] a million Iranians under Khomeini's power [will] invade Mesopotamia all the way to Egypt.

Then came the 1991 (the fourth) printing of his very successful book, after the massive Iranian invasion had failed to take place. This edition had seven pages of revised text, with another anti-Christ in the person of Saddam Hussein—substituted for the Ayatollah Khomeini, who had inconsiderately died rather than fulfilling Nostradamus's plan for him—and omitted completely the above-quoted prediction along with another Hogue had made for a specifically dated alliance of the superpowers. Blank spots replaced the previous entries.

One thing, however, remained the same in both editions: the portrait of Nostradamus clutching a telescope, an instrument that had not yet been invented when the seer died.

numerology The mystical attraction of basic qualities of numbers resulted in strange theories about magical powers that could be invoked or discovered by carrying out certain arithmetical operations. Such a belief, based on an idea of **Pythagoras** that all facts can be reduced to numbers, results from a failure to understand the true nature of the concept of number.

In applying numerology to a person's name, for example, there are many different systems in this "art" for assigning numbers to the letters of the alphabet, adding them up and arriving at a series of qualities, characteristics, and specific facts that are said to apply to that person. The dubious nature of the practice becomes obvious.

Three of the most popular systems among many, many such systems to determine "name numbers" are shown here:

A	=	1	1	1
B	=	2	5	2
C	=	3	6	3
D	=	4	9	4
E	=	5	3	5
F	=	8	8	6
G	=	3	8	7
H	=	5	3	8
I	=	1	9	9

J	=	1	9	1
K	=	2	6	2
L	=	3	5	3
M	=	4	7	4
N	=	5	7	5
O	=	7	1	6
P	=	8	5	7
Q	=	1	6	8
R	=	2	9	9
S	=	3	3	1
T	=	4	8	2
U	=	6	8	3
V	=	6	3	4
W	=	6	3	5
X	=	0	9	6
Y	=	1	6	7
Z	=	7	5	8

The third column of numbers represents what is known as the Pythagorean system. All of these systems require the user to add together each of the digits representing each letter in the name, then to add the digits of the resulting number, and repeat that process until a number less than 10 has been arrived at. This final digit is interpreted according to the following table:

1 — action, aggression, ambition, leadership, purpose

2 — balance, passivity, receptivity

3 — brilliance, gaiety, versatility

4 — dullness, endurance, steadiness

5 — adventure, instability, sexuality

6 — dependability, domesticity, harmony

7 — knowledge, mystery, solitariness

8 — material success, worldly involvement

9 — great achievement, inspiration, spirituality

It can be seen that there is no standard and no consistency in numerology—let alone rationality—but it provides an easy method for the naive person to play a satisfying game without having to apply any intellectual powers to the matter.

Gematria is a form of numerology which employs the Hebrew alphabet, in which all the letters also have numerical values.

Modern numerologists, quick to adopt new technologies to prove and enlarge old claptrap, have now turned to a computer number system, the American Standard for Coded Interchange of Information (ASCII), for further deep meaning of the alphabet.

See also **kabala.**

nymph An **elemental spirit** of the water. In the real world, the immature form of the dragonfly and certain other insects, or a young woman with robust sexual interests. Take your choice.

O

OBE— *see* out-of-body experience.

obeah A magic cult found in the West Indies, particularly in Jamaica, and similar to **voodoo.**

obsession From the Latin *ob-sedere* meaning "sit outside," this refers to the besiegement of a person by a **devil, demon,** or **spirit.** It differs from **possession** in that the agent does not take up residence *inside* the body, but assails it from outside. Saints and especially holy persons are said to be safe against possession, but not against obsession. Partially reassuring.

Occam's razor — *see* parsimony.

occult From the Latin *occulere,* meaning "to cover up." Used as an adjective, *mysterious, not revealed, secret,* and *obscure* are all synonyms.

odic force From the name of the Norse god Odin. The name given by Baron Karl von Reichenbach (1788-1869) to an unmeasurable and undetectable energy that he imagined came from **crystals,** magnets, and the bodies of certain **adepts.** This was a precursor to the notion of the equally imaginary **aura.**

ointment In **witchcraft,** any substance to be rubbed on the flesh to produce **magical** results. There were many formulas for **flying** ointment, for poisonous ointment, and for aphrodisiacs. A special flying ointment was prepared by boiling the fat from newborn, unbaptized children. It did not work.

Olcott, Henry Steel (1832-1906/7) An otherwise respected agriculturist who took up the cause and theories of **H. P. Blavatsky** and cofounded the religion known as **Theosophy.**

om (or "aum") A Sanskrit word often used in **mantras** and which is pronounced at the beginning and at the end of every lesson of the Vedas, the four sacred books of Hinduism. The *Katha-Upanishad* of Hinduism says of "om" that "whoever knows this syllable obtains whatever he wishes." Well, now *you* know it, too. Good luck.

omens In attempts to discover meaning in every natural event or condition, we have used considerable imagination. There are many genuine clues provided by nature: The changing angle of the Sun charts the changing of the seasons, the reappearance of migratory birds heralds the advent of spring, and behavioral differences—what we could call "symptoms"—in animals and humans can indicate physiological situations.

We should not be too surprised to find that our forefathers extended their observations beyond reasonable limits, believing that almost everything that occurred bore some relationship to upcoming events. Thus, not only the position of the Sun, but the configurations of the stars and the planets were also thought to hold significance. Even the general flight patterns of birds and indeed the arrangement and variations of their internal organs took on meaning to observers. Chosen "sacred" animals, by their most minor behavioral meanderings in a temple court, indicated important conditions that could be interpreted, with enough skill. Thereby were born such arts as **astrology, phrenology, palmistry** and **augury**.

It might be hoped that we are now free of such impediments to progress. Not so. Most major modern office buildings omit the thirteenth floor, and highly paid lawyers and bankers avoid ladders and black cats. Astrology, worldwide, is a billion-dollar business. Palm readers are sought out by Wall Street brokers, and otherwise bright folks call unseen "certified **psychics**" by phone to ask their advice.

Progress is often difficult to define. Perhaps it should involve the process known as growing up, as well.

one-ahead method In spiritualistic circles, a "sealed billet-reading" procedure is often used to convince the audience. One popular system for producing this effect is known as "one-ahead."

A **sitter** is told, as he enters the room or church, to write out a question or phrase he wishes to be answered or interpreted, and is told to seal it in an envelope. Often he also writes his initials on the outside of that envelope. The **medium** accepts a basket full of these envelopes, takes one, and holds it to her head. She announces the contents and comments appropriately on the question or phrase. The medium then tears open the envelope to check how correct she was, then repeats the process with another sealed envelope.

The trick lies in the fact that before accepting the basket of envelopes, the medium has secretly obtained one, opened it, and memorized the contents. It has then been destroyed. Upon picking up the first envelope, the medium misidentifies it as the one secretly peeked at. Opening the envelope as if to check, the medium is now aware of the actual contents of that envelope, and represents that data as belonging to the next one. She is always working "one-ahead."

This method is worked in every country, even to this day, and is very effective as a convincer.

OOBE — *see* out-of-body experience.

open medium A term in opposition to **closed medium**. The open medium may seek assistance from, and cooperate with, others. He or she is totally aware of the flummery involved. The considerable amount of data available from the **Blue Book** is contributed to the publisher by the open mediums and used by them. Though the closed performer may compile his or her own data, they are not made available to others.

Order of the Golden Dawn (more correctly, Hermetic Order of the Golden Dawn) Founded in 1888 in London, this was a secret society that boasted as members Irish poet William Butler Yeats (1865-1939), Mrs. Constance Wilde (wife of Oscar Wilde), and **Aleister Crowley**. Founder S. L. MacGregor Mathers said that he obtained his esoteric

An icon of the Order of the Golden Dawn, incorporating symbols used by the Rosicrucians.

knowledge for the order from "Secret Chiefs" and "Masters" while in **trance**.

The order broke up in 1900.

orgone A name given by psychologist Wilhelm Reich (1892-1957) to an imaginary substance he believed was normally evenly distributed about the body, but gathered into the genital area during orgasm, then was redistributed after that event. Lack of proper, satisfying orgasms, he said, led to orgone imbalance and attendant negative symptoms of every sort.

Reich preached that cancer was caused by a lack of orgone.

In 1940 he built and marketed a box he called an Orgone Accumulator, and sales were brisk. It was simply a three-foot-square box made of two layers, wood on the outside and metal on the inside. The natural orgone from the sky, he said, was soaked up by the wood and transmitted to the metal and thus to the body of the owner, crouched inside. Orgone Blankets followed, as well as small orgone "shooters" that were said to direct concentrated orgone to needed areas.

Only fourteen years later, in 1954, ever-vigilant investigators for the U.S. Food and Drug Administration discovered these devices and obtained an injunction against Reich selling his products. However, Reich continued, and in 1956 was tried, convicted, and sentenced to a $10,000 fine plus two years in prison. He died in prison, praised by his followers as a persecuted pioneer of progress.

Ouija board Bearing a name said to be derived from the French and German words for "yes," the Ouija board is simply a flat, smooth board bearing the letters of the alphabet, numbers, and often the words "Yes," "No," "Maybe," and "Goodbye." A hand-sized, heart-shaped device perched upon three

The planchette used as an automatic writing device.

short legs, each of which has a pad or wheel to enable the instrument to slide freely across the board, is known as the **planchette**. This is used as a pointer, the tapered end of the heart shape indicating letters on the board.

One or more operators sit around the board, each lightly resting fingers upon the top of the planchette. It is said that **spirits** or other entities cause the planchette to move about the board, spelling out messages and answers to questions posed by the operators. (This process is a form of "dactylomancy," or divination by means of finger motions.)

Actually, the movement is due to the **ideomotor effect** and this can be shown by the fact that when the operator is properly blindfolded, only gibberish is produced.

The Ouija board was patented in 1892 by a Maryland novelty company. *See also* **planchette**.

Ouspensky, Peter Demianovich (1878-1947) A Russian mathematician and mystic, Ouspensky is best known for his interest in **George Ivanovitch Gurdjieff** (1877?-1949) and for his explanations of Gurdjieff's teachings. He also wrote on the **Tarot,** and in his most popular work, *Tertium Organum,* he tried to reconcile Western rationalism with Eastern mysticism.

He met Gurdjieff in 1915, was profoundly impressed, and became a disciple, but broke with him in 1924.

out-of-body experience (also OBE or OOBE) Mentioned in 2 Corinthians 12:2-4 by Saint Paul:

I know a Christian man who fourteen years ago (whether in the body or out of it, I do not know— God knows) was caught up as far as the third heaven.

The word *ecstasy* is derived from the Greek, meaning "out of place" or "out of body."

Parapsychologist Charles Tart has defined the phenomenon as

> an event in which the experiencer (1) seems to perceive some portion of some environment which could not possibly be perceived from where his physical body is known to be at the time; and (2) knows *at the time* that he is not dreaming or fantasizing.

However, this definition also matches (1) the experience anyone has of listening on the telephone, watching a television broadcast, or hearing a radio program, and (2) it is difficult to imagine how one can *know* that he "is not dreaming or fantasizing," if Webster's definition of an hallucination is the apparent real perception of sights, sounds, etc., that are not actually present.

Given the exceedingly complex nature of the cognitive process in human beings, it cannot be said with any degree of certainty that sensory/perception malfunctions do not occur that give the strong impression of being "real" while in actuality there is no corresponding situation or event.

Parapsychologist **Susan Blackmore** covered the subject thoroughly in her books *Parapsychology and Out-of-the-Body Experiences* (1978) and *Beyond the Body* (1982).

P

Palladino, Eusapia (née Palladino, then Signora Raphael Delgaiz, 1854-1918) Born in southern Italy, **spirit medium** Palladino was accepted by many scientists, particularly those like **Charles Richet** and **Schrenck-Notzing**, who were devout believers in all **spiritualistic** claims. She specialized in **levitation** of tables.

A cantankerous, vain, difficult person, she became an international celebrity, and sometimes sat for tests, though she was often caught **cheating** on these occasions and on other non-controlled **sittings** as well. The prominent investigator Hereward Carrington (né Hubert Lavington, 1880-1958) brought her to America, became her manager, and took her on tour. In America she continued to be caught cheating, and Carrington came to the conclusion that she sometimes cheated (when she was caught), but that the rest of her performance (when she was not caught) was genuine.

Part of her success was probably due to her petulant attitude, which she used to discourage proper examination of her performances. As with others in her trade, she needed to control the circumstances around her and managed to do so very effectively, throwing temper tantrums and walking out of tests when things were not to her liking. She was also noted among investigators for her seeming lack of acquaintance with soap-and-water, being the source of a heavy variety of unpleasant body odors, especially in the closed **séance room**. She provided her examiners with plentiful reasons to regret having taken on such a formidable woman.

In spite of all this, and her repeated exposures, Carrington remained thoroughly convinced for the rest of his life that Palladino was genuinely in touch with **Summerland**.

palmistry (also chiromancy or chirognomy) An ancient notion that says a person's character, health, and destiny are portrayed in the folds, shape, size, and lines of the palm. In the nineteenth century, the writings of William Benham and Louis Harmon revived interest in the idea, which had somewhat waned since earlier times. **William Warner**, as Cheiro, was the great palmist at the turn of this century.

An interesting variation of the art, and every bit as accurate, is

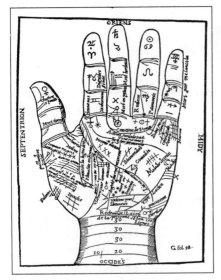

Lines, mounds, and proportions of the hand, shown with zodiacal and planetary signs. Used in palmistry.

"podoscopy," reading fortunes from the sole of the foot. It is popular in China.

In the same way that **reflexology, iridology, physiognomy,** and similar systems try to establish that information is available in physical features, palmistry satisfies the human need to look for meaning in any sort of natural pattern.

Paracelsus (circa 1493-1541) He was grandly named Theophrastus Philippus Aureolus Bombast von Hohenheim, a Swiss scholar/physician/mystic who called himself Paracelsus (*para* Celsus meaning "beyond" Celsus, an early Platonist and anti-Christian philosopher). Paracelsus was born to educated parents in Switzerland and was admitted to the University of Basel at age sixteen.

His life's work took him to Croatia, France, Germany, Greece, Italy, Poland, Portugal, Russia, Scandinavia, Spain, and Turkey. His philosophy was a curious mixture of mystical notions and hard thinking. He added a few facts to chemical knowledge, made some of the earliest attempts to organize medical information, and was among the first to use nonorganic chemicals to treat disorders, but by most measures he was a superstitious, argumentative, offensive braggart who alienated everyone with whom he came in contact.

True to his calling as a physician of that day, he insisted upon applying his knowledge of **astrological** aspects to all healing processes. On a more realistic bent, he laid the basis for an understanding of psychologically based illness by teaching that negative attitudes and stress can invoke certain problems, while a positive attitude is more conducive to avoidance of those conditions and/or to recovery. That glimmering of the basic idea of psychological/psychosomatic causes and effects, widely accepted today, was expressed by Paracelsus thus: "A powerful will may cure, where a doubt will end in failure."

Paracelsus favored the use of magnets in curing patients, and was in that respect the inspiration for Franz Anton **Mesmer,** the French mountebank who, two hundred years later, discovered the principles of what we now call **hypnosis,** or suggestion. Mesmer at first believed that magnets were necessary for his induction of the **"trance"** state, but soon found that what became known as Mesmerism worked just as well without such aid.

Paracelsus studied and recorded methods of discovering and recovering metals from the earth. In that time, diviners (**dowsers**) used their forked sticks, **pendulums,** and other devices in attempts to find not only water, but metallic ores. Then, as now, any success they enjoyed was due either to their knowledge of geology or just dumb luck.

A natural wanderer and vagabond, this scholar managed to lose every friend he ever made, and his superiority complex soon earned him a terrible reputation. That reputation was well earned, as indicated in the preface to one of his books. He wrote:

> In this midcentury, monarchy of all the arts pertains to me, Theophrastus Paracelsus, prince of philosophy and medicine. For to this am I chosen by God that I may extinguish all fantasies of all far-fetched, false and putative works and presumptuous words, be they of Aristotle, Galen, Avicenna, Mesue, or any of their adherents.

As a result of this attitude, though he taught at various centers of learning, Paracelsus stayed at each for only short periods of time before his superiors and his students decided they'd had enough of him.

He tried to change even the primitive notions of what made up the basic elements of the Renaissance universe. He disallowed the four **elements** of fire, earth, water, and air, replacing them with sulfur,

mercury, and salt. However, even in this matter he seems not to have ever made up his mind.

In 1536 he published his *Prognosticatio,* a book of thirty-two illustrations that very much resemble the well-known **Tarot** cards. He claimed that the line drawings were **magical,** and wrote accompanying captions for them which he said were **prophecies.** Allegorical and sym-

Paracelsus, the flamboyant early scientist who revolutionized the medical treatment of his day.

bolic in nature, these drawings and texts are as enigmatic as the **Nostradamus** writings, and may well have inspired the French seer in his style, since they were available to him well before he even produced his first almanac. This work of Paracelsus was referred to by his great admirer, another mystic named **Éliphas Lévi,** as "the most astounding monument and indisputable proof of the reality and existence of the gift of natural prophecy."

Along with descriptions of strictly magical procedures that he took as having some value, Paracelsus made observations which indicated his grasp of both human nature and correct methodical thinking. Though he was inescapably subject to the superstitions of his day and the necessity of catering to popular prejudices—including a tendency to immolate those who doubted scriptural declarations—he was frequently able to rise above those burdens, as when he discoursed on medical matters and public attitudes. In his fourth book on diseases, *A Paramiric Treatise,* he closed with these words:

> You have seen how natural bodies, through their own natural forces, cause many things [believed to be] miraculous among the common people. Many have interpreted these effects as the work of saints; others have ascribed them to the Devil; one has called them sorcery, others witchcraft, and all have entertained superstitious beliefs and paganism. I have shown what to think of all that.

One might believe those to be the thoughts of a thinker of this century.

paranormal An adjective referring to events, abilities, and matters not yet defined or explained by **science**. From the Greek, it translates as "beside/beyond normal." All of what is popularly classified as **psychic** can be placed in this

class, though serious **parapsychologists** may choose to exclude some, like spoon-bending.

Parapsychological Association

Founded in 1957, the PA is a private international nonprofit organization of some three hundred scientists devoted to the study of **psi** and related subjects. The PA was admitted to membership in the American Association for the Advancement of Science in 1969. The Association

> seeks to increase knowledge and obtain a better understanding of the full extent of humankind's potential for awareness, communication and action. The primary emphasis of the membership involves the investigation of psi . . .

parapsychologist A properly qualified scientist who works in **parapsychology**. More strictly, a full member of the **Parapsychological Association**.

parapsychology Among all the **sciences**, there is one known as parapsychology. It studies certain reported but unsubstantiated events (such as **ESP, psychokinesis, dowsing, prophecy**) that have no presently known explanation. Like all other sciences, it develops theories to explain these claimed events and attempts to test those theories by experimentation. *See* **science**.

However, unlike in other sciences, none of the parapsychologists' experiments have both shown positive results and have been replicated by independent researchers.

Even the *Guinness Book of Records*, listing the single most astonishing performance in ESP, apologizes and reports that the episode fails to meet even their standards. Data in some important basic parapsychological experiments that yielded apparently positive results have been shown to be falsified—though parapsychology is not alone in this respect.

Some students of **paranormal** matters say that such claims cannot be examined rationally. If that is the case, then their studies do not belong with science, but in the same category as flat-Earth theories and perpetual-motion machines, none of which can have the slightest importance to anyone except, perhaps, students of abnormal psychology or editors of the sensational press.

Psychologist Dr. David Marks, who has done extensive investigation of the parapsychologists' work, has said:

> Parascience has so far failed to produce a single repeatable finding and, until it does, will continue to be viewed as an incoherent collection of belief systems steeped in fantasy, illusion and error.

The U.S. National Research Council in 1988 concluded a well-funded two-year study by a special committee and published a report, *Enhancing Human Performance,* which concluded:

> The committee finds no scientific justification from research conducted over a period of 130 years,

for the existence of parapsychological phenomena. In the committee's view, the best scientific evidence does not justify the conclusion that ESP—that is, gathering information about objects or thoughts without the intervention of known sensory mechanisms—exists. Nor does scientific evidence offer support for the existence of psychokinesis—that is, the influence of thoughts upon objects without the intervention of known physical processes.

Nonetheless, courses in parapsychology are offered in more than two hundred colleges and universities in the United States alone, and degrees in parapsychology are offered at several schools, in particular at **John F. Kennedy University** in Orinda, California. Their Graduate School of Consciousness Studies offers a parapsychology master of science degree.

parsimony Aside from its usual meaning of "frugality," this word expresses a very important philosophical and logical concept. Also known as Occam's (or Ockham's) razor, it is a philosophical principle usually credited to William of Occam (1285-1347/9), though Galileo used it before Occam when he preferred the heliocentric solar system over a geocentric one. Sir W. Hamilton (1788-1856) stated it:

> The law of Parcimony [sic], which forbids, without necessity, the multiplication of entities, powers, prin-

ciples, or causes; above all, the postulation of an unknown force, where a known impotence can account for the effect.

(The rule was originally stated by Occam as, "*Entia non sunt multiplicanda praeter necessitatem.*")

In effect, this rule states that if there exists two answers to a problem or a question, and if, for one answer to be true, well-established laws of logic and science must be re-written, ignored, or suspended in order to allow it to be true, and for the other answer to be true no such accommodation need be made, then the simpler—the second—of the two answers is much more likely to be correct.

Here is an example of a problem:

The claim: that a person can cause an ordinary spoon to bend merely by looking at it, using psychic powers that have not been established and which would violate many known rules (conservation and transfer of energy, etc.) and cause those basic laws of science to be rewritten.

There are two explanations available: one says that these basic physical laws *have* been suspended in this case—a unique event never before known in history—and the other says that the performer has employed sleight of hand and/or deceptive optical principles and/or psychological misdirection to provide the illusion of the spoon bending without the use of ordinary physical force.

The second of the two explanations is much more likely to be true.

To substitute another phenomenon for the previous example:

The claim: that a magician can saw a woman in two pieces and then restore her using magical powers that have not been established and which would violate many known rules (physiological, biological, etc.) and cause those basic laws of science to be rewritten.

There are two explanations available: one says that these basic physical laws *have* been suspended in this case—a unique event never before known in history—and the other says that the performer has employed deceptive optical and/or mechanical principles to provide the illusion of the woman having been sawn in two and then restored alive.

In this case, which explanation is much more likely to be true? Is the likelihood not just as strong in both cases?

pendulum One method of **divination** uses a pendulum. A weight of any kind, the bob, is suspended at the end of a string or chain: **crystals**, real or fake, are currently popular. The device is held over a map or other object, and various movements of the bob are interpreted in different ways by different operators. Most pendulum swingers say that the bob swings clockwise over a person's right hand and counterclockwise over the left. They say that it swings to and fro over a male's body and in a circular pattern over a female's. But some of them say exactly the opposite.

In this phenomenon, it can *always* be seen that the subject moves his or her hand to set the pendulum swinging, though this will be vehemently denied. The event is a perfect example of **ideomotor reaction.** To-and-fro motions and circles are produced, often in answer to questions directed by the dowser at the pendulum itself. The operator speaks to the pendulum. Really.

The bob of the pendulum is often hollow so that diverse substances— solid or liquid—can be retained inside, the idea being that the device will thereby become more sensitive to the contained substance. The French, who dignify the process with the term *radioaesthesia,* produce a wide selection of screw-together pendulums in various colors made of metal, wood, or plastic.

See also **dowsing** *and* **map dowsing.**

pentacle/pentagram A five-pointed figure used as a **talisman,** with magic symbols. Also, a figure chalked on the floor by a **magician,** inside which he stands while invoking a **demon** or other dangerous entity; since the entity cannot enter that space, the magician is protected. Not proven.

See **magic circle.**

perpetual motion This is a pervasive notion that has probably cost more time, money, and mental effort for the crackpots than any other pursuit except for the **philosopher's stone.**

The idea that a device, machine, or engine can be designed whereby free energy or work can be obtained simply by setting it into motion has preoccupied inventors for centuries. While "free" power is available through such forces as solar radiation, ocean tides, changes in atmospheric pressure, and flowing water, no device can be constructed that will operate without energy input or by using stored energy, or that will generate an energy output greater than that required to operate it.

In 1678, the Abbé John of Hautefeuille (1647-1724) designed a machine that would perform continually as a result of the energy provided by warping pine boards subjected to natural changes in humidity, and in 1751 a St. Petersburg inventor named Kratzenstein came up with a thermal energy scheme. These, of course, did not come under the definition of perpetual motion machines since they depended on a natural energy source, in the same way that solar cells, hydroelectric, and various wave- and tidal-change systems do. Similarly, several kinds of timepieces such as the Atmos clock perform continually, powered by changes in barometric pressure.

By far the larger proportion of inventors of such devices are self-deluded. The rest are intentional frauds. Somewhere in between are those who sincerely believe that their ideas are workable, but are not averse to improving the performance of their creations by means of a little hidden support.

One of the most famous—and successful—of the fraudulent class of

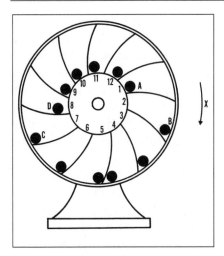

One of the basic ideas for a perpetual motion device. The wheel, mounted vertically and rotating freely about the central axis, has a number of compartments (1-12 here) each containing a heavy ball. The theory is that the wheel is turning in the direction X. Ball A, as it falls into position B, overbalances the wheel and causes it to turn further, one-twelfth of a rotation, so that ball C now moves into position D. This puts it closer to the axis, giving it less force to prevent the rotation of the wheel. Balls in compartments 9,10,11,12, and 1 will cancel one another's effect. Balls in 2 and 7, and in 4 and 5, also cancel one another. The slight negative advantage of 8 is offset by the positive advantage of 3 over 6. The wheel will turn in direction X, say the perpetual motionists, because A slams into position B as it changes position, while ball C slowly rolls over into position D. While this is an intuitive feeling, the potential energy of this system and its kinetic result are actually zero.

inventors was John Worrell Keely (1837-1898), a Boston man of no appreciable education who managed to raise vast amounts of money from investors who witnessed, at Keely's home, a model of his machine—the Hydro-Pneumatic-Pulsating-Vacuo-Engine—merrily whirring away without an apparent source of energy. Though he spent a short time in prison, he died wealthy and only after his house was torn down was it discovered that a flywheel in the basement connected to concealed tubes in the floors and walls had delivered compressed air to power this secretly and several other models of marvelous machines he had designed.

The U.S. Patent Office, much to its shame, has actually issued patents on perpetual motion devices and systems, though these "inventions" have never been shown to work. This, in spite of a decision years ago that no patent for such a device would be considered unless a working model was submitted. Recently, a Mississippi man named Joe W. Newman actually obtained signatures from thirty scientists who said his "free energy" machine, which is in actuality a huge direct-current motor powered by a massive stack of batteries, is a valid invention. Newman himself says that when his creation is finally able to be put to work,

there will be no more pollution, no more Ethiopias. Deserts will become oases. People will work only one hour a week and have all the material goods they need. Children will have hope. There is absolutely no doubt in my mind that my machine is going to bring peace, prosperity and happiness.

Newman, who holds other valid patents for ideas that really do work—one is a cigarette-making machine, thus showing another of his contributions to mankind—refuses to accept the "perpetual motion" label for his design, insisting that it is a "free energy" idea. However, if the output of his machine is simply connected to the input, he should have an ever-running system. This he has apparently never managed—or tried—to do.

Perpetual motion/free energy remains a vain notion in the minds of eccentric folks who are intent upon wasting their time and other people's money on a dream. As Arthur Ord-Hume, in his fascinating book *Perpetual Motion—the History of an Obsession,* says:

> There must be something in the make-up of the perpetual motionist which, while urging him on in his quest for the impossible, encourages him not to deviate from the well-trodden path to certain failure. . . . Even the alchemist . . . knew when he was beaten.

Petrie, Sir William Matthew Flinders

(1853-1942) A genuinely talented archaeologist who laid the foundation for much of today's methodology in excavation techniques, Sir William was also a mystic who believed that the **Great Pyramid** of Egypt was constructed in the form of a **prophetic** message, with the entire past, present, and future of Earth represented in the structure and design. Some religious sects such as the **Jehovah's Witnesses** have adopted this notion as part of their philosophy.

phantom leaf effect — *see* **Kirlian photography.**

philosopher's stone (also azoth, Elixir of Life, Grand Catholicon, Lapis Philosophicus, Powder of Projection, Prima Materia, Universal Alkahest) The substance, spirit, or symbol by which base metals—iron, lead, copper—can be changed into gold or silver. It also imparts **immortality,** cures disease, and performs other miracles. It is said to be the material from which all metals derive. A charming **alchemical** notion not supported by reality.

The search for the elusive substance has led to the discovery of several processes of variable merit: the German Bötticher developed the method of making what is now known as Dresden porcelain, **Roger Bacon** came up with an improved form of gunpowder, and Johann Rudolf Glauber invented Glauber Salts.

See also **alchemy.**

philtre — *see* **potion.**

phrenology The German physician Franz Joseph Gall (1758-1828) invented the idea of studying the bumps on the human head, from which he believed character traits could be read. His theory of phrenology (meaning "mind system") was first known as "organology" and was announced by Gall in Vienna in 1796, when he mapped twenty-six areas of the head that he said were assigned to certain aspects of human personality.

After a falling-out with Gall, Dr. Johann Kaspar Spurzheim, a disciple of Gall's, took his own version of phrenology to America, where it became very popular, now with thirty-five areas of the head marked out. U.S. President Martin Van Buren, Henry Ward Beecher, Walt Whitman, and Daniel Webster endorsed it. Horace Mann declared:

> I look upon phrenology as the guide to philosophy and the hand maid of Christianity. Whoever disseminates true phrenology is a public benefactor.

Jurist Oliver Wendell Holmes, known for his common sense, denounced the whole idea.

In 1836, the Fowler brothers, Orson and Lorenzo, started a publishing house for the *American Phrenology Journal*. The business was expanded to include instruction centers, a museum, and all manner of props and devices. It continued to flourish until 1932 under the name Fowler & Wells, and original phrenological busts in porcelain made by the firm are sought after by modern devotees of the idea.

A ponderous machine called the Psycograph was soon developed. It

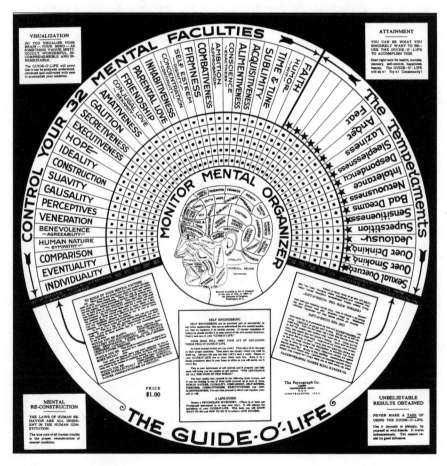

consisted of a large hemispherical frame with thirty-two probes pointing inward at the victim's head. The contraption produced a printed tape that evaluated the character of the person whose head had been poked at. Several varieties of the machine are still in operation at the Museum of Questionable Medical Devices in Minneapolis, Minnesota, where genial proprietor Robert McCoy demonstrates a variety of admittedly **quack** devices.

An exceptionally fatuous notion popular well into this century, totally unsupported by the most superficial examination of the evidence but therefore still quite popular among the uninformed, phrenol-

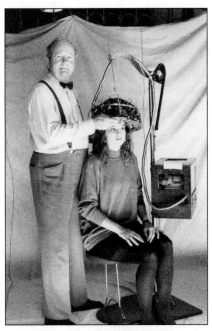

"Dr." Robert McCoy applies the Psycograph to a young woman who obviously needs her head examined. The 32 probes extend to touch the scalp, then register an "analysis" on the recorder.

ogy is another **"science"** that seems to satisfy the human need to solve the enigmas of character and fate.

physiognomy The art of reading character and fate from the features of the face. It was once widely believed that one's true qualities were mirrored in the configuration, size, and condition of the facial features. Criminologists of the nineteenth century seized upon this possibility and squandered a great amount of study and money on the shape of the criminal ear.

The Oscar Wilde story *The Picture of Dorian Gray* (1891) was based on the premise that a highly realistic painting of a young man, rather than the man himself, took on all the physiognomical changes associated with an evil life.

See also **Adamantius.**

Piddington, Sydney and Lesley (1918-1991 and 1925-) In their heyday during the 1940s, the Piddingtons had England thoroughly convinced that they were able to read one another's minds. Aside from their great skill, the fact that they were able to make use of radio exposure (in 1949) was a strong reason for their success. At a period when the notion of ESP was being referred to as "mental radio," the Piddingtons were regarded by many as probably able to converse by telepathy. They were careful to disavow any such idea.

During their time, these performers were the subjects of much scientific controversy, though their attitude convinced most academics that they were entertainers and nothing more, which was exactly the case.

Pike, Bishop James A. (1913-1969)

Episcopalian Bishop James Pike became a devoted supporter of **spiritualism,** convinced by the **spirit medium Arthur Ford** that he'd been contacted by his deceased son Jim. In 1966, at age twenty, Pike's son had shot himself in a New York hotel room. Pike even wrote a book about the personal evidence that Ford had offered him to prove the contact, and various bits of "proof" he'd discovered himself.

Pike was deeply impressed by what he described as "evidential" events such as one day finding a safety pin on the floor which was open at an angle which he said was exactly the angle formed by the hands of a clock at the hour his son had died. It is little wonder that Pike accepted everything else offered him to establish the reality of **survival after death.** One wonders what would have happened had his son died at six o'clock.

Such persons often become interested in survival-after-death ideas when a loved one dies, as was also the case with **Sir Arthur Conan Doyle** and with **Sir William Crookes.** Pike was unaware of such advantages as the **Blue Book** and Ford's own personal research files, which enabled the medium to produce all sorts of apparently evidential material of a personal nature to support his claims.

Pike died tragically in 1969 in Israel during a "spiritual pilgrimage" in the desert.

Piper, Leonora E. (1857-1950)

A Boston housewife who said she discovered her power as a **spirit medium** at age twenty-seven, Mrs. Piper told of an Indian **spirit guide** with the unlikely name of Chlorine who was aided by another guide named Dr. Phinuit, which she pronounced "finny." Strangely, this French doctor knew only a little French and less about medicine.

The mediumship of Mrs. Piper, which involved dramatic teeth-gnashing, moaning, and thrashing about, was enthusiastically supported by the famous psychologist/philosopher William James. The fact that she regularly spoke with Longfellow and Bach (the latter spoke no German in **Summerland**) provided James with excellent methods for testing the medium, but such tests were not done.

Mrs. Piper began featuring **automatic writing,** and then in 1911 abandoned her **séances** altogether and concentrated solely on the automatic writing.

She was investigated by Richard Hodgson, a member of the **American Society for Psychical Research,** for eighteen years. He became convinced of her legitimacy, and he was very pleased when she told him that he would have a long life, would soon marry, and would have two children. Hodgson died a few months later, unmarried and childless.

PK — *see* **psychokinesis.**

placebo effect Miraculous recoveries, unexplained cessation of pain, and termination of certain medical conditions in **faith healing** and other such procedures is often believed to be either due to occult forces or to divine intervention. More likely, this could be due to the well-known placebo effect.

Some recent studies indicate that in cases of neuroses and depression, almost any type of therapy is better than none at all. The word *placebo* is Latin and means "I shall please." It is defined by Webster's as

a process or substance, of little or no known worth in itself, which is applied to a problem in order to produce an encouraging or "pleasing" result.

This phenomenon takes place when a patient is exposed to a satisfactory "bedside manner" and/or when medication, manipulation, passing of the hands, **prayer,** or other means (any or all of which may be entirely ineffectual in themselves, but are seen by the recipient as unique, special, or advanced) are applied to the problem. Such effects may also take place when the patient feels in control of his situation or when he has surrendered that control to another in whom he has confidence. This is a simple case of what is known as "transference." Encouragement leads to hope, and hope to better self-care and self-interest.

Many types of chronic pain, because of the emotional condition of the sufferer, are associated with chronic anxiety. An efficient and caring physician, knowledgeable about the placebo effect, can largely alleviate that anxiety and thus improve at least the symptoms of certain ailments.

Even American jurist Oliver Wendell Holmes had an opinion on this matter:

Healing is a living process, greatly under the influence of mental conditions. It has often been found that the same wound found received in battle will do well in the soldiers that have beaten, that would prove fatal in those that have just been defeated.

It is well to consider the possibility of this powerful psychological effect when evaluating some claims of "miraculous" healing.

planchette The heart-shaped pointer device often said to have been invented in 1852 by a man named Planchette, but this seems highly unlikely, given that the French word *planche* means "board," and thus *planchette* means "small board."

This device is usually used with a **Ouija board,** the point of the heart moving over the board to indicate the letters or numbers. It is supported above the board or paper on three short legs equipped with tiny casters or other bearings. If equipped with a pencil at the pointed end as a support, it can be used over a piece of paper in **automatic writing.**

The *Daily News* of London in 1896, describing in an obituary the life and work of a hare-brained socialite of the day, was well aware of the real value of the device:

For nine years, he toyed with the planchette, the turned tables, in short used the familiar, hanky-panky means of communication with the unseen world.

See also **Ouija board.**

police dowsers (*First see* **dowsing.**) These are dowsers who claim they assist the police by sensing the presence of bodies or murderers while consulting maps. This is only a variety of the **police psychics** phenomenon, but shows some specifically unique aspects. An example follows.

One of the most prominent serial killer mysteries ever to take place in the United States became known as the Hillside Strangler case. Over a long period of time, a number of women had been murdered in southern California and the police were baffled. California dowser Verne McGuire, who used a **pendulum** swinging over a map, confidently told a writer for the Ridgecrest *Daily Independent* newspaper how he had helped to solve that case. McGuire told the *Independent* that the police refused to listen to him at first, but that finally he and his dowser friends

> got the Los Angeles police and sheriff's department, the Marshall Service and the Federal Bureau of Investigation. They told us that if we knew where the Hillside Strangler was, we must be involved with him. To prove we weren't involved, we had to find him in such a way that it was impossible we could be involved, so we moved in with some cops. Then he killed again. Because he would now be on the run, we thought this was the best time to look for him.

These amateurs proposed to find the strangler by using their pendulums over a map of the area. According to McGuire, they actually located him by this means and sent the police to a certain spot on the map, where he was found in his car sitting at a service station, and in the trunk of the car were articles of clothing and a purse belonging to one of his victims. When the murderer was arrested, said McGuire, "He knew they had him. We were vindicated."

Not according to the police, who in fact solved the case by totally different means. First of all, the Hillside Strangler turned out to be two persons working together, not just one. The U.S. Marshal's Office was not involved at all in the investigation, nor was the FBI. As for the Los Angeles police, who actually solved the case, they reported that McGuire's description of how and where the killers were found is quite fictional:

> McGuire's statements concerning the "Hillside Strangler" case and his involvement are in conflict with what occurred. One of the suspects was arrested in Bellingham, Washington, and the second was arrested at his place of business in the City of Glendale. No clothing belonging to any of the victims was ever found.

The case provides an excellent example of unchallenged claims uncritically published by the media, the kind of claims which unfortunately are usually not again examined and which thus go into the literature of the paranormal as factual. In this case, Mr. David J. Simmons contacted the editor of the Ridgecrest *Daily Independent* newspaper and informed him of the facts. The editor ignored this and neither acknowledged the contribution of Mr. Simmons nor published it. The *Independent* continues to report unproven claims.

police psychics (*First see* **psychometry**.) There are some psychometrists who claim they can handle items connected with crimes, particularly violent crimes, and can obtain, by their powers, impressions that help the police in the solutions of these crimes. These people are sometimes called in by the police, but more often it turns out that they themselves have contacted the police, have said that they know something about a crime, and are thus invited to make a statement. The police, by the very nature of their duties, must choose to record any volunteered information.

In one case in the United States within recent years, police listened with more than usual interest to a **psychic** who told them about a serious industrial fire that he not only had predicted with great accuracy, but about which he had supplied important details after the event, details which it appeared he could only know as a result of his special powers. His account was so accurate that he was immediately arrested and an investigation soon revealed that he'd had no need of paranormal powers to produce his visions. His information was essentially first-hand: He himself was the arsonist.

If there is any ability on the part of a psychic to supply law enforcement officials with relevant data which might assist in obtaining the solution to a crime, that ability should be cultivated and used. To find out if psychics could assist the police, American psychologist Dr. Martin Reiser conducted two extensive investigations into the use of psychics by the Los Angeles Police Department for that purpose. After several years of research, his conclusion was that psychics could contribute nothing useful to police work. "Psychics come out of the woodwork during cases which the media become heavily involved in," he says.

Part of Dr. Reiser's experimentation involved weapons used in homicide cases. These were mixed in with "virgin" items as controls, and it was found that the psychics were unable to differentiate among them.

Inspector Edward Ellison of the U.K.'s Scotland Yard, in response to statements by psychics that they regularly worked with them, reported that:

1. Scotland Yard never approach psychics for information.

2. There are no official "police psychics" in England.

3. The Yard does not endorse psychics in any way.

4. There is no recorded instance in England of any psychic solving a criminal case or providing evidence or information that led directly to its solution.

Inspector Ellison had canvassed his department to find out if any police officers had consulted psychics or were able to benefit from the use of psychics. In all of the eight districts of London that the Yard covers, he made inquiries, and he found that rather than the officers seeking out the psychics, it was the other way around. Said Ellison, "They've [the police] been approached, is the answer.

"I've had a psychologist and a statistician standing by since last August, and so far, nothing reported," said the inspector. His inquiry ended in August 1991. The results were negative.

The famous Yorkshire Ripper case in the U.K. was a bonanza for the psychics, and for the sensational newspapers as well. The *Sunday People* newspaper consulted Britain's then-leading psychic/**medium** who provided what she said were psychic drawings of the Ripper's friends, relatives, and even his car mechanic. All this information was not only useless, but was quite wrong.

Mr. Bob Baxter, chief press officer for the West Yorkshire police, made a statement about the hundreds of persons who offered clues in the Yorkshire Ripper case:

Many people contacted us during the Ripper inquiry. Many of them were mediums or people professing to have psychic powers. However, nothing that any of these people told us has any bearing on the outcome of the case. We certainly did not discuss our investigations with them.

This is in sharp contrast with the numerous claims made by psychics who said they helped solve the matter.

In 1980/81, a series of murders of young black men in Atlanta, Georgia, attracted the attention of psychics, who sent in more than nineteen thousand letters and over two thousand drawings that attempted to identify the killer. Most of those described or drawn were white men, but the murderer turned out to be a young Afro-American. None of the drawings or letters properly described the murderer or gave his correct name, though many names were tried.

poltergeist   Derived from the German words *polter* for "commotion" and *geist* for "spirit," a poltergeist is a **ghost** of mischievous character, usually throwing things about and damaging the surroundings. Martin Luther referred to this type of manifestation and declared it to be the product of **demons**.

Poltergeists usually show up in homes where a discontented adolescent lives, and the phenomena seem to take place only when that individual is present. When the discontent is relieved, the mischief ceases. It is interesting to note that in a significant percentage of these cases, the child is also adopted or living in a foster home.

A modern case of such a haunting took place in Columbus, Ohio, at the home of the Resch family in 1984. *See* **Columbus poltergeist**.

poppet   Another name for the wax doll used in **voodoo**.

possession The literal occupation of a person's body by a **devil, demon,** or **spirit** is believed in by several religions, even today. It is said that the possessed person speaks in a different voice and often in an unknown tongue. The 1972 film *The Exorcist* popularized the idea and gave rise to dozens of suddenly popular **exorcisms.**

See **glossolalia** *and* **obsession.**

potion A mixture or liquid, usually to be ingested, made to serve a magical function. Also known as a philter, especially when used to win the object of one's affection or to bring about an erotic or emotional effect on the subject. *See also* **ointment.**

Poughkeepsie seer — *see* **Davis, Andrew Jackson.**

Prabhupada, Swami — *see* **Hare Krishna.**

prayer A recited **incantation** designed to force or cajole a deity or deities into changing the normal, existing, or probable course of events in the universe, obtain an advantage, or avoid a divine penalty. Also an expression of gratitude or adulation, or an affirmation of continual fear, made to a deity.

A prayer is often accompanied by a promise or a sacrifice (the firstborn, money, giving up a favorite vice, not lying, a select bit of food the priests can eat) to seal or satisfy the agreement. A **spell.**

precognition Knowledge of a future event or circumstance not obtained through inference or deduction, but by **paranormal** means.

prediction — *see* **prophecy.**

Premanand B. Premanand is a prominent leader of the Indian Committee for Scientific Investigation of Claims of the Paranormal. He publishes the *Indian Skeptic,* a monthly journal of the committee. Premanand tours the subcontinent and around the world demonstrating how the Indian **fakirs** and "godmen" do their conjuring tricks, and he constantly questions claims of **kundalini** and other powers said to be possessed by the many Indian performers.

premonition — *see* **prophecy.**

Presidential Curse Beginning in 1840 with William Henry Harrison, and at twenty-year intervals up until 1960, each president of the United States elected or reelected in those years died in office. Fans of this notion choose to ignore the fact that President Zachary Taylor, elected in 1848 (not a twenty-year interval) died sixteen months after taking office, on July 9, 1850. He does not fit the expectation, so is excluded.

Those who search for cycles confidently expected Ronald Reagan, elected in 1980, to suffer the same fate. Reagan, it seems, has broken the "curse." Thank you, Mr. President.

See also **Jeane Dixon.**

Price, Harry (1881-1948) A prominent British "ghost hunter" whose major investigation was of **Borley Rectory,** Price lived a life which was a strange mixture of fact and fraud. He claimed to be descended from an aristocratic family, to have inherited wealth, and to be an expert archaeologist, bibliographer, numismatist, and—most importantly—a **psychic** researcher.

Price organized the National Laboratory of Psychical Research in 1927, in direct opposition to the London-based **Society for Psychical Research.** He wrote on numismatics for a short time, and then extensively on his psychic interests. Among his books are *Leaves from a Psychist's Case-Book* (1933), *Confessions of a Ghost-Hunter* (1936), *Fifty Years of Psychical Research* (1939), *The Most Haunted House in England* (1940), *Search for Truth* (autobiography, 1942), and *The End of Borley Rectory* (1946).

Among the many rare books in Price's extensive library were several volumes dealing with **conjuring,** and a number that discussed specific techniques applicable to the **spiritualistic** type of trickery that can be used to approximate ghost phenomena. Price was well versed in conjuring, belonged to a well-known conjurors' organization, and served there as a librarian.

Even during his lifetime, Price was exposed as a charlatan. A brilliant and competent researcher, he apparently wished to add to his reputation by fraud. Following his death, investigations showed that Price had been more of an adventurer than what he had purported to be. He had faked, plagiarized, and bluffed his way into

the confidence of his many and enthusiastic supporters, along the way accomplishing some valuable and genuine research.

To quote **Dr. Eric J. Dingwall,** who knew and collaborated with Price on various projects:

> When I first knew him [Price] showed no signs of the ability to present psychic material in a way which appealed not only to the popular press but to the intelligent general reader who wanted to know what was being done in this field. At the end of his life he was by far the greatest master of this type of narrative. The most trivial incident or haphazard meeting could be made into an enthralling tale through the imaginative pen of Harry Price.

His very extensive and valuable library, amounting to 4,376 books and thousands of pamphlets, photographs, and periodicals, filled eighty-seven packing cases when it was accepted by the University of London, where it resides today.

Project Alpha — *see* **psychokinete.**

prophecy This general term encompasses a wide range of claimed phenomena—prediction, premonition, prognostication—all of which can be defined as the ability to foretell events, more limited to an ability not related to induction or deduction from known facts. Many studies have been made to determine whether the ability exists, and if so, how accurate it might be. One of the most extensive is the Premonition

Registry, where records are kept of thousands of predictions that are sent in. Not much has been heard from the registry in recent years.

Research in this matter is subject to the element of selective recall, whereby individuals tend to remember when a dream or hunch turns out correctly and forget it if it fails. Therefore, anecdotal reports are not of much value.

In 1983, an examination was made of the evidence offered by 127 persons who responded to a U.K. newspaper feature on premonitions. A questionnaire was accompanied by a personality test. Most who answered were female, average age was forty-six years, and 80 percent of them said that they were correct 70 percent of the time. The personality test showed that these persons were significantly more neurotic than average and scored high on a "lie scale." Some 85 percent of their predictions involved death or other tragedies. The investigator concluded that the ability to have premonitions is important since it warns females and thereby provides a "survival advantage to the species." No comment.

Large-scale studies of prophetic ability have failed to provide sufficient dependable data to support claims that it is valid. Mystics have offered strange rationalizations of this fact, as demonstrated in *The Magician's Companion,* a comprehensive volume by Bill Whitcomb dealing with magical formulas and systems. Mr. Whitcomb observes:

One point to remember is that the probability of an event changes as soon as a prophecy (or divination) exists. . . . The accuracy or outcome of any prophecy is altered by the desires and attachments of the seer and those who hear the prophecy.

The obvious paradox provided by these caveats is quite acceptable in the pursuit of **magic,** it seems.

The prophecy business was once fraught with danger. While modern practitioners are forgiven over and over again for failures, Henry VIII of England meted out a nasty death to Elizabeth Barton, the "Holy Maid of Kent" who predicted His Majesty's immediate death for having married Anne Boleyn. The punishment was for treason, not for having been wrong by fourteen years.

Of the thirty-nine books of the *Old Testament,* eighteen are ascribed to prophets. The Hebrews, Muslims, and Mormons all have strong dependence upon the teachings of prophets.

See also **astrology, Cayce,** *I Ching,* **Jeane Dixon, Nostradamus, palmistry,** *and* **scrying.**

prophet — *see* prophecy.

Prophet, Elizabeth Clare (1940-) President of the Church Universal and Triumphant, founded in 1958 with her husband, Mark Prophet (1918-1973). The church moved its headquarters from Malibu, California, to Montana, where a massive underground bunkerlike construction has been established, with tons of arms and food supplies saved against an **Armageddon** that has been promised several times but somehow delayed. The dismantlement of the Soviet Union has essentially dampened Ms. Prophet's hopes for doom, since she had designated that political entity as The Enemy.

The church now claims that their chanting of mantras and use of "Violet Flame Decrees" has forestalled global disaster. Maybe. We'll see. If so, thanks, Liz

psi The twenty-third letter of the Greek alphabet (pronounced *sy* in America, but often *p-sy* in Europe) suggested by psychologists **R. H. Thouless** and **W. P.** Weisner in 1944 to denote **paranormal** events, abilities, and studies. Defined by the **Parapsychological Association** as

> the apparent ability of human beings and other species to acquire information about their environment and to affect it physically without the use of currently understood mechanisms.

One **parapsychologist** who expresses disenchantment with psi is **Dr. Susan Blackmore.** Perhaps her opinion is best expressed in her own words:

> My ten years of research have left me an open-minded skeptic rather than a disbeliever, but I have come to one conclusion: The notion of psi is remarkably unhelpful. If we want to understand the higher potentials of human experience, we need a better notion.

psi gap Borrowed from such expressions as "technology gap," popular during the Cold War to denote the discrepancy between an advantage obtained or held by the Soviet or by the Western powers, the "psi gap" was used as a scare technique by the **parapsychologists** and the **psychics**. It was largely fed by various hoaxes such as those perpetrated by a reporter working for syndicated Washington columnist Jack Anderson. He had "psychotechtronic weapons" such as the "hyperspatial howitzer" and "SADDOR"—a satellite-borne mechanical **dowsing rod**— striking fear into the public mind.

A leading **psychic** of the day, **Uri Geller,** was actively promoting interest in the psi gap, urging members of the U.S. Congress to invest in probing these mysteries as a defense mode, until the Soviet Union collapsed and relations between the powers relaxed. It has since been determined that neither side had anything even vaguely resembling a psi weapon, psi technology, or psi power.

psychic As an adjective, describes a variety of supernatural forces, events, or powers. **Telepathy, extrasensory perception** (ESP), **clairvoyance, spiritualistic phenomena, magical** or **divine healing, psychokinesis, levitation, prophecy,** or **fortune-telling** could come under this label. As a noun, it designates a person said to be able to call upon any of many psychic forces.

In this book, the word should always be viewed as if enclosed in quote marks.

psychic criminology — *see* police psychics.

psychic portraits Some persons who believe they have psychic powers produce what they call "psychic portraits" of dead persons. They say that the evidence they have that the persons so represented have ever lived is the acceptance of the sitters for whom the images were produced, and they usually say that they are unable to produce a likeness of any specific person upon request.

Frequently a sitter will accept a likeness as representing someone they have known. Since these performances are usually done for very large audiences and all present are challenged to come up with a correspondence between the portrait and someone who looked like the artwork, it is likely that the attempt will be successful. Sometimes sitters who are interviewed admit that they "went along" with the artist in order not to cause any conflict. They are, after all, believers, otherwise they most probably would not pay to attend such a gathering. Having paid their money, they have an interest in the performance being successful and want it to be a positive experience. Going along with it seems harmless enough and moves things forward.

See also **cold reading.**

psychic surgery Every week, increasing numbers of people from all over the world arrive in Manila, capital of the Republic of the Philippines, seeking **magical** aid from the *curanderos,* who claim they can heal every sort of malady. Apparently by means of **psychic**— or divine—powers, these **native healers** can reach their hands into the bodies of clients, extracting deadly tumors and other substances, along with quantities of blood. In most cases, there is no trace of an incision on the body of the patient.

To any experienced **conjuror,** the methods by which these seeming miracles are produced are very obvious. But inexperienced observers quite naturally do not see the trickery, and if they are predisposed to believe in magic, they are prepared to accept that something supernatural has taken place.

There are two distinct classes of this performance, which is now known as "psychic surgery." The most common form is relatively free of direct and immediate physical damage and risk to the person treated. It consists of secretly introducing the blood and other materials onto the surface of the body by means of sleight of hand. No incision takes place, and any infection which occurs does so through minor abrasions or scratches. The second form is simply a direct invasion of the body by means of small, shallow incisions, often made unobserved, under cover of distraction— in exactly the way that a conjuror would perform.

This Filipino practice has spread worldwide now, and in the states of California and Florida, psychic surgeons regularly visit on tour, untroubled by law enforcement agencies under the protection of the principle of Freedom of Religion. Since actual incisions are seldom made, the risk of infection is small. These practitioners, often assuming the titles "Reverend," "Brother," or "Doctor," typically charge $100 per minute for their services. In other cases, they make no formal charge, but accept sizable "donations" that are carefully suggested by them, in writing, to their victims.

One variety of "operation" performed by these people is actually a medieval procedure that involves actual invasion of the body. Known as "cupping," it consists of first making a tiny incision with a knife, usually without any sterilization, anesthetic, or antiseptic. Then a bit of cotton wool soaked in alcohol is placed upon a coin near or upon the cut, and the cotton is ignited. A small glass is then quickly inverted over the site. At this point the area is often covered with a cloth, as if performing a conjuring trick and thus concealing from sight the process that now takes place inside the inverted glass.

As the oxygen is consumed by the flame, a partial vacuum is created, drawing the flesh up into the glass. This causes the wound to bleed, and when the partial vacuum is thus equalized, the cloth is removed so that one can see that about one-fifth of the volume of the glass is now filled with blood. This process will, to an uninformed person, appear as if some magical force had brought the blood from the wound.

psychography — *see* **automatic writing.**

psychokinesis (PK) Once known as "telekinesis," PK is the claimed power to affect matter by mind alone. Such feats as spoon bending, moving small objects, causing items to fall over or fly through the air, or changing the quality or quantity of any substance are included in this category.

Many explanations have been offered for such feats, including certain mythic energies such as "ectenic force," said to come from the body of the **spirit medium** during a **séance,** resulting in **table tipping** and **apports.** (The word *ectenic* was coined by two Swiss scientists, Count de Gasparin and Professor Thury, who convinced themselves that table tippers were generating a special force, rather than simply pushing the table about. This postulation denies the existence of **ectoplasm** and its more divine origins.) *See also* **parapsychology.**

psychokinete A term for a gifted person who can produce **psychokinetic** effects, invented by **parapsychologist** Michael Thalbourne to describe two young subjects, Michael Edwards and Steve Shaw, who in 1982 convinced parapsychologists at the McDonnell Laboratory for Psychical Research (MacLab) in St. Louis, Missouri, that they could bend metal, impress images on photographic film, move objects, and use ESP.

The psychokinetes proved to be ringers, sent in to show that simple **conjuring** techniques were sufficient to deceive the scientists. The parapsychologists easily accepted the boys as genuine psychics and until the hoax was voluntarily exposed in 1983 by the boys themselves, the scientists were sure they had proven the existence of supernatural forces and prepared a scientific paper on their investigation.

Project Alpha, as the matter became known, was designed to show that some scientists are easily deceived and that they usually have no adequate knowledge of conjuring techniques. Alpha cast no aspersions on the honesty of the researchers, but did question their competence. It was a great success and has resulted in some parapsychologists being more careful about their conclusions. Following the revelation of the hoax, the MacLab closed permanently.

Though Mike Edwards got a real, traditional job and only performs occasionally in **magic,** Steve Shaw has gone on to become a ranking professional **mentalist.** He has been "buried alive" on network television and escaped from six feet down in the ground. In 1984 he performed another such stunt, being dug up after three days. He has developed many new angles to standard methods of the mentalists, and as a result has traveled internationally with his very clever and entertaining act.

See also **Beloff, John** .

psychometry/psychometrist It is a

common notion that "psychic vibrations"—of some unspecified and undefined nature—can be absorbed by places and by objects, particularly objects made of metal.

This is referred to as "psychometry." It was "discovered" by a Dr. J. R. Buchanan, who named it and called it a **science.**

Many persons have had the experience of returning to a childhood location and feeling the "chill" of returning memories from long ago. Standing before an ancient monument can bring on strange feelings that seem to be the result of the edifice itself, and not merely of an awareness of the history and the personalities involved with that monument. It would be difficult to walk through Westminster Abbey and fail to be stirred by the memories thus invoked of famous persons.

It is said that certain persons have an ability whereby they can sense **vibrations** taken up by objects, absorbed from persons and events that have been associated with those objects. If psychometry actually works, it should be possible for a practitioner (known as a "psychometrist") to "read" vibrations from objects which have been intimately associated with a specific person, and to differentiate them from other similar objects owned by another person. The claim has been thoroughly tested and found false.

The psychometrists claim that by "reading" these vibrations, they can obtain information, and they also use it for diagnosing illness, with the same degree of success.

psychotronics A "science" that

includes **dowsing,** radionics, and the construction and, as of 1974, the use of various "machines" that are said to focus and concentrate psychic powers. This is currently a very popular fad in Russia, though scientists there insist that the devices cannot be tested because of their esoteric nature. For the same reason, they also cannot be demonstrated. All rests on faith.

See also **Drown, Ruth.**

Puharich, Dr. Andrija (Henry K. Puharich, 1918-) A medical doctor who has never practiced except as an intern, Puharich served the U.S. Army in several functions.

In 1959, he wrote *The Sacred Mushroom, Key to the Door of Eternity,* about his adventures with peyote and other hallucinogenic substances. In Hawaii, he was appointed to be a "grand kahuna," or mystical chief. Then, in the early 1970s, he met **Uri Geller,** and the result was another book, *Uri: A Journal of the Mystery of Uri Geller.* A very strange book relating highly unlikely events (dematerializations, disembodied voices, and **teleportations**), it was endorsed enthusiastically by its subject, who declared that "every word [of the book] is true!"

In Brazil, Puharich investigated the work of the **psychic surgeon** named **Arigó** and wrote an afterword to a naive book on the subject, *Arigó, Surgeon of the Rusty Knife.*

pyramid inch A unit of measurement proposed by Charles Piazzi Smyth, a Scottish astronomer who was obsessed with the **Great Pyramid of Giza** (*which see*). The original outside "casing" layer of stones that had covered the Great Pyramid had been carted away over the ages, so that the true dimensions were unknown until investigators began finding a few of the stones buried at the foot of the structure. Smyth measured the first casing stone that was uncovered, divided the width by twenty-five (the reason for choosing 25 was never given), and obtained what he called the basic unit used in the pyramid's construction, the pyramid inch. This was just slightly greater than the English inch.

Though it was soon found that other casing stones measured different widths, Smyth's definition was retained by believers in the myth, and it is still used today by those who accept that the Great Pyramid is a tool of **prophecy.**

pyramid power A book by author Pat Flanagan, *Pyramid Power,* citing unknown and untraceable sources, claimed that wonderful forces were at work in the **Great Pyramid,** forces that could be tapped by those who would purchase from him miniature replicas of the monument.

In 1973, U.K. author Lyall Watson told of placing a dead cat inside a model of the **Great Pyramid** and thus preserving it. He later endorsed a process discovered by a Czech engineer named Drbal whereby it was claimed that razor blades placed in a small pyramid remained sharp despite use.

The craze for pyramid devices lasted through the seventies, though simple tests of the claims easily showed them to be spurious.

Pythagoras (circa 580-500 B.C.) A prominent Greek philosopher/mathematician who developed intricate mystical theories involving the basic qualities of numbers. He taught that "number is all."

Pythagoras contributed greatly to an understanding of musical harmonies and their mathematical sources, and this gave rise to his ideas of corresponding cosmic harmonies. "Harmony of the Spheres" is the term used to designate that notion. Those views, though they were expressed mystically by the philosopher, are basically sound. Unfortunately but understandably, the valuable elementary truths were smothered in abstract attributions such as good and evil, male and female, positive and negative.

The school he left behind him continued to generate ideas and formulations that have often been attributed directly to him. The famous Pythagorean theorem—that the square on the hypotenuse of a right-angled triangle is equal in area to the sum of the squares on the other two sides—is probably a discovery made well after his death, but using the methods he had advocated.

Q

qabala — *see* kabala.

qi (pronounced *chee*; the Japanese equivalent is "*ki*") The poorly defined substance, the "life force" believed by the ancient Chinese—and many **new agers**—to circulate in the body through the **meridians.** Balancing the **yin and yang,** the two different forms of qi—feminine and masculine—is a process said to bring about harmony of body and spirit. There are thirty-two different kinds of qi, all essential to all forms of life.

Since belief in this substance is very widespread in Asia, it has become a firm article of cultural acceptance, and there is great reluctance there to examine the matter closely. Fortunately, the Chinese have accepted other, more Occidental forms of medical treatment and have incorporated those into their system.

See also **acupuncture.**

qi gong (pronounced *chee-gung*) One claim made by practitioners of this art is "remote diagnosis," in which the diagnoser needs only the name of the patient in order to correctly state what ailments are afflicting that person. Since patients seldom, if ever, report results, the practitioner has no means for assessing his or her success. This claim, and the many other aspects of qi gong, have been tested many, many times and have failed eloquently. For a fuller discussion of qi gong, *see* **acupuncture.**

quack An ignorant person who pretends to have knowledge of medicine and wondrous remedies. The word is short for *quacksalver,* meaning, one who "quacks" (makes a loud noise) about a remedy (a salve).

Though a multitude of quacks have been exposed and convicted for their activities, the support of their dupes is eternal. An early American scientist/philosopher offered a more specific comment on the breed. Ben Franklin was aware of that strange quirk of human nature that elects the victim as chief supporter of the trickster. He said:

> There are no greater liars in the world than quacks—except for their patients.

One prominent British quack of the 1830s who went by the title of

St. John Long, developed a salve that he claimed indicated disease by raising a rash on any afflicted body part to which he applied it. The means of using this salve need hardly be puzzled over for long. This fraud was convicted of manslaughter and was fined for causing the death of one patient, then the following year he was brought up on another such charge and acquitted. This time he was driven in triumph from the courthouse in a nobleman's carriage and cheered by the crowds.

At this writing, quackery is becoming more and more popular worldwide, particularly in the United States, and threatens to supersede much of modern medicine. Political and legal considerations have prevented open discussion or even the questioning of procedures that are clearly without merit. The highly litigious nature of American society has effectively provided the quacks with protection, and the public suffers because it cannot afford to defend itself, and politicians fear censure.

R

radionics — *see* **Drown, Ruth.**

Rampa, Tuesday Lobsang (Cyril Henry Hoskin, 1911-1981, also Dr. Carl Kuon Suo) A Surrey plumber's assistant who in 1956 published a romantic tale, *The Third Eye,* dealing with a Tibetan youth from Lhasa who had a hole poked in his forehead—an operation to open the "third eye"—and thereby became gifted with all manner of mystic powers, had encounters with the **Abominable Snowman,** and performed levitation. Hoskin said that he was the chosen youth.

The book was a best-seller in twelve countries and was followed by *The Cave of the Ancients.* When it developed that the author spoke not a word of Tibetan, had not ever owned a passport, and certainly had not been a hero of the Chinese air force battling the Japanese—as he'd claimed—the inventive Hoskin came out with two more books, *Doctor from Lhasa* and *The Rampa Story,* which explained all by saying that the real Rampa had occupied the body of the otherwise ordinary plumber's assistant. Believers gladly accepted this illumination of what had appeared to be a refutation of the Rampa history.

Hoskin produced several more books, including *My Visit to Venus,* in which he described a trip in a flying saucer in the company of two Venusians named Tall One and Broad One.

Having no adequate knowledge of **science,** Hoskin produced some classic blunders. In his 1955 book *Flying Saucer from Mars,* he explained that UFOs do not land on Earth because they are made of anti-matter, which upon contact with regular, terrestrial matter would produce a spectacular explosion resulting in the mutual annihilation of both the substances involved. He failed to recognize that air itself would bring that about.

Hoskins's books are of course still very popular and widely sold.

Ramtha — *see* **Knight, J. Z.**

rapping A phenomenon first widely exhibited in 1848 by the **Fox sisters** in which raps are made to come from the floor, a table, or a wall. There are those who believe these are signals originating with **spirits.** Such tintinnabulation is very popular at **séances,** and incidentally also very easy to accomplish by trickery, if the real thing is not available at the moment.

There are various mechanisms available for this purpose, but the basic trick can be accomplished by a person who has the ability to crack the toe joints. While the person is standing, this gives rise to a distinct thump on the floor. In the time of the Fox sisters, one Reverend Eli Noyes discovered and demonstrated seventeen different methods of producing raps without mechanisms. His raps were indistinguishable from "real" spirit communications.

The stunt is not original with the Fox sisters. A 1528 book published in Paris described the spirit of Sister Alis de Tellieux, who had lived in a monastery where she swiped some relics and was thus doomed to walk around the place as a ghost. The book describes what followed:

> A number of years afterwards, when the monastery was occupied by other and better nuns, one of their number, a girl of about eighteen years, was aroused from her sleep by the apparition of Sister Alis. For some time afterwards the spirit haunted her wherever she went, continually rapping on the ground where she stood.

It appears that this neat trick has a long history.

Rasputin (Né Grigory Yefimovich Novykh, 1872?-1916)

A mystic popularly referred to as the "mad monk" who was very popular at the court of Nicholas II of Russia because of his attempts to heal the Czar's son, a hemophiliac.

Rasputin was also known as a notorious lecher; he espoused a religious philosophy that dictated sexual exhaustion as a means of liberation and revelation. His adopted name, Rasputin, means "debauched one."

He became very influential at the Russian court, particularly with the Empress Alexandra. He appointed ministers and used large quantities of treasury money for his projects. There were many attempts to assassinate him, only one achieving any success. In December 1916 at St. Petersburg, a determined group of nobles led by Vladimir Pureskivich poisoned him, clubbed and shot him, and finally drowned him. His death preceded by a few weeks the takeover of the empire by the revolutionaries and the murder of the Czar and his family. Doubtless the failure of the Czar to anticipate the revolution was due to his loss of the services of his mystic.

reflexology

The art of diagnosing ailments by examination of the sole of the foot, and of treating the patient by manipulation of parts of the foot that are said to relate to corresponding body parts and areas. Similarly to such notions as **palmistry,** ear **acupuncture,** and **iridology,** the foot in reflexology is believed to represent a **homunculus:** The great toe is the head, the next toe is the right arm, and so on.

Reflexology could be regarded as simple **sympathetic magic** except for one saving factor: treatment is effected by massaging the foot, and that usually feels rather good. As a

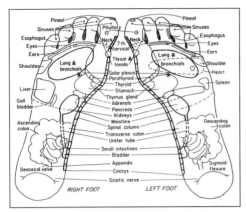

A diagram of the soles of the feet, indicating specific areas ("reflex points") related to organs and parts of the body, according to the theory. Relief is achieved, say the practitioners, by pressing these points to "stimulate blocked nerve ending." This is nonsensical jargon.

medical tool for treating specific ailments not connected with the pedal extremities, however, it is useless.

Reich, Wilhelm — *see* orgone.

reincarnation

The idea that the spirit of a person leaves the body at death and is reborn into another. It is claimed, in some versions, that the spirit must wait a certain period before entering the next body.

In some Indian religions, the spirit passes either to a higher or lower form of life, depending on the righteousness of the life just left. This obviously encourages righteousness.

The idea is a very important part of the **Theosophical** religion, which teaches that there are a series of reincarnations necessary for the **spirit** to attain The Path of Perfection.

See also **karma.**

relics

(religious) Though all the Protestant denominations have historically condemned the veneration of holy objects/relics and their use in healing, the Catholic church—at one time—preferred to depend entirely upon the **magical** qualities attributed to the possessions or actual physical parts of various saints and biblical characters for healing. The Vatican not only permitted but encouraged this practice, which entered history in the third century.

Catholic churches and private collections still overflow with hundreds of thousands of relics. Included are pieces of the True Cross (enough to build a few log cabins), hundreds of thorns from the mock crown placed upon Christ, bones of the children slain by King Herod, the toenails and bones of Saint Peter, the bones of the Three Wise Kings and of Saint Stephen (as well as his complete corpse, including another complete skeleton!), jars of the Virgin Mary's milk, the bones and several entire heads and pieces thereof that were allegedly once atop John the Baptist, sixteen foreskins of Christ, Mary Magdalene's entire skeleton (with two right feet), scraps of bread and fish left over from feeding the five thousand, a crust of bread from the Last Supper, and a hair from Christ's beard—not to mention a few **shrouds,** including the one at Turin, Italy.

A church just outside Moscow holds the fourteenth-century bones, it is said, of three Russian saints: Bishop John, Saint Euphemia and Saint Euphrosinia. Alas, examination shows that Saint Euphemia has been assembled from three different skeletons (one of them a child's) and has far too many ribs and several other extra bones. And all of these three assemblages are the remains of Mongols; the three saints were not Mongols. This may be a miracle.

One avid German collector claimed to have more than 17,000 of these objects, which inspired Pope Leo X to calculate that the man had saved himself exactly 694,779,550½ days in purgatory by such pious devotion to his hobby. But this man's efforts were dwarfed by the collection at the Schlosskirche at Halle, Germany, which boasted 21,483 relics in its vaults.

See also **Januarius, Saint.**

remote viewing This phenomenon first became a celebrated subject after **parapsychologists** Harold Puthoff and Russell Targ published a scientific paper which reported on experiments in which a remote location had been chosen, an experimenter visited there, and a subject recorded his or her psychic impressions of the spot. Their results seemed to prove that a "remote sensing" faculty did exist.

Subsequently, properly controlled tests were done by several other researchers, eliminating several sources of cuing and extraneous evidence that had been present in the tests. These new tests produced negative results. The data of Puthoff and Targ were reexamined by the other researchers, and it was found that their students were able to solve the locations without use of any psy-

chic powers, using only the clues that had inadvertently been included in the Puthoff and Targ transcripts.

rhabdomancy Also known as "water witching," "divining," and **dowsing,** *which see.* More strictly speaking, rhabdomancy is an art of throwing sticks, rods, or arrows on the ground to interpret the plans of nature. It has a parallel in "throwing the wands" in the process of *I Ching* fortune-telling.

Rhine, Dr. Joseph Banks (1896-1980) Dr. Rhine originally planned to enter the ministry, but graduated in botany at the University of Chicago. In 1922 he attended a lecture on **spiritualism** by **Sir Arthur Conan Doyle** and became interested in the subject, an interest that was furthered when he read *The Survival of Man,* a book by **Sir Oliver Lodge** on his supposed communications with deceased persons through **séances.**

In 1926, Rhine became acquainted with Dr. William McDougall, and the next year he left botany behind him and began to study **paranormal** claims. On one of his first investigations, Rhine discovered the medium **Margery Crandon** in fraud, and when he reported that fact, he was castigated by Conan Doyle and the other leaders of the spiritualists.

By 1930, Rhine and McDougall had begun studies at a psychology lab at Duke University in Durham, North Carolina. A colleague, **Dr. Karl Zener,** developed the set of five-symbol cards now known as Zener cards, for Rhine to use in testing **psychic** powers. By 1935, Rhine had established the Duke University **Parapsychology** Laboratory at Durham.

Dr. Rhine invented the term **extrasensory perception** (ESP) in one of his first books on the subject. He and his wife, **Dr. Louisa Rhine**, became known as the paramount experts on the subject of ESP.

Though there are in the literature many impressive reports of Rhine's successes with "gifted" subjects, it later developed that he had allowed himself to ignore much of the data he gathered, reporting the positive results and ignoring the failures. Very early in his career, he had been taken in by a "telepathic" horse named **Lady Wonder,** much to the embarrassment of his colleagues.

The final blow to Rhine occurred when **Dr. Walter Levy,** a trusted colleague at the Foundation for Research on the Nature of Man (FRNM), a private organization established by Rhine in 1962, was discovered to be **cheating** on an impressive animal-ESP test that had been reported as a huge success. Levy confessed and was fired.

At this point in time, Rhine's work, though pioneering and well intentioned, is not looked upon as definitive in any way. His understandable errors, given his lack of sophistication in handling and understanding people, give ample reason for rejecting his conclusions. As with all the exciting breakthroughs regularly announced by parapsychologists, flaws developed that put the work beyond serious acceptance.

Unlike some research projects in parapsychology, no hint of dishonesty on Rhine's part has ever been seriously suggested, though it may be that a certain amount of trickery was introduced into his lab without his knowledge. Though proponents of ESP are fond of quoting the immense odds against success in ESP tests by chance alone, those figures mean nothing at all if the experiments are not properly conducted.

See **Lady Wonder** *and* **Levy.**

Rhine, Dr. Louisa Ella (1891-1983)

Née Weckesser, Mrs. Rhine was the wife of **Dr. Joseph Banks Rhine** and was his closest collaborator. From the time of their marriage in 1920, when they were both students of biology at the University of Chicago, they worked together on developing test procedures and amassing data on ESP. Mrs. Rhine contributed many books to the study of psi, including *ESP in Life and Lab: Tracing Hidden Channels, Hidden Channels of the Mind, Mind Over Matter* (one of at least eleven books that have borne this title), *Psi: What Is It?* and *The Invisible Picture.*

Richet, Dr. Charles (1850-1935)

Richet was one of the most influential and important scientists who endorsed the claims of the **spirit mediums.** He was a Nobel laureate (1913, in physiology and medicine).

Though his accounts of **sittings** with such mediums as **Eva C.** and **William Eglinton** appear rather naive today, they were taken as proof by his readers of the period. He wrote that the reality of "[spiritual] **materialization** is as certainly established as any fact in science." However, Richet was not at all convinced by the performances of medium **Eusapia Palladino,** whom he also witnessed.

Roberts, Jane — *see* Seth.

Roll, William G. A parapsychologist associated with the Foundation for Research on the Nature of Man (FRNM), in Durham, North Carolina. He has specialized in the study of **poltergeist** phenomena and is the author of *The Poltergeist* (Nelson-Doubleday 1972). *See also* **Columbus poltergeist.**

Romany — *see* Gypsy.

Rosicrucians A mystical order said to have been started by Christian Rosenkreutz (1378-1484?) whose name translates as "Rosy Cross."

Very little is actually known about the origins of the group, though the modern Rosicrucians claim to be direct inheritors of the original purposes and philosophy. It appears to have an anti-Catholic outlook.

The Rosicrucian order first came to the attention of the world in Paris in 1623, when anonymous leaflets were distributed around the city announcing the "invisible college" that had materialized there. It is perhaps no coincidence that a new booklet titled *Fama Fraternitatis* dealing with the life of the previously-unknown Christian Rosenkreutz had

just been published by a Paris bookseller.

A modern revival, the Ancient and Mystical Order of the Rosy Cross (AMORC) was begun in 1909 by H. Spencer Lewis, an advertising man in California. Lewis actually purported to change zinc into gold during a demonstration of **alchemy** before the press in 1916.

AMORC continues today, operating from its base in San Jose, California, home of Rose-Croix University, complete with an Egyptian museum, sphinxes, a planetarium, and classrooms for studying **science** and **parapsychology.** The movement has advertised in every sort of magazine and newspaper, a major departure from the original "invisible college," and teaches such subjects as universal peace, harmony, willpower, and wisdom.

As with many political and religious groups, this sort of promise appeals to persons who feel alone and withdrawn from the world around them. It gives them a rather exclusive peer group, with a membership card, secret handshake, and secret passwords. Followers are told that they will develop exotic **psychic** powers and insights after studying—in person or by mail—the lessons offered. Much of the idea and theory being taught is based on alchemy.

royal touch Part of the tradition of divine healing through the touch of special persons is validated from scriptural references to such healings by Christ and the disciples and in direct instruction from Christ to his disciples in Matthew 10:8:

Heal the sick, raise the dead, cleanse the lepers, cast out devils.

European royalty decided that because they claimed to rule by divine right they could also claim to have the divine ability to heal. As early as 1307, people in need of healing were visiting Philip the Fair, King of France, for his holy touch. Soon, beginning with Edward the Confessor (ruled 1042-1066) the English kings were "touching" for scrofula, a tubercular inflammation of the lymph nodes often confused with similar afflictions of the face and eyes. Thus originated the "royal touch," which was said to be effective against this condition, and the disease became known in those days as the "king's evil." The last person said to have been "touched" in England was Dr. Samuel Johnson, in 1712, by queen Anne. He was only thirty months old, so could not have known better than to participate.

The presence and involvement of kings doubtless had an effect upon people with psychosomatic and quite imaginary ailments, and subjects eagerly provided affidavits to the monarchs in support of strong belief in this sort of healing.

In the eighteenth century, the Earl of Chesterfield took it up, much to the embarrassment of his friends.

runes A general term applied to a form of sticklike writing of Anglo-Saxon, Germanic, and Scandinavian origins. Probably because of the primitive flavor of the symbols, **magical** qualities have been ascribed to them. Runes have been found on many Old World megaliths and grave sites, and reportedly on some in the New World. It is highly doubtful that any of the latter are genuine.

Runes are used in **divination**. Letters are inscribed on wooden blocks, which are then thrown like dice to come up with random words that can then be interpreted.

Russell, Charles Taze — *see* **Jehovah's Witnesses.**

S

sabbat An assembly of **witches** and wizards, held every three months on February 2, **Walpurgis Night** (May Day Eve), Midsummer's Eve, and November Eve. Anointed with the appropriate substance made of the fat of murdered (preferably unbaptized) children, and using belladonna and aconite (*see also* **flying** *and* **ointment**) the attendees arrive flying on goats, broomsticks, rakes, and other unlikely conveyances. **Satan** himself presides, often in the form of a crow, cat, or goat. Nakedness is the accepted costume for the occasion.

Sai Baba (Sri Satya Sai Baba, 1926-). The word *baba* is derived from the Turkish word for "papa." Born Sathyanarayana Ratnakaru Raju, this modern Indian **yogi** has a large following all over the world, among them Harry Saltzman, producer of the James Bond films. His organization is ruled from his ashram Prasanti Nilayam (meaning "abode of great peace") at Puttaparti. He claims to be the **reincarnation** of Sai Baba of Shirdi (1856-1916).

His followers claim that he can produce *vibhuti* ("holy ash"), gold rings, and even modern Seiko wristwatches for them by simply reaching into the air. There are claims that he has raised the dead, levitated, healed cancer, and even done his version of the loaves-and-fishes miracle. These are referred to as **siddhis.**

Examination of films and videotapes of Sai Baba's actual performances show them to be simple sleight of hand, exactly the same as the sort used by the other Indian *jaduwallahs,* or "street conjurors." Sai Baba has never submitted to an examination of his abilities under controls, so his claims are totally unproven. **Parsimony** applies here.

India's leading debunker of the claims of the god-men who infest that country, the famous **Premanand,** has duplicated all of Sai Baba's tricks and tours the world demonstrating these feats.

Saint Elmo's fire Named after Saint Erasmus (a corruption of the name), patron saint of Mediterranean sailors, this is a natural high-voltage effect sometimes seen on the mast and spars of a sailing ship during calms, considered to be a benevolent warning of an impending storm. Blue halos in the form of flamelike discharges are seen at the tips of the rigging and are due to charges between the earth (water) and the atmosphere leaking off into the surrounding air. *See also* **Kirlian photography.**

Saint Germain, Claude Louis, Compte de (1710?-1784)

Attached to the court of Louis XV of France, Saint Germain claimed he was two thousand years old. More sober, but not more convincing sources put his age at either 188 or 223 when he died in 1784.

It was believed that he had mastered **alchemy** in all its facets, could make himself invisible, knew the secret of eternal life, and could speak all languages. He said he'd known Solomon and the Queen of Sheba.

British author Horace Walpole (1717-1779) reported that Saint Germain was in London in 1743, after which he was in France in the service of Louis. In France he had some political problems and fled to St. Petersburg. In Germany he claimed to have founded freemasonry and to have initiated **Cagliostro** into that brotherhood.

An amusing anecdote about Saint Germain has survived: Since he claimed to have discovered the secret of immortality, his valet also claimed to share that treasured knowledge with him. When asked by a visitor whether it was true, as his master had claimed, that he'd been present at the marriage at Cana in Galilee when Jesus Christ turned water into wine (John 2:1), the valet responded, "You forget, sir, that I have only been in the Comte's service for a century."

The **Rosicrucians** claim that Saint Germain is still alive and that he was once known as Sir **Francis Bacon** (1561-1626).

Saint Joseph of Copertino

A monk who is reputed to have flown forty feet from the middle of a church to the high altar. Doubtful. *See* **flying.**

Saint Malachy's prophecies

St. Malachy (1094-1148) was an Irish Benedictine bishop who is said to have predicted, by means of brief phrases for each one, a characteristic feature of the reign of every Roman Catholic pope, from the beginning of the papacy to the very end. A total of 112 popes were listed in what is believed to be his only publication, a book published by Benedictine friar Arnold Wion in the year 1590.

Some of the predictions are obviously very general, as illustrated by the listing for Pope John XXIII (reigned 1958-1963): "Shepherd and navigator." Since all popes are, by definition, figurative shepherds and are charged with directing the church, this fits any and all popes. Another prophecy, this one for Gregory X (reigned 1271-1276) designated him as "Man of the serpent" and his coat of arms featured a serpent. However, though most of the phrases published by Wion that refer to popes who reigned *before* he published are surprisingly accurate, those that follow are quite generalized.

The suspicion is that the prophecies of St. Malachy were invented in Wion's time. The authenticity of the book has been doubted since the seventeenth century. Certainly St. Malachy had nothing to do with the prophecies.

Wion's book calls for pope number 112, "Peter of Rome," to be the last to reign. After that, it says, Rome "will be destroyed and the awful judge will pass judgement on his people." John Paul II is pope number 110.

salamander An elemental spirit of fire, or a lizard-like creature that was believed to be able to live in fire. Not in any way related to the innocent amphibian creature *caudata,* a legitimate entity, not in any way fireproof. *See also* **fire-eating** and **fire walking**.

Salem witch trials The notion of **witchcraft** was first officially recognized in America in 1692 in the town of Salem, Massachusetts, when governor Sir William Phipps became aware of charges against several servants of African heritage. The situation rapidly escalated when the **Mather** family, fanatical Puritans, became involved.

Increase Mather, president of Harvard College, and his son **Cotton** prosecuted huge numbers of accused **witches,** and the gallows were busy. The Mathers, according to writer Lewis Spence,

> displayed an extraordinary amount of ingenuity and an equally great lack of anything like sound judgement.

Local children were encouraged to relate tales of wild orgies and evil deeds, and their stories were eagerly accepted as true.

(This is very much the manner in which American children today are being mercilessly interrogated by "therapists," sometimes over several months, and subjected to suggestions and leading questions about Satanic practices and sexual abuse, until they produce the stories that their inquisitors require of them. Adults who have been named in these procedures have been imprisoned and their lives ruined by the same methods in use three hundred years ago. Apparently we have not learned much in this respect in those three centuries. Things are not quite as bad today, however. In old Salem, anyone who even *doubted* the validity of witchcraft or of the guilt of those accused was also hanged. Today they are only looked upon as eccentrics.)

In 1692, even pet dogs and cats were put on trial and executed for witchcraft. But when the Mathers eventually accused the wife of Governor Phipps of being a witch, Phipps began to have doubts about the wisdom of allowing things to get any worse, and he put an end to it.

The Salem witch trials stand as one of the most disgraceful episodes in the history of America, yet there is still today a firm belief in the basic claims and procedures that continue to condemn innocent victims.

Samhain — *see* **Halloween**.

Sasquatch — *see* **Abominable Snowman**.

Satan The Devil, in Christian belief the opposite in every way to Jesus Christ, and the ruler of the region of hell. Satan is known by many other names, such as Lucifer ("Light-bearer"), Asmodeus ("Creature of Judgment"), The Adversary, Behemoth ("Beast"), Diabolus, Belial, and Beelzebub ("Lord of the Flies"). These names are often used for various **demons** as well and are not necessarily applied to the King of Demons. Demonology is not an exact science.

Satanism This belief is a directly opposing power structure to Christianity. The **Devil** replaces Jesus Christ, **demons** replace **angels**. The kingdom of Satan is below the Earth, that of Christ above it.

Satanism was so strongly accepted as real by ecclesiastics in the fifteenth, sixteenth, and seventeenth centuries that they declared some fifty specific prohibitions against it. Though simple banishment was sometimes the penalty for convicted Satanists, burning alive was the more frequent punishment. For the church, that has always been an effective deterrent to opposition and/or rivalry.

Today, the **new agers** and other such dilettantes toy with the naughty notion. Trashy magazines and tabloids feature advertisements and lurid articles dealing with the Dark Powers, confident that there are enough silly people around to support a limited industry devoted to Satanism. Their confidence has not been poorly placed.

scapulimancy — *see* **I Ching**.

scarab An ancient Egyptian rendering of the common scarab beetle, often fashioned of green stone, marble, or limestone, was usually buried with the deceased as part of the interment ceremony. It was placed in the position formerly occupied by the heart of the person, which had been removed during the embalming process.

The scarab, also known as the dung beetle, is often seen in nature rolling a small sphere of cattle dung into its nest. This event was perhaps taken by the Egyptians to symbolize the passage of the sun across the sky, and in their writings and decorative motifs they represented the scarab as holding the sun-disk between its legs, in a similar pose to that they had observed in nature.

Carved scarabs, in all sizes from one centimeter to more than a meter in length, are seen in museums around the world and small versions are still sold to unsuspecting tourists at souvenir stands in Egypt, and in **new age** bookshops.

Schmeidler, Dr. Gertrude A **parapsychologist** known for her discovery of the "sheep/goats effect" in ESP testing. She found that believers ("sheep") doing standard card-guessing tests had 0.4 percent *more* "hits" than nonbelievers ("goats"), who obtained 0.3 percent *less* than what would be expected by chance alone. The total number of tests was 250,875 guesses.

Schneider, Rudi (1909-1957) An Austrian-born **spirit medium** who became famous for **psychokinetic**

phenomena. He had two brothers, Karl and Willi, who also claimed mediumistic powers.

Rudi was extensively tested by **Eric J. Dingwall, Schrenck-Notzing** and others. He claimed to be in a **trance** when he caused objects to move in the **séance room,** often while he was secured and controlled by the **sitters.**

Later in his career, when more stringent controls were applied to him to guard against trickery during his demonstrations, and perhaps as a direct result of these controls, Schneider's phenomena dramatically decreased in regularity and effectiveness. With the decline in Rudi Schneider's ability to produce physical phenomena began the end of the "golden age" of **spiritualism.**

Schrenck-Notzing, Dr. Albert Freiherr von (1862-1929)

An undistinguished German medical doctor who married into a very wealthy family, Schrenck-Notzing was able to devote himself entirely to his hobby, **psychic** research. He had a penchant for flamboyance and was a devoted self-publicist and a dilettante without peer.

Séances held at the Schrenck-Notzing home in Munich were much more entertainments than serious investigations. They were attended by royalty and the cream of German society, in a period when séances were popular evening pastimes and these people could afford the heavy fees demanded by the performers.

Schrenck-Notzing flitted blissfully from **medium** to medium, seeing such sought-after celebrities as **Eva C.** and Willi and **Rudi Schneider,** and pompously declared them all to be absolutely genuine. When damning evidence of fraud was produced by other investigators, Schrenck-Notzing was able to rationalize away the contrary data in ingenious ways and to influence researchers into suppressing the awkward data. He also occupied a position which made him impervious to criticism; he had no fear of losing sponsors.

In spite of his obvious lack of expertise and his consummate, willful gullibility, Schrenck-Notzing's observations were quoted by others and accepted as positive evidence of the phenomena he was presenting.

science From the Latin *scientia,* meaning "knowledge." Science is a search for knowledge of the universe.

Scientists observe, draw conclusions from their observations, design experiments to examine those conclusions, and end up stating a theory which should express a new fact or idea. But if newer or better evidence comes along, they must either discard that theory or amend it to accommodate the new evidence.

In effect, science is a process of arriving, but it never quite arrives. A theory can perhaps be disproved, but it can never really be "proved." Only the probability of a theory being correct can ever be properly stated. Fortunately, most of science consists of theories that are correct to a very high degree of probability; scientists can only establish a fact to the point that it would be obstinate and foolish to deny it. Since new data are constantly being presented, a theory or observation may have to be refined, repudiated, modified, or added to in order to agree with the new data.

True science recognizes its own defects. That willingness to admit limitations, errors, and the tentative quality of any conclusion arrived at is one of the strengths of science. It is a procedure not available to those who profess to do science but do not: the abundant and prolific pseudoscientists and crackpots.

And there is an important difference between pseudoscience and crackpot science: The former has some of the trappings, generally the appearance and much of the language used by real science, while the latter has no pretensions at all of appearing to be science. The present German fascination with imaginary **E-rays** and the speculations on how **dowsing** is supposed to work are pseudoscience; most **perpetual motion** ideas and things like **reflexology, palmistry,** and **psychometry** are crackpot science.

Scientists aren't always right. And they don't always follow the rules exactly. The monk Gregor Mendel, performing his experiments in the mid-1880s which established the fundamental laws of heredity, apparently altered his figures slightly so that the results were somewhat more convincing—but in the long run, despite this "honest" fiddling with his data, he was right. The fact that other researchers can, even today, replicate his experiments and

thus validate his conclusions has provided us with firmly established basic scientific laws about heredity.

Newton, Kepler, Einstein, Curie, Galileo, and hundreds of other men and women of science—though they made some errors along the way—have provided mankind with knowledge that has made life richer, fuller, and more productive.

Science and **magic** are exact opposites.

See also **testing psychic claims.**

Scientology — *see* Hubbard.

Scot, Michael (1175?-1234?)
Scottish **astrologer/magician** who translated Aristotle's works and wrote on **alchemy** and on occult sciences. He was said to possess a **demon** horse and a demon ship. It is said that he accurately predicted his own death. Records on the man are at best sketchy.

Scot, Reginald (1538?-1599) In
English writer Reginald Scot's *The Discouerie* [sic] *of Witchcraft* (1584), we find an in-depth serious attempt to refute the superstitious belief in **witchcraft, demons,** and **devils.** The book, written in the vernacular, consists of sixteen divisions, with the last four devoted to **charms** and the tricks of jugglers and **conjurors**; in the sixteenth century, even street performers were suspected of demonic powers, and Scot wished to show that what they did was merely clever trickery.

Conjurors recognize many familiar and still-popular tricks among those Scot mentioned: swallowing a knife, burning a playing card and reproducing it from the spectator's pocket, transferring a coin from one pocket to another, converting coins into tokens and back again into money, making a coin appear in a spectator's hand, passing a coin through a tabletop, making a coin vanish when wrapped into a handkerchief, tying a knot into a handkerchief and making it untie itself, removing beads threaded onto a cord while both ends of the cord are held, transferring rice from one container to another, turning wheat into flour, burning a thread and restoring it, pulling yards of ribbon from the mouth, sticking a knife into the arm, passing a ring through the cheek, and decapitating a person

The title page of Scot's 1584 book, a later (1665) edition.

and restoring him. Wow. Let's hear that applause.

Scot's book is very rare in its first edition, because when James I of England succeeded Elizabeth I to the throne in 1603, he ordered all copies burned. James was most eager to hang anyone suspected of witchcraft, and since Scot claimed that belief in witches was silly and illogical, that might have interfered with James's religious work. It was sixty-seven years later, in 1651, that Scot's book again appeared in print, well after the death of King James.

See also **conjuring, Johannes Weyer, witchcraft.**

scrying The process of gazing into a crystal, mirror, bowl of water, shiny metal object, or other device to see visions of the past, present, or future. Said to be an aid to **clairvoyance.**

See also **Dr. John Dee.**

séance Correctly spelled "séance," rather than "seance," this word is from the French, derived from the Latin verb *sedere* ("to sit") and meaning "a sitting." It is a session during which attempts are made to contact departed **spirits.** A person who attends is referred to as a **sitter.** The person calling up spirits is called the **medium.**

Séances are held by a group of persons usually seated about a table in the dark or semi-darkness. The medium is believed to go into a **trance** state in which he or she is able to contact dead persons. Various noises such as creaks, raps, clicks, and voices are said to come from beyond the grave. Props such as tambourines, horns, guitars, and drums are heard to play, and it is believed that they have been handled by spirits.

Materializations, performed by only the most skilled mediums, are occasionally seen. Often a glowing figure, said to be made of **ecto-plasm,** can be seen and felt moving about. A materialization séance is mentioned in the *Bible*, in 1 Samuel.

séance room   The location of the séance. Each **medium** has his or her own requirements for this setup, and often the **sitters** are forced to use a room within the house of the medium, which of course provides opportunities for specialized preparation, if **cheating** were to take place. Curtains are often hung about the walls, even covering doors, and total darkness can be achieved easily. *See also* **Palladino, D. D. Hume, Lodge.**

second sight   This was the designation of the act whereby two partners were seemingly able to know one another's thoughts. The team of Mercedes and Mlle. Stantone headlined vaudeville with an act in which Mlle. Stantone, seated onstage at a piano, was able to play any tune whispered to her partner in the audience. Similarly, the Svengali Trio used the musical idiom in such an act from 1900 to 1925, playing the United States and Europe. An American act, Liz and Tom Tucker, were equally successful with this sort of performance, until quite recently appearing on television to the acclaim of both press and public.

From a less realistic point of view, the term "second sight" refers to **clairvoyance,** often claimed by Scottish Highlanders. The Gaels called it "shadow-sight," or "tais-chitaraugh."
See also **Zancig.**

Secret Gospel   The Secret Gospel refers to a document rediscovered in 1958 by Dr. Morton Smith of Columbia University, the brilliant biblical scholar who upset many previous views of the life of Jesus Christ. It is a lost portion of the St. Mark Gospel, and the contents can be disturbing, according to one's personal philosophy and interpretation of what appears there.

The Secret Gospel appears to repeat the story of the raising of Lazarus from the dead (as told in John) but without using the name. It also adds an event not previously known and certainly not included in the Gideon's *Bible*. To quote:

> . . . going in where the youth was, [Jesus] stretched forth his hand and raised him, seizing his hand. But the youth, looking upon him, loved him and began to beseech him that he might be with him. And going out of the tomb they came into the house of the youth, for he was rich. And after six days Jesus told him what to do and in the evening the youth [came] to him, wearing a linen cloth over his naked body. And he remained with him that night, for Jesus taught him the mystery of the kingdom of God.

Clement of Alexandria, one of the early fathers of the church, writing in the late eighteenth century about this document (only part of which has been recovered), tells his reader that other references to "'naked man with naked man' . . . are not found [in his copy]." He adds that he has found in his copy the statement:

And the sister of the youth whom Jesus loved and his mother and Salome were there, and Jesus did not receive them.

He went on to give his own interpretation of the story, "the true explanation and that which accords with the true philosophy." He was anxious to deny any support that this document might offer the Carpocratians, a **Gnostic** sect that he particularly detested. The faction was prominent in the second century and taught that the Earth was made by **angels,** but more importantly that one should abandon oneself to every lust with indifference, since by experiencing all varieties of sin, one could become satiated and therefore free of further desire for such activities.

This notion has been diligently pursued by many, not all of them Carpocratians.

Serios, Ted — *see* thoughtography.

Seth   A spirit **channeled** through author Jane Roberts (1929-1984), who taught that each person creates a separate reality by desires and needs. Because of the nature of this claim, it is an ideal **new age** notion in that it cannot be examined, proven, or disproven.

Roberts, using a **Ouija board,** said that Seth was an "energy personality essence" that had been a caveman, a pope, a Roman, a citizen of Atlantis, and a "Lemurian," in its various lives.

Roberts dictated the Seth material at weekly sessions of the course in creative writing that she taught.

shaman   Originally referring to a Siberian or generally north or central Asian **witch doctor, sorcerer,** or medicine man, the term is now also used for anyone working for his social group to cast fortunes, go into **trance** to **divine** the future, diagnose illness, or perform other **magical** services. The trance can be brought about by fasting or by hallucinogenic substances. The purpose of the trance is to contact **spiritual** forces or entities, often in the form of animals.

The shaman is essentially a "wise man," one sought out for advice and healing. The position is often hereditary, though by experiencing certain "ecstatic" experiences, a tribal member can be elected to the post. When a youth becomes alienated from his family and tribe, wanders away and seeks solitude for long periods, or exhibits severe antisocial behavior, he may be expected to become a shaman.

There are emotional and sociological problems common to all cultures, and it appears that some individuals subject to these differences find the position of shaman to be a release from the restrictions imposed upon other tribe members. The shaman is sometimes a socially

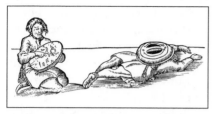

The Lapp shaman with his magical drum inscribed with figures. At right, he has fallen into an ecstatic state with his shield on his back.

inept or poorly integrated citizen, often homosexual, crippled, or epileptic, and the exalted station of shaman allows him to fit into the social picture and survive. This would seem to be an excellent method of providing for and accommodating those with disabilities and/or unique lifestyles.

The shaman is an integral and honored member of most American Indian tribes, and as such serves an important function.

Shaw, Steve (1960-) — *see* **psychokinete.**

SHC — *see* **spontaneous human combustion.**

shiatsu — *see* **acupuncture.**

Shipton, Mother   No reference to Mother Shipton prior to 1641 is in existence. It is thus difficult to determine whether this English **prophet** actually existed as she is represented in folklore, though writings seriously ascribed to her are being reproduced even today. There were several women who claimed to be her, but it is a Yorkshire claimant who has won the title.

Mother Shipton was Ursula Southill (or Sowthiel, or Southiel), the incredibly ugly daughter of Agatha Southill, known locally herself as a powerful **witch**. She is supposed to have been born in a cave at Dropping Well, Knaresborough, Yorkshire, in 1488, and because of her unfortunate appearance and reputed powers, was widely rumored to be the child of **Satan**.

Sometime about 1512, she married a wealthy builder from York named Tobias Shipton. She soon attained considerable notoriety throughout England as "The Northern Prophetess," and her prognostications received great public attention, were printed in pamphlets, and were widely distributed. Though copies of these publications still exist, most of what can be found today are mere forgeries, and many meteorological and astrological almanacs published as late as the nineteenth century used Mother Shipton's name freely. An 1838 book gives an idea of the overblown claims made for such tomes. It is titled *The New Universal Dream-Book; or The Dreamer's Sure Guide to the Hidden Mysteries of Futurity — By Mother Shipton.*

A 1686 book attributed to Edwin Pearson, *The Strange and Wonderful History of Mother Shipton,* because of its similarity to another book, *Life and Death of Mother Shipton,* was probably actually written by Richard Head, who also wrote *The English Rogue,* a racy account of his experiences with various tricksters, cheats, and rascals of his day.

Many localized prophecies were invented to use the Shipton name to advantage. In a 1740 book by John Tyrrel, *Past, Present and To Come: or, Mother Shipton's Yorkshire Prophecy,* is quoted what might well have been issued as a genuinely pre-event prediction:

Time shall happen A Ship shall sail upon the River Thames, till it reach the City of London, the Master shall weep, and cry out, Ah! What a flourishing City was this when I left it! Unequalled throughout the World! But now scarce a House is left to entertain us with a Flagon.

This prophecy has all of recorded time in which to be fulfilled, since no date is given or even suggested. Also, no cause of this calamity is specified. War, earthquake, or fire could all produce the cited effect. In fact, no disaster of a physical nature is inferred. Believers have declared that this is a prophecy of the Great Fire of London (1666), which is also said to have been foretold by **Nostradamus** and other seers.

A perfect example of an unquestionably true Shipton "prediction" is the often-quoted and misquoted:

Eighteen hundred and thirty-five,
Which of us shall be alive?
Many a king shall end his reign
Many a knave his end shall gain.

Though one can hardly argue with this question and the two statements, the verse was resurrected at the end of 1934 with the change of "Eighteen" to "Nineteen."

The famous seeress died at age seventy-three in 1561 and is believed to be buried at Clifton, just outside the city of York. On her memorial is carved:

Here lies she who never ly'd
Whose skill so often has been try'd
Her prophecies shall still survive
And ever keep her name alive.

This is said to be the only such tribute to a witch in all of England, since the usual memorial—if there is any—consists of nothing more than a cairn of stones to mark the spot where such a person was hanged or burned.

New inventions on behalf of Mother Shipton continue to be published even today.

Showers, Mary Rosina (circa 1890-?)

Born in India, the teenage daughter of a military family, Mary Showers was a **spirit medium** who worked with **Florence Cook**. She was famous for her "full-form" spirit **materializations,** done under very unsatisfactory (for the skeptic, but ideal for her) conditions. When placed under adequate controls, Showers failed to produce and was, in fact, exposed as a **cheater**.

Both mediums, Showers and Cook, were known for producing spirit forms that were indistinguishable from real people. In fact, **sitters** often remarked that their ghosts not only looked, felt, walked, smelled, and behaved exactly like the mediums themselves, but were identical to them in every possible way, except for costume. The message inherent in that observation seems to have escaped the believers.

In March 1874, Cook and

Showers gave a demonstration, a **séance,** for **Sir William Crookes** at his home. This was attended by several witnesses, among them Sergeant E. W. Cox. Such a séance always took place in a dimly lit room, a curtained-off section at one end in which the medium, usually dressed in black, either sat in a chair or reclined on a couch, supposedly in a **trance.** The ghost, garbed in white, would either peek through the curtain or actually emerge and walk about among the spectators.

Following this séance, Sergeant Cox felt called upon to clearly state his observations. In *The Spiritualist* (a prominent journal of the day) of May 15 of that year, he reported of the supposed ghost forms:

They were solid flesh and blood and bone. They breathed, and perspired, and ate. . . . Not merely did they resemble their respective mediums, they were facsimiles of them—alike in face, hair, complexion, teeth, eyes, hands, and movements of the body. . . . No person would have doubted for a moment that the two girls who had been placed behind the curtain were now standing [in person] before the curtain playing very prettily the character of ghost. . . . There was nothing to avoid this conclusion but the bare assertion of the forms in white that they were not what they appeared to be, but two other beings in the likeness of Miss Cook and Miss Showers; and that the real ladies were at this moment asleep on the sofa behind the curtain. But of this their assertion no proof

whatever was given or offered or permitted. The fact might have been established in a moment beyond all doubt by the simple process of opening the curtain and exhibiting the two ladies then and there upon the sofa, wearing their black gowns. But this only certain evidence was not proffered, nor, indeed, was it allowed us—the conditions exacted from us being that we should do nothing by which, if it were a trick, we should have been enabled to discover it.

Cox's report effectively put an end to belief in the validity of the séances offered by these two charlatans. In a further report, he described an 1894 séance during which he and a spectator had actually pulled aside the curtain and all present discovered Miss Showers wearing a headdress, poking her head through the curtain. The chair in which she was supposed to be sitting, in a trance, was empty. Following this debacle, Cox made the incredible statement that he believed that on this occasion, Showers had been "entranced" and had donned the headdress unconsciously.

It is not recorded whether Sergeant Cox was awarded the Supreme Gullibility Medal for 1894.

Shroud of Turin   One of several cloths said to be the burial shroud of Jesus Christ, this is by far the most famous. It consists of a large linen cloth bearing a very faint image outline of a human figure that is said to be that of Jesus Christ, deposited there by some unknown process.

The object first showed up in 1355 as a relic in the Church of Our Lady of Lirey in north-central France. It became an object of veneration, and pilgrims flocked from all over Europe to view it and to ask for miracles in its presence. From Lirey it traveled all over France, passing from church to church, being purchased, donated, and repurchased by the pious rich who wanted recognition. It eventually (1578) ended up in Turin (Torino) in Italy, where it still resides.

Much has been made of the fact that when a photographic negative of the image on the cloth is viewed, it appears much more "lifelike." All the expected wounds of the crucifixion process, along with bloodstains, appear on the cloth.

Definitive tests prove absolutely that it is a forgery. The evidence shows:

1. The cloth itself could not date from the correct period or from that area of the world, simply because that particular weave of cloth was not made then or there.

2. Wrapping of a body in that size and shape of cloth was not done in Palestine at that period. Such wrapping disagrees with the biblical description as well.

3. The representation of the face of Christ on this cloth and in all paintings and sculptures is and always has been a formalized guess. This version matches the "accepted" one. We know nothing about Christ's actual appearance.

4. Carbon dating of the fabric, done in three independent labs, showed that the linen fabric was woven about the year 1350.

5. The "bloodstains" are not only red in color (they could not be, after that period of time), but they were shown by chemical analysis to be paint of the composition used in the fourteenth century.

6. The bishop of Troyes (Lirey) knew who the artist was who painted the cloth and when and how he did it, and so reported to Pope Clement VII. The document still exists and has been shown to be unquestionably authentic.

In spite of this (and *much* more) evidence that the Shroud of Turin is merely an artifact turned out by an artist, there is a large group of "sindonologists"—a special designation for those who believe this object to be genuine—who continue to insist on its validity. A *New York Times* editorial of December 4, 1981, quoted some of the evidence that the shroud was a fake, then added:

> We excel over our medieval forebears in many things, no doubt, but should try not to outdo them in credulity.

shut-eye medium A trade term for the **closed medium** who is innocent and believes in his or her powers. *See also* **open medium.**

siddhis A series of supernatural abilities that certain **gurus** claim to teach disciples, notably in the

Transcendental Meditation movement. **Clairvoyance,** invisibility, invulnerability, levitation, super strength, **telepathy,** and other wonderful powers taken from Book III of the third century B.C. guru Patanjali's *Yoga Aphorisms* are taught by various mystic movements, but *none* have so far been observed to work.

sign, astrological — *see* zodiac.

Silva Mind Control A system developed by José Silva (1914-) that claims to develop improved memory, learning ability, and **paranormal** powers like **telepathy.** Much of the course consists of "visiting" absent persons imagined by students and performing diagnoses on them. No tests of the validity of this practice have been done; such tests are discouraged by the teachers of the system.

Simon Magus (Simon the Magician) The *Bible* mentions the Samaritan **magician** Simon in Acts 8:10, saying that he used **sorcery** to bewitch the people of Samaria. His teacher was said to be Dositheus, and he was believed to have many magical powers, among them invisibility, being able to pass through fire, the ability to cure the sick and to raise the dead, and the ability to **fly.**

Simon Peter (Saint Peter) followed him around, outmiracling him at every opportunity and finally encountering him in Rome. In desperation, Simon Magus announced that he would fly to heaven from a specially erected tower in the Campus Martius. Despite his claims to flight, he fell from the tower when Saint Peter prayed to have him fail in his attempt. Simon broke both legs and subsequently died of his injuries.

In Irish folklore, Simon Magus appears associated with Druidic practices and is referred to there as Simon the Druid.

sitter A person who participates, usually as a paying customer, at a **séance** or other **spiritualistic** procedure. He or she is warned to maintain unwavering faith in the observed phenomena, to never touch the **medium** or the **ectoplasm,** and to cooperate fully with instructions from those in charge

Skeptics Society An international organization that sponsors a monthly lecture series at the California Institute of Technology and publishes *Skeptic Magazine*, devoted to the investigation of fringe groups, extraordinary claims, and revolutionary ideas, and the promotion of science and critical thinking. *Skeptic* has investigated such fringe groups as the Holocaust deniers and controversial subjects such as cryonics, Afrocentrism, race, intelligence and I.Q., and the relationship of science and religion.

The Skeptics Society can be reached at: 2761 N. Marengo Avenue, Altadena, CA 91001. E-mail: SKEPTICMAG@AOL.COM.

Slade, Dr. Henry (1840-1905) "Dr." Henry Slade developed the art of **slate writing** and toured all over the world with his act. Slade was a **spiritualist** faker who could produce apparently spirit-written messages on school slates that had been washed and then sealed together, face-to-face. The trick was a simple one, but it fooled several scientists, including a prominent German astrophysicist named Zöllner, who even wrote a comprehensive book, *Transcendental Physics,* based on his observations of Slade's tricks and his firm belief that they were *not* tricks.

In 1876, the famous British conjuror J. N. Maskelyne was a prominent witness against Henry Slade when Slade was charged in the U.K. with fraud. The court case caused great excitement, and though the renowned physicist Lord Rayleigh (1842-1919) had publicly declared Slade to be genuine, Maskelyne was easily able to demonstrate to the satisfaction of the court that Slade's slate writing was brought about by trickery.

Henry Slade lost a case brought against him by prominent U.K. conjuror J.N. Maskelyne (seen at left) who demonstrated to the court how Slade used trickery to produce writing on common school-slates.

Slade was convicted and sentenced to three months at hard labor, but a technicality in the way the charge was worded caused a mistrial, and Slade left England hurriedly before a new trial could get under way. He never returned to the British Isles.

In Europe and in America, Slade was a great success until repeated exposures brought about his downfall. He finally signed a definitive confession of his fakery, faded from view, and at last died in a sanitarium in Michigan.

slate writing — *see* Slade, Dr. Henry.

Smith, Hélène — *see* automatic writing.

Smith, Joseph (1805-1844) Joseph Smith, who was to become founder of the Mormon church, worked at first as a **conjuror** in New York State. At one point, he was charged and convicted in court with being "a disorderly person and an imposter," having claimed to be able to **divine** "hidden treasures in the bowels of the earth," booty to which he said he could direct any willing and paying clients. There were many.

Then he claimed that at age twenty-two he had unearthed some "plates of gold" which bore "revised Egyptian hieroglyphics" that told the story of a lost book of the *Bible,* which he called *The Book of Mormon.* Fortunately there were two special optical instruments found with the plates, which enabled Smith to dictate to chosen scribes a translation of the sacred

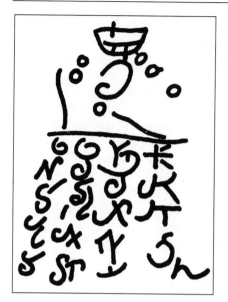

A drawing of the strange figures on one of the mythical golden plates Joseph Smith said were given him by an angel. He said this was writing in Assyrian, Chaldean, and Egyptian.

text. He did this from behind a curtain, since he was the only person privileged to see the plates or to see or handle the instruments. Indeed, to this very day, no one else has ever seen either the plates or the instruments. Where could they be?

In 1830 he founded the Mormon church, which went through many difficulties, as did Smith. While he was held in prison at Carthage, Illinois, a mob attacked and lynched him.

See also **The Book of Coming Forth by Day.**

Smyth, Charles Piazzi — *see* **Great Pyramid of Giza.**

Soal, Dr. Samuel George (1889-1975) Dr. Soal was a mathematician who became president of the Society for Psychical Research (SPR) in 1950. He studied **spirit materialization, mediumship, automatic writing, telepathy,** and **clairvoyance.**

In the period 1936-39, Soal began replicating the experiments of the American **Dr. J. B. Rhine,** who he greatly admired. His results were astonishingly good, and he enjoyed considerable fame as a result. Soon, skeptics began to question his methods, offering many theories on how errors—or cheating—could have taken place. But it was only after Soal's death in 1975 that a well-meaning supporter of his at the Society for Psychical Research, seeking to remove the suspicions that had been expressed, found instead through a computer program that Soal had cheated in grand style by changing the figures on the score sheets.

Soal's later work (in 1955) with two thirteen-year-old Welsh boys, Glyn and Ieuan Jones, showed that apparently he, too, could be deceived. The boys performed astonishing tests with Soal, being paid well for their success, and the result was *The Mind Readers,* a highly naive book by Soal that was a best-seller sensation overnight. **Sir Cyril Burt** raved over the work, which he accepted completely.

The Jones boys could transmit to one another—apparently by ESP—words, numbers, and the names of cards with animal pictures. The protocol used was farcical, with so many possibilities for communication between the two boys that one cannot believe that Soal was actually fooled. Whenever conditions were improved to defeat signaling, the score dropped to chance and the boys complained loudly. Immediately, the protocol would be relaxed and the scoring would improve.

But, said Soal:

> We [the experimenters] were perfectly aware that boys of the calibre of Glyn and Ieuan could never hope to deceive us for more than a few minutes.

The reference to the "calibre" of the boys no doubt refers to the fact that they were country folks, and therefore probably not very smart, certainly not as smart as the scientist Soal.

Eventually the protocol for the tests was tightened to the point where the boys could not signal one another, and in the opinion of the investigators, they had suddenly "lost" their powers.

All of Soal's work is now considered valueless.

Society for Psychical Research (SPR) This British group, the parent organization of the **American Society for Psychical Research** (ASPR), was founded in 1882 in London as an offshoot of the British National Association of Spiritualists, itself founded in 1873. The SPR is located at 1 Adam & Eve Mews, London W8 6UG, U.K. *See also* **American Society for Psychical Research**.

sorcery The word is derived from the same root as **sortilege** (*sortiarius,* Latin for "one who casts lots") and refers to the use of **magic** methods, through evil **spirits,** for obtaining power over others. This would include the selling of one's soul, consulting with the dead (**necromancy**), and other such improbabilities.

sortilege A variety of **divination** by means of dice, bones, stones, sticks, or other objects being cast upon the ground in patterns. In a way, the gaming houses in Las Vegas use sortilege when dice are thrown to divine whether the customer will lose his money.

See also **I Ching.**

Soubirous, Bernadette (1844-1879) Most who uncritically accept the miracles of **Lourdes** (*which see*) are unaware of what occurred to young Bernadette Soubirous, the originator of the story of the vision in the grotto. She herself never made any claim that the entity she said she had seen there had promised cures at the shrine. In fact, she called the vision the local French equivalent of "the lady" and the identification of the figure with the Virgin Mary was made by others.

On one occasion, Bernadette was asked by an English visitor about certain miracles that had been reported during her last visit to the shrine. She replied, "There's no truth in all that." Asked about cures at the shrine, she answered, "I have been told that there have been miracles, but . . . I have not seen them."

Bernadette was herself chronically ill, and she chose to visit hot springs in another town to treat her ailments. She was taken into a convent and died slowly and painfully in 1879, at age thirty-five, of tuberculosis, asthma, and several complications. Her own father, crippled and partially blind, died still afflicted.

Southcott, Joanna — *see* Appendix II, year 1774.

speaking in tongues — *see* **glossolalia**.

speculum (plural, speculi) Any mirror, crystal, shiny stone, or metal surface which can be used for **scrying**.

spell A written or spoken **incantation** used in an attempt to produce magical effects. Not at all dependable.

spirit Derived from the Latin word for "breath." A soul, or an immaterial substance, entity, or pattern said to inhabit a living creature. It can be coerced out of the body or will voluntarily leave the body for various reasons. However, it leaves involuntarily upon death and survives.

No really good evidence for spirits is currently available.

spirit bell The great conjuror Robert-Houdin is credited with having originated this trick, in which a small bell contained under an inverted glass cover rings in response to questions posed by the audience. The trick is still sold today from magic catalogs, in various forms. **Spiritualistic mediums** have used the device to produce answers to questions posed by **sitters** and have represented the effect as a genuine spirit phenomenon.

spirit guide Also known as "spirit helper." This is the claimed **spirit/ ghost/angel** that a **spirit medium** says is serving as a go-between with the "other world." In America during the heyday of **spiritualism**, Native Americans were said to be the most common guides, since so many of them had "gone into spirit" (died) during the occupation of the continent. The fact that no **sitter** was likely to speak an American Indian tongue, also worked in favor of the mediums.

spirit medium A person who claims to be able to call up **ghosts**, usually by going into some sort of **trance** in a darkened room. Mediums were very common in the United States up until the 1950s, when the interest in **spiritualism** and séances began to wane, though some are still doing business in England in a limited fashion.

spirit photography The **spiritualists** have long embraced a physical phenomenon that they believe proves their basic premise of **survival-after-death**. They call it "spirit photography."

It all began in 1861, when a Boston engraver named William H. Mumler discovered extra images of persons on an amateur photograph he took of an associate. Mumler went into business as a **medium/ photographer**, snapping photos of well-paying clients who recognized deceased celebrities, strangers, and friends in the extra images recorded on the portraits of themselves.

Then two years after he'd begun the business, Mumler was exposed when some of his "extras" were recognized as living Bostonians. He moved off to New York, reestablished his business, and was once again accused of fraud. His career ended after a trial in 1869, and he died in poverty in 1884.

An Englishman named Hudson, inspired by Mumler's idea, began taking spirit photos. It was clearly shown that he was producing double exposures and even posing himself, in disguise, for some of the "extras." However, he was endorsed entirely by **Reverend William Stainton Moses,** who declared his work to be an "unassailable demonstration" of the existence of survival after death.

A Frenchman, Buguet, entered the trade in 1874 in London, but was soon arrested for fraud and made a full confession. At the trial, his victims swore they had recognized their loved ones in photos of dummy "prop" heads that the police had seized at Buguet's studio. Reverend Moses had also endorsed Buguet's work just a month before the photographer's arrest.

Many examples of so-called spirit photography have been published. Several offered by believers as proof of the validity of the phenomenon show a likeness of **Sir Arthur Conan Doyle,** since he was a champion of the spiritualist cause. The spook-snappers claimed to have summoned him up after his death in 1930, and he was by far the most popular target for their cameras. The most used "spirit" photo of Sir Arthur is an ordinary one of that author in his prime, a photo that was and still is widely published and easily available. The "spirit" photo that are offered agree in detail,

lighting, and expression with this original. In a few cases the "spirit" photo is obviously a cutout of that photo simply reversed and placed in what appears to be cotton wool.

spirit portraits   Certain **spiritualists** claim that they can produce a drawn or painted portrait of a departed person that will be specifically identified by the intended **sitter.** Many tests of that claim have been made, one of them on a television series in the U.K. for Granada TV in 1991.

Coral Polge is a U.K. spiritualist who makes her living producing pastel portraits of people who she vaguely defines as some sort of ambiguous entities. During her demonstration in Manchester for Granada, Ms. Polge skillfully drew in brown chalk the face of a middle-aged, rather ordinary lady that could be any one of a half dozen such women that the average person has encountered at one time or another. However, no one in the studio audience of ninety persons was able to identify with both the portrait that Coral Polge drew, and the description that she had verbally offered in a rambling, disconnected series of guesses and **try-ons.**

When a vote was asked for on whether anyone could recognize the face Ms. Polge had drawn, the response was eleven percent yes. No two people in that audience should have recognized that person—unless they both had known her—and the generality of the drawing served to bring enough recognition votes that the scenario Ms. Polge was trying to build—that of a distinct person "coming through" for a specific member of the audience—was not at all established.

The production of spirit portraits is a form of Rorschach ink blot test.

spiritism A philosophy very popular in nineteenth-century France which was very similar to **spiritualism** except that it taught **reincarnation** as well.

spiritualism (sometimes with an initial capital, to denote the formal church) There is confusion in the use of this term. More correctly, it would be reserved for designating one who follows the *religion* which teaches that **ghosts** can be summoned up by **spirit mediums** and communicated with, and that these ghosts can even touch, move, and physically affect objects and persons.

It began with the performances of the **Fox sisters** and is still an important religion in England. The correct term for one who merely believes in calling up spirits, asking them questions and receiving inane answers, could be *spiritist*. However, the longer word is more impressive and is now almost universally used.

The oldest spiritualist group still in existence is the National Spiritualist Association of Churches, which dates from 1893. In the United States, the National Spiritualist Alliance was founded in 1913.

spiritualitis A term coined by author L. Sprague de Camp for the condition afflicting researchers into **spiritualism**. He defines it thus:

The symptoms of this malady are a tendency to sneer at the "limited range of view" and "dreary agnosticism" of unbelievers; to defend mediums as "men of high intelligence and probity" or "simple, honest, kind-hearted people" whose feats, even after exposure, "remain to this day absolutely inexplicable"; to blame exposures on evil spirits or a Jesuit plot; and to assert sweepingly but untruthfully that "every trained observer" who has investigated the phenomena has either been converted "or has been forced to admit that the phenomena are at present wholly inexplicable."

spondylotherapy — *see* **Abrams**.

spontaneous human combustion (SHC) A not-too-well-explained phenomenon in which solitary humans have, in some unknown manner, burned up almost entirely, usually in a closed room, without setting fire to the room beyond a possible hole in the floor, a chair, and some nearby furnishings.

Often, the subject is an alcoholic, usually elderly and smoking, sometimes known to regularly take sleeping pills. It is not difficult to see that such a combination could lead to the person catching fire. Forensic scientists point out that the "candle effect" may be responsible for the dramatically complete burning that often takes place in SHC. This effect is the result of human fat percolating out of a burning body, permeating the clothing and the stuffing of a chair, and thus burning as a giant candle wick.

Some point to the fact that the room—and house!—do not also burn, but this may be a case of selective reasoning; when the house *does* burn down, the question does not arise, and that condition is far more likely to exist than the alternate.

An excellent discussion of this phenomenon is the book of Joe Nickell and John F. Fischer, *Secrets of the Supernatural,* 1991.

spoon-bending — *see* psychokinesis.

SPR — *see* Society for Psychical Research.

sprite   A small **demon, fairy,** or other spirit with some supernatural powers, though on a minor scale. Little is known or said about the sexuality, if any, of sprites. Probably not much to say, really.

Steiner, Rudolf (1861-1925) — *see* Anthroposophy.

stigmata   As religious phenomena, spontaneous wounds of the hands, feet, and right side of the body—corresponding to the traditional wounds on the body of Jesus Christ—first were reported by a chronicler of Saint Francis of Assisi in 1229.

Among modern stigmatists—and there are many—were Padre Pio da Pietralcini (né Francesco Forgione, 1890-1968) and Teresa Neumann (1898-1962). These people exhibited the wounds to varying degrees, Ms. Neumann even crying tears of blood. When she was in a coherent state, she claimed that she had survived only on sacramental wafers and a sip of wine each day for thirty-five years.

Since twenty-four-hour-a-day surveillance would be necessary to establish the validity of these phenomena as miracles, no case of stigmata exists that can be said to be free of suspicion. The attitude of church officials who looked into the Neumann claim that wounds appeared in her palms spontaneously, reflects the general indifference to rigor exhibited in such inquiries. One investigator, Father P. Siwek, S.J., wrote that though he had "the gravest doubts about the genuineness of the marvels attributed to Teresa," those doubts did not exclude the possibility of "solid Christian virtues and genuine mystical states."

It is also interesting to note that in all such cases, the wounds in the hands appear at the palms, which agrees with religious paintings but not with the actualities of crucifixion; the wounds should appear at the wrists.

Stokes, Doris (1919-1987) Primarily as a **clairaudient,** U.K. psychic performer Ms. Stokes became very popular in Australia in the 1980s. Her techniques were essentially **cold reading,** though she also depended on obtaining information in person in advance from her clients, who were then encouraged to show up at her public appearances, at which time the information could be given back to them as if received psychically from the Great Beyond.

Subuh, Pak Muhammad (1901-1983?)   An Indonesian monk who began a movement called Subud (a contraction of three mystical Sanskrit words: *sushila, budhi,* and *dharma*) in which a mystical phenomenon known as "latihan" was said to come to followers who studied under an appropriately trained disciple. The latihan occurred after a few moments, days, months, or even years of study.

In the late 1950s, U.K. mathematician/author J. G. Bennett, a devotee of **Gurdjieff**—who had just died—came under the influence of Pak Subuh, brought him to England, and financed his career, believing him to be the New Messiah. Movie actress Eva Bartok, recovering from personal tragedies, joined the movement in 1957 and brought with her a covey of admirers and sycophants. Two years later, the **guru** was so popular that a congress at Coombe Springs (near Salisbury) attracted more than four hundred delegates from forty countries.

By 1960, interest in the cult had faded, Pak Subuh moved back to Indonesia and J. G. Bennett left the group and became a convert to Roman Catholicism.

succubus (plural "succubi") A female demon that copulates with men. The princess of all the succubi is Nahemah, believed by the profane to have now retired from royalty and to have opened an all-night diner in Red Bank, New Jersey.

Summerland The expression used by **spirit medium** "The Poughkeepsie Seer" **Andrew Jackson Davis** to denote the place where one "goes" at death. The term was free of religious requirements, thus satisfying those who wished to embrace **spiritualism** without those entanglements.

survival-after-death There is probably no question which has preoccupied our species more than whether we can survive after clinical death. It is believed that other species are not aware of their own mortality, though that seems difficult to establish with any certainty.

Over the years, famous figures like **Sir William Crookes,** Sir Arthur Eddington, inventor Thomas Edison, magician **Harry Houdini,** philosopher **David Hume,** and **Sir Oliver Lodge** occupied themselves with looking into this eternal question. But one figure in recent history stands out as the most important and influential advocate of the reality of life after death: **Sir Arthur Conan Doyle,** the internationally famed creator of Sherlock Holmes and an ardent promoter of **spiritualistic** matters, accepted claims that full-form **materializations** of the dead could be produced during **séances** and that survival after death had been firmly established.

Swedenborg, Emanuel (1688-1772) A Swedish mystic who had a great influence on the thinking of the muddle-headed. He was born into a well-to-do family of theologians and was well traveled and well educated. Though a brilliant man in most ways—as a statesman, mathematician and engineer—his search for the secrets of the universe led him to have visions, and he decided that the answers lay in studying the relationship between the soul and the body.

Swedenborg designed a syrupy theology that sounded elegant but was based on huge presumptions of his own insight, which he never doubted for an instant. He was sure he knew all about matters far beyond his perception, such as the nature of the planets. He had them peopled with life very similar to that on Earth, in most ways, but sufficiently exotic to appeal to the mystic sense.

Of the inhabitants of Venus, Swedenborg said:

> They are of two kinds; some are gentle and benevolent, others wild, cruel and of gigantic stature. The latter rob and plunder, and live by this means; the former have so great a degree of gentleness and kindness that they are always beloved by the good; thus they often see the Lord appear in their own form on their earth.

The mystic averred, of course, that the Venusians (and all others in the solar system) shared one God. Of the Moon he revealed that

> The inhabitants of the Moon are small, like children of six or seven years old; at the same time they have the strength of men like ourselves. Their voice rolls like thunder, and the sound proceeds from the belly, because the Moon is in quite a different atmosphere from the other planets.

Perhaps small folks living in a vacuum have to speak from the belly, especially to make those thunderous sounds.

sylph An **elemental spirit** of the air. Seldom—if ever—seen.

sympathetic magic (also known as image magic) Best exemplified by the myth of the **voodoo** doll, usually made of wax or clay, in which injuries inflicted upon a figure representing the victim are simultaneously experienced by the real person. Thorns, pins, or needles are stuck into the doll, which has been identified specifically with the subject by having incorporated in it scraps of clothing, hair, fingernail or toenail parings, or other personal substances of the victim, or by being baptized in that person's name.

Such dolls were also used in ancient Assyria and Egypt as early as the reign of Rameses III in the twelfth century B.C. The Greeks and Romans were also familiar with the practice. The Greek sorcerer Theocritus was said to have killed his enemies by performing **magic** rites over their images. In Latin, the dolls are called *imaguncula*.

Another example of this sort of thinking was first written about by Baptista Porta in his *Magiae Naturalis* (1558), when he described "magic needles." He wrote that if two needles were prepared from the same piece of iron then magnetized and placed upon pivots like compass needles, one needle would follow the same direction as the other if it were moved, no matter what distance was between the two. Cardinal Richelieu of France accepted this idea. The cardinal accepted almost anything.

The Celtic witches used figures this way, and the Scots called them "clay bodies." Today in Malaya magicians still use such images.

T

---

tabard Ceremonial robe worn during magic ceremonies. It consists of two rectangles sewn together at the top corners and then belted. Not flattering to the average sorcerer, nor practical in breezy weather.

table tipping (Also, table tilting, table turning) Known as a form of "dactylomancy," along with the **Ouija board** and other notions which make use of the **ideomotor effect.**

This phenomenon takes place with one or more persons seated about a table, often a light card table. Placing their hands flat upon the surface, they "will" the table to move. In response, it either rises, tilts, or rotates. It can be found by experimentation that drawing back or pushing forward, horizontally, will cause the table to tilt up on two legs. Two persons seated at adjacent or opposite sides doing this together can cause the table to move even more dramatically.

The scientist/inventor Michael Faraday devised an elegant system for demonstrating that table tipping was often an ideomotor effect. Unknown to the **sitters,** he placed a second wooden tabletop over the first one, separated from it by thin, round wooden rods the ends of which passed behind an adjacent curtain and were equipped with pointers. When the sitters attempted to make the table move, those pointers turned, showing that, unconsciously, horizontal pressure was being applied by the sitters, though they denied that they did so.

A simple control method consists of placing pieces of smooth paper beneath the hands of the sitters. Since no grip can be obtained on the surface, the table does not move.

Of course, other methods can be used, as when **Palladino** did her effective table tipping. In her case, she wore custom-made boots with wide soles that protruded beyond

Three Belgian mediums seated around a three-legged wooden table. Any one of them will have little trouble causing it to tilt simply by pressing down.

the edges of the boots. The edge could have been hooked beneath a leg of the table, the hand located over the leg pressing down, forming what is known in the trade as the "human clamp." This is a means for lifting straight up on a table, a seemingly impossible maneuver.

There are other methods, too, for moving and lifting a table, even a heavy one. Some are one-person methods, and some require a confederate.

taboo Any prohibition of a motion, a gesture, an item of clothing, a word or phrase, use of a substance, or indeed almost any human action which is thought to provoke a deity, a class of person, a demon, or any other entity.

Many religions and other belief systems are loaded with such taboos as appearing outdoors with the head uncovered, eating certain foods on certain days of the week, allowing a cat (especially a black one) to cross one's path, showing the sole of one's foot to another person, or living on the thirteenth floor of a building. Entire books have been written listing improper actions, from simple discussions of table manners to serious warnings about divine retribution applied for transgressions.

talisman A disk, stone, or medal designed to confer some sort of power, as opposed to an **amulet,** which has more of protective purpose. The sale of talismans, as well as of books describing their manufacture and use, provided much of

the income for those who dealt in such malarkey. In fact, it still does. **New age** and religious-goods shops deal in talismans.

See also **charms.**

talking plants — *see* Backster, Cleve.

tantra A term referring to the sexual aspects of various Eastern religions, mostly concerned with conserving sexual energies and desires and directing them to other purposes. As might be expected, failure to attain this goal is frequent among practitioners. In the Western world, tantric arguments are often employed, by enthusiastic disciples, to rationalize a seduction.

Tarot cards A set of seventy-eight playing cards decorated with a variable set of fantastic and mystical diagrams, symbols, and illustrations. The earliest deck still in existence is dated circa 1432. Researcher Norman Schwarz has dated the Tarot to between 312 and 64 B.C., from various clues such as the inclusion of earlier astronomical constellations (such as the Lovers and the King).

The cards are grouped into the Major Arcana (twenty-two trump cards) and the Minor Arcana (fifty-six suit cards). The four suits consist of fourteen cards each, ace through ten, page, knight, queen, and king. These cards were first in use in the mid-1400s and have been used ever since by gullible persons to cast fortunes.

The modern deck of fifty-two

cards used in gambling was derived from the Tarot deck, the suits being transmuted so that "swords" became spades, "cups" became hearts, "wands" became clubs, and "coins" (or "pentacles") became diamonds. (In Spain, these suits were "*palomas*," "*rosas*," "*conejos*," and "*dineros*"; in France, "*piques*," "*choer*," "*trèfles*," and "*carreaux*.") These are the cards that were called the Minor Arcana. Originally, there were four "court" cards, but the knight (or cavalli) card was dropped in the modern deck, resulting in 4 x 13 cards, while the Tarot retained 4 x 14.

One of the familiar Tarot cards, number zero in the Grand Arcana.

The Major Arcana of twenty-two cards are individual figures:

0	The Fool
I	The Magician
II	The High Priestess
III	The Empress
IV	The Emperor
V	The Pope
VI	The Lovers
VII	The Chariot
VIII	Justice
IX	The Hermit
X	The Wheel of Fortune
XI	Strength
XII	The Hanged Man
XIII	Death
XIV	Temperance
XV	The Devil
XVI	The House of God
XVII	The Star
XVIII	The Moon
XIX	The Sun
XX	Judgement
XXI	The World

(In some versions of the Tarot, the Fool is given the number XXI and the World becomes XXII. There is no known difference in accuracy between the two systems as far as prophetic value is concerned.)

For use as a **divinatory** device, the Tarot deck is dealt out in various patterns and interpreted by a gifted "reader." The fact that the deck is not dealt out into the same pattern fifteen minutes later is rationalized by the occultists by claiming that in that short span of time, a person's fortune can change, too. That would seem to call for rather frequent readings if the system is to be of any use whatsoever.

The form of deck most used today is the Golden Dawn, designed by A. E. Waite, a mystic, and drawn by artist Pamela Coleman Smith about 1900. The art of reading the cards has been referred to as the "*ars notoria.*"

Tart, Dr. Charles (1937-   )

Parapsychologist/psychologist at the University of California at Davis, Dr. Tart obtained his degree at Duke University under the prominent psychologist Norman Gutman.

Dr. Tart has contributed much to parapsychology, including a "10-choice Trainer" which he constructed to test ESP. This setup consisted of two isolation booths and a system whereby one of ten digits was randomly chosen by an experimenter in the first booth and then transmitted to a subject in the other booth by ESP.

After his book on the experiments appeared reporting successful results and causing a great sensation in **psi** circles, an independent, skeptical researcher visited the laboratory and examined the device and how it was used. He pointed out that there were methods by which sensory leakage might have occurred during the tests. Then mathematicians at Davis discovered that there were faults with the randomizer of exactly the nature that would tend to produce positively biased results. And there were several modes available if the subjects chose to **cheat**.

Dr. Tart's book on the Trainer experiments continues in circulation and is still quoted in the literature to prove the existence of ESP.

tea leaf reading (also tasseography)

An old, quaint notion that the patterns formed by tea leaves in a cup are indicators of a deeper truth. The tea is drunk and the cup is drained, inverted, and turned around three times left to right, using the left hand. (This turning process, whether done with either hand or a foot, does not in any way redistribute the tea leaves, but it can't hurt, either.) The reader then examines the leaves and prognosticates.

Leaves on the bottom, we're told, indicate the distant future, those on the rim the immediate future. Tea leaf stems represent persons. Fat stems are fat people, for example.

The use of tea bags has not only made the art more difficult, but less accurate. Coffee grounds are also read, but there is no record of Shredded Wheat or coleslaw being so employed.

Not yet.

telekinesis — *see* psychokinesis.

telepathy

Often redundantly referred to as "mental telepathy." The term was originated by researcher F. W. Myers (1843-1901) in 1882. It refers to the supposed ability of humans or animals to perceive the thoughts or emotions of others without the use of the recognized senses. It is one of the specific facets of **extrasensory perception** (ESP).

teleportation

The ability to transport oneself from place to place **magically**. Not well established by evidence.

See also **apport.**

Tenhaeff, Wilhelm (1894-1981)

Chairman of the **parapsychology** department at Utrecht University, this cantankerous Dutch investigator had all sorts of problems getting along with his colleagues, who always suspected him of hyperbole in matters of **psychic** reporting. Nonetheless, he was widely published in parapsychology.

He took as a pet the **clairvoyant/police psychic** and general performer **Gerard Croiset** (1909-1980), for whom he obtained considerable media coverage. For years, parapsychologists and general believers in psychic matters pointed to the exploits of Croiset as examples of undoubted powers, in particular his work as a police psychic. Then Dutch journalist Piet Hein Hoebens looked into the reports that Tenhaeff had made, and discovered that he had exaggerated them and in some cases had lied. There were many examples in which Tenhaeff had solved a trick method used by Croiset and had chosen not to report it.

Tenhaeff died a few months after his protégé, revealed as a fraud.

testing psychic claims It has been said that it would be very difficult to design a test for psychic claims. Not knowing very much about how proper **scientific** tests are designed, objectors have claimed that it would be impossible to come up with a test that would be satisfying to "both sides," as if a scientific experiment should or could have two "sides." A properly designed test has no preferred results, and no decision in advance—or bias—is allowed to influence the design or conduct of the test, nor the reporting of the results. These provisions *must* be written into any proper scientific test, in advance. The result obtained

must be accepted and binding to "both sides."

If any claim is so vague, imprecise, and/or ambiguous that it cannot be examined rationally, then it cannot be tested and it probably cannot have the slightest importance to anyone except students of abnormal psychology. And it most probably has no merit whatsoever.

Tetragrammaton In the **kabala**, this is the term for the four-letter name of God. In effect, it is the name of a name.

It varies from text to text. Some versions are JHVH, IHVH, JHWH, YHVH, and YHWH. Since these are too sacred to be spoken aloud, the word **"Adoni"** is used when the name is spoken. This has led to a serious misunderstanding, since in Hebrew texts only the vowels of Adoni (or of "Elohim"—this makes it more confusing) are printed. Thus are produced the reconstructions such as Yahweh or Jehovah.

thaumaturgy The general, and poorly limited, term covering almost all practices such as **witchcraft, sorcery,** or **magic.** Often wrongly and facetiously used by eighteenth-century **conjurors** to describe their art.

Theosophy Formed from the Greek words *theos* meaning "god" and *sophia* meaning "wisdom." The religion founded in 1875 by **H.P. Blavatsky** teaching that matter, spirit, and consciousness are the basis for the universe and the individual. Borrowing from the **kabala** and Indian religious ideas, Theosophy rails at Christianity and most other organized religions and invokes images of secret societies, "Tibetan Masters," "lost" Indian philosophy, and "ancient wisdom." Madame Blavatsky was constantly being visited by **astral** beings and other **spirits** who imparted to her the rules of the religion. **Astrology, clairvoyance,** and other powers are not only automatically accepted in Theosophy, but are important factors in its dogma. *See also* **Blavatsky.**

thoughtography   Ted Serios (born circa 1920) is said to have the ability to project his thoughts onto the film inside a Polaroid camera.

There is a method involving a simple handheld optical device that can accomplish this by trickery. If Mr. Serios used such a method, the trick managed to convince a Freudian psychiatrist named Jule Eisenbud (1908-), several **parapsychologists,** and a number of other persons, in spite of definitive exposure of the trick. If Mr. Serios did not use a trick method, all the rules of physics, particularly of optics, everything developed by **science** over the past several centuries, must be rewritten to accommodate Eisenbud's opinion. No such revisions have been found necessary.

In Dr. Eisenbud's 1967 book *The World of Ted Serios,* the photographs shown are stark evidence, not only of the very strong indication that the simple handheld optical device was indeed used by Mr. Serios, but also of the wishful, convoluted reasoning process by which parapsychologists sometimes decide

in favor of **paranormal** explanations. This is a valuable book in this regard.

Thouless, Robert Henry (1894-1984) Thouless was a well-known British psychologist who turned, in his later years, to **parapsychology.** He became well known for his most successful book, *Straight and Crooked Thinking* (1930), which in the United States was titled *How to Think Straight.*

Thouless's attempts to reproduce the **Dr. Joseph Banks Rhine** ESP card tests failed, and he was far from satisfied with the standards adopted by parapsychologists in their laboratory protocols. He was one of the first to discover that early versions of the famous **Zener** symbol cards favored by Rhine in his ESP tests could actually be read from the backs of the cards. He also introduced the term **psi** to parapsychology.

Although he was still unsatisfied with experimental procedures that were being used, Dr. Thouless became convinced of the existence of ESP. He became president of the **Society for Psychical Research** in 1942.

In 1948, he established a "survival" test. Similar tests had been set up by **Sir Oliver Lodge,** F. W. H. Myers, **Houdini** and others, and all had failed. The Thouless test specified that his test of survival after death was designed so that:

1. The test would have no concealed object or writing that might be determined by subterfuge or by clairvoyance.

2. It would "allow the possibility of an indefinitely large number of checks of the attempted solutions."

3. It would provide for any solution to be quite definitely "right" or "wrong," without any ambiguity.

4. It would leave no uncertainty about whether or not the solution was the correct one.

This test consisted of two "Vigenere" cipher code passages:

> INXPH CJKGM JIRPR FBCVY
> WYWES NOECN
> SCVHE GYRJQ TEBJM TGXAT
> TWPNH CNYBC
> FNXPF LFXRV QWQL

and

> BTYRR OOFLH KCDXK FWPCZ
> KTADR GFHKA
> HTYXO ALZUP PYPVF AYMMF
> SDLR UVUB

It was stated in the Thouless challenge that a third set of characters would provide the key to understand these lines. This third set was not recorded in writing, since Thouless feared the possibility, as stated in his first provision, that some gifted **clairvoyant** might sense such a record, thus destroying the "survival" aspect of the test. Also:

> The key to the first is a continuous passage of poetry or prose which may be indicated by referring to its title, and the key to the second consists of two words.

The first cipher was quickly solved (the "key" word was SURPRISE) and Thouless withdrew it from the test, but the second remains unsolved.

Dr. Thouless considered the development of this test his greatest contribution to parapsychology. To date, no one, alive or dead, has succeeded in solving the second message. Of course, the failure does not mean that Thouless did *not* survive death.

Many **sittings** with **spirit mediums** attempting to obtain the two key words from the ghost of Dr. Thouless have failed; though the mediums claim they make contact with the ghost, it tells them it has forgotten the two words. That seems strange, since Dr. Thouless wrote, in his description of the test, that those two words were "easy to remember." The ghost is able to recall all other aspects of Thouless's life, such as names, addresses, events, and quotations—all details that are easily available to anyone who might want to know them—but not the two simple words upon which the entire test—and proof of survival—depend.

Any attempts at a solution should be sent to: Society for Psychical Research, 1 Adam & Eve Mews, London W8 6UG, U.K.

thumb writer A device fitting on the end of the thumb (or, as with the "finger writer," on a finger, usually the index) which enables a **medium** to secretly inscribe writing upon a pad, card, or slate. Often, the performer will pretend to write a name or number, then place the pad (for example) facedown upon a table, ask the **sitter** to reveal the word or number sought, and upon picking up the pad will use the writer to quickly and secretly write out the word or number. The pad is then shown, as if the word had been written there previously.

trance A poorly defined "altered state" of consciousness loosely described as a sleeplike condition, daze, or stupor. In some definitions, voluntary action is suspended. No definition of the **hypnotic** trance has been arrived at, nor are there tests to establish it. **Psychics** and **spirit mediums** usually claim to be "in trance" when they work, but there is no good evidence for this.

Transcendental Meditation (TM) Becoming very popular after its introduction outside of India by the Maharishi Mahesh Yogi (1918?-) in the 1960s, TM requires devotees to **meditate** twice daily, repeating their individually assigned **mantras**. TM is a philosophy that also teaches **siddhis** such as levitation (flying in the air by mind power) and invulnerability (safety from all assault, physical and spiritual) along with an assortment of other supernatural claims.

Study of the siddhis is an aspect of the Maharishi's **"Science** of Creative Intelligence," which has no scientific characteristics at all. Though wide claims have been made for the effect of TM on the world, none of the claims have stood examination. One of the Maharishi's attractive analogies—in which he equates the solar system with the structure of the atom —is not only crackpot science; it is very bad crackpot.

TM obtained a brief surge of great interest when the Beatles embraced the idea for a few months in 1967. They were quickly disillusioned when the promises of the Maharishi went unfulfilled, and dropped out. However, Beatle George Harrison has again joined the TM political party and he ran for Parliament in the U.K. in 1992, as did many other TMers, including Canadian **conjuror** Doug Henning. None of the TM candidates won office, though they'd been told by the Maharishi that their election was assured. In 1993, Henning tried for political position as a TM candidate again, this time in Canada; he was unsuccessful.

The Maharishi claims to have discovered the secret of age reversal, though his own ripening process appears to be continuing at the expected rate. Tens of thousands of students have taken his course in levitation, but none have flown, which would appear to have been the eventual goal. And tests of the "invulnerable" siddhi have not been successfully conducted, as far as is known, in spite of the fact that such a test would appear to be easily designed and implemented.

Currently, the growth of TM has slowed, though Maharishi International University in Fairfield, Iowa, still functions as the center of the movement in the United States.

transvection — *see* **flying**.

trial by ordeal An early system of judgment in which the accused was pitted against a person who had been appointed by the court or by the accuser himself, in combat or some other form of competition. Divine powers were believed to regulate the outcome. In cases where, for example, a maiden was unable to battle with a man, a "champion" might be assigned to her. Other ordeals, such as handling hot metal, plunging a hand into burning embers, or being submerged under water might also be ordered by the court. In tests of **witches,** if the accused survived the ordeal, he or she was guilty; if not, he or she was innocent. The testing process was not an ideal one.

*See also **Bible.***

trigram A set of three parallel lines, either broken or solid, which can be combined with another set to form a **hexagram.** *See also **I Ching.***

try-ons In the process of **cold reading,** this is a subtle prompting technique whereby the **medium** introduces an uncertainty to the statement, an unspoken invitation to the **sitter** to direct the attempt. Such phrases as these are used:

> I want to say that . . .
> I feel that . . .
> Possibly . . .
> It might be that . . .
> I'm led to say that . . .
> I get the feeling that . . .
> I'm being told that . . .
> Why do I say that . . .
> Why do I feel that . . .

Tut, Curse of King An international myth started by the press and carefully nurtured by them ever since.

When the tomb of a minor pharaoh of Egypt, Tutankhamen (circa 1350 B.C., died age 19), was discovered and opened in 1922, it was a major archaeological event. In order to keep the press at bay and yet allow them a sensational aspect with which to deal, the head of the excavation team, Howard Carter, put out a story that a curse had been placed upon anyone who violated the repose of the boy-king. The fact that this "curse" was accepted as traditional for all royal tombs escaped the notice of the eager press.

The man who had financed the project was Lord Carnavon (né Herbert, 1866-1923), and after he died in Cairo the following year, the Curse of the Pharaoh came into full bloom. The fact that Carnavon was chronically ill, and particularly so when he arrived in Egypt from England to view the tomb, was ignored. Since the electricity in Cairo also went out that same night (it frequently failed at that period in the city's history), the curse seemed to be working very well.

The story arose that many of those who had been connected with the tomb died violently and prematurely. The awkward facts are that the average *duration of life* for the twenty-two nonnative persons (those who can be traced) who might be said to have had anything to do with the tomb opening or excavation—those who should have suffered the ancient curse—was *more than twenty-three years* after the "curse" was supposed to become effective. Lady Evelyn Herbert, Carnavon's daughter, died in 1980, a full fifty-seven years later.

Howard Carter, who not only discovered the tomb and physically opened it, but also removed the mummy of Tutankhamen from the sarcophagus, lived until 1939, sixteen years after that event, and British soldier Richard Adamson, who slept in the tomb as a guard for seven years following the opening, was alive and well in 1980, fifty-seven years after his violation of the tomb.

This group died at an average age of seventy-three-plus years, beating the actuarial tables for persons of that period and social class by about a year. The Curse of the Pharaoh is a beneficial curse, it would appear.

See Appendix I for more information.

twenty-year curse — *see* Presidential Curse.

~ U ~

UFO   Acronym for Unidentified Flying Object, and also, after the first reported sighting in June 1947 by pilot **Kenneth Arnold** of "saucer-shaped" flying objects, known as a "flying saucer."

Since that time, endless reports of UFOs have come in, most of them actually of weather balloons, science projects, meteors, regular airline flights, and other relatively mundane events. In most cases, sizes and distances have been given, though such figures simply cannot be determined without the use of proper instrumentation, a comparison object, or another properly recorded, independent report. It is a delusion most people have that they can tell the size and/or the distance of an object without these advantages, and it is just not true.

The viewing of an unknown object or image in the sky has almost automatically brought in suggestions of extraterrestrial origins. While there can hardly be any doubt that because of the vastness involved, other forms of life must exist in the universe besides those of which we are already aware, that fact does not imply that a viewed UFO is a manifestation of such life.

It is simply what its name implies: an object or other phenomenon seen in the sky, apparently flying, and of unknown origin and nature, at that time and place, to that observer.

The currently favorite UFO claim is that of "abduction," in which "abductees" report to the media—in considerable detail—how they were whisked away by alien craft as biological specimens. Almost invariably we hear that the UFO occupants carefully examined the genitals of the victims, who delight to dwell on that factor. The *Journal of Irreproducible Results* in the United States awarded their 1993 "Ig Nobel Prize" to scientists John Mack of Harvard Medical School and David Jacobs of Temple University in Philadelphia for their joint conclusion that people who believe they were kidnapped by aliens from outer space probably were, and that the purpose of the abduction is the production of children. The opinion of Mack and Jacobs on the Tooth Fairy was not revealed.

Significantly, many persons who believe they are abductees also believe they have lived former lives and can recall them.

Umbanda A Brazilian combination of the ideas of **Allan Kardec** and the teachings of Candomblé, which is a religion of African origin presided over by women. Created about 1920, Umbanda is often incorrectly referred to as Macumba. It is popular and highly respected in Brazil.

unicorn A mythical animal resembling a small horse with a beardlike appendage and a long, spiral, tapering horn (known as an alicorn) projecting from the forehead. The only person who can tame a unicorn, it is said, is a virgin. A virgin is recommended as necessary for capturing the beast. None of the beasts has been captured.

The Chinese have long recognized this beast in their mythology. They refer to it as *ch'i-lin*, which translates as "male-female." The earliest Greek reference to a unicorn (by Ctesias) is in 400 B.C. and may have actually referred to the Indian rhinoceros. It is described there as having the legs of a buck deer, the head and body of a horse, and the tail of a lion. The horn is said to be white at the base, black in the middle, and red at the tip. Its body is white, the head red, and the eyes blue. This description was largely ignored and an all-white beast became accepted as typical.

In early Greek writings on animal husbandry there is a description of the process whereby horn buds of a goat kid are extracted and one of them is implanted at the center of the forehead. This produces in the mature goat the appearance of a small unicorn. The simple operation has also been done, first in 1933, with an Ayrshire calf. Since then, angora goats thus modified have been offered for sale as novelties.

Powdered unicorn horn was said to neutralize poisons and cure dropsy, epilepsy, gout, and many other ailments, and it was sold for those purposes by early apothecaries. The substance thus offered was probably narwhal horn, actually a form of specialized tooth growing from the mouth of the male narwhal, a small whale that is found in Arctic waters. (Incredibly, a powdered horn substance is still available in oriental pharmacies in the form of rhinoceros horn, which is extolled as an aphrodisiac. This is yet another fallacy that shows clearly the manner in which ignorance and greed by humans are destroying the assets of our planet, in this case leading inexorably to the extinction of the white rhinoceros.)

The **demon** Amduscias, Grand Duke of Hades, is said to have the form of a unicorn.

V

vampire Known in Poland as an *upir* and in Greece as a *brucolaca*. In Slavic countries, it has been believed that a child born with a tooth already developed will become a vampire.

Traditionally, the vampire is an "undead" person, often a suicide, who survives ordinary death by feeding on human blood, that of beautiful young maidens being much preferred. The blood is ingested through a bite wound on the victim's neck. It is said that some new vampires are the result of infection brought about from such a bite.

The person thus affected must sleep by day in a coffin in contact with earth from his or her mother country in order to sustain the pseudo-life state. Sunlight is invariably fatal to vampires. Only that, a stake through the heart, a silver bullet in the heart, or the destruction or sealing up of the resting place can finally kill a vampire. They do not cast shadows, nor do they have reflections in a mirror.

In 1730, there was a widespread panic in Hungary, where the legend was very strong. Adolescent girls reported nightly visitations from these creatures, much to the concern of the church.

Bram Stoker's novel *Dracula* (1897) benefited from the fact that the vampire bat *(Desmodus rotundus)* had been discovered and studied in South America and seemed to provide an animal counterpart to the legend. In fact, the bat took its name from the mythical monster.

vibration An object or substance which oscillates from a neutral position (node) to positions (crests) on either side of the node is said to vibrate. An example would be the movement of the tines of a tuning fork, of a violin string, or of a pendulum (all "transverse" vibrations), or the compression effect on air or another medium when it vibrates with sound waves, an example of a "longitudinal" wave. The general condition of such oscillation, or a single cycle, is known as a vibration.

Occultists have used the word *vibration* freely but without much notion of its meaning or respect for its true nature. It is a highly popular catchall description for imaginary forces, powers, or influences.

Von Däniken, Erich (1935-) Former Swiss bank employee and author of *Chariots of the Gods?*, *Gold of the*

Gods, and others, books in which he attempted to establish that UFOs were spacecraft described in ancient writings and mythology. Over thirty-six million copies of his books have been sold, and they are still on bookstands.

Von Däniken's work does not survive even cursory examination. His calculations are wrong, his facts are misquoted or invented, and he has admitted, during a 1978 PBS *Nova* television program, that some of his claims, conversations, and research did not take place at all; he simply invented material via what he termed "writer's license." Nonetheless, his books continue to sell by the millions all over the world, in several different languages.

Perhaps the greatest weakness of Von Däniken's arguments is that though he cites the varied marvelous accomplishments of brown-, yellow-, or black-skinned races, he expresses his doubt that they could have constructed these wonders (the Egyptian pyramids, Easter Island statues, Nazca [Peru] lines, for example) without extraterrestrial help. He never mentions Stonehenge, Chartres Cathedral, the Parthenon, or any other wonders created by white-skinned races.

voodoo A religion of the West Indies, and specifically Haiti, origi-nating with the slaves imported from Africa, who combined their gods with the Christian religious figures and through Macumba, Obeah (Jamaica), and other variations of this process created a great number of specific religions now popular in the Caribbean.

Voodoo itself is most well-known for its use of the wax doll to effect changes on a subject. A doll, preferably made using the hair, nail parings, and/or clothing of the intended subject, and baptized in that name, is subjected to various procedures such as pin-pricking, melting, or being submerged in water. The subject is said to undergo the actual experiences to which the doll has been exposed.

Though there is no evidence that such a system works, it has been postulated by modern authorities that perhaps a process of suggestion is involved, *if* the subject is informed of what has been intended and believes that it can work.

See also **sympathetic magic.**

voodoo doll — *see* **voodoo** *and* **sympathetic magic.**

vril An imaginary "occult essence," the invention of mystic/ novelist Bulwer-Lytton (1831-1891), who headed up a **magic** center in London and was a colleague of **Éliphas Lévi.**

W

Waldorf schools — *see* **anthroposophy.**

Walpurgis Nacht (night) The night of April 30, also known as May Day Eve and Beltane. (Beltane, in Ireland, is celebrated on June 21.) The Celtic beginning of summer. Traditionally the date of an important **witch** festival, or **sabbat.** The name Beltane derives from Baal, the name of an early Semitic fertility god of decidedly priapic nature. X-rated.

warlock — *see* **witch.**

Warner, William (1867-1936) Warner liked to claim he was Count Louis le Warner de Hamon. Better known under his professional name, Cheiro, he was an Irishman who claimed to have discovered a rare book, written on human skin, about **palmistry,** and then to have studied in Egypt and in India to perfect his knowledge of the art. He opened an elegant salon in New Bond Street, London, and soon became the leading palmist of his time.

Flamboyant, and with a skill for self-promotion, Warner claimed to have had a love affair with the fabulous spy Mata Hari, to have obtained validation from the British intelligence services, and to have had a 1904 encounter with the Russian Czar and a battle of wills with the monk **Rasputin.** These claims were unsubstantiated, but of course added substantially to his reputation.

Warner traveled the world with great success. Celebrities of all sorts were his clients, British Prime Minister Arthur Balfour, U.S. President Grover Cleveland, Kings Edward VII and VIII of England, General Horatio Herbert Kitchener, Leopold of Belgium, the Shah of Persia, Mark Twain, and Oscar Wilde among them. The fact that he may have performed his service for them, of course, does not imply their endorsements.

He died poverty-stricken in Hollywood, California, in 1936, his popularity having waned. Books on palmistry bearing his name are still sold.

water-witching — *see* **dowsing.**

weeping statues From time to time, reports of weeping or bleeding religious statues, icons, or paintings are featured in the media. There is no specific season for this phenomenon, but Christmas and Easter are slightly favored.

The Christmas season of 1986 brought a media blitz of articles and interviews about another variety of the miracle, this one of a Virgin Mary painting in Chicago that was said by church authorities to exude "a very thin, oily sweet substance very similar to the [liquid] we use to baptize children or [administer] unction for the sick." These authorities firmly declined to have the "tears" examined by chemists, saying that

> to further analyze [this phenomenon] would be almost blasphemy. The Archdiocese thinks [investigators] should not subject [the substance] to a scientific analysis, which is not a very religious procedure.

The previous year, a similarly attractive myth had collapsed when another religious figure, in Montreal, Canada—this time a combination weeping/bleeding statue—turned out to have been smeared with a quite mundane mixture of the owner's own blood and K-Mart shaving lotion. The resulting fuss was no surprise to experienced observers of these matters. Media exposure of the hoax brought a barrage of hate mail to the local bishop. The letter writers felt that in spite of the evidence—a direct confession from the hoaxer—the bishop still should have declared the event a genuine miracle.

Ordinary atmospheric condensation, encouraged by the increased number of candles offered at the site, as well as the exhalation of the large crowds, can often result in "tears" on a plaster figure. And it is obvious that any person armed with a concealed syringe or other similar device can surreptitiously project the required liquid onto the figure. Since proper examination of the site and of the substances involved are forbidden and discouraged, there is little to be gained merely by theorizing on the modus operandi that might have been used. Certainly, no assumption of a miracle would be **parsimonious**.

werewolf (also werwolf; In French, *loup-garou* or *bisclaveret;* in Spanish, *lobombre;* in Italian, *lupo mannaro*) The myth says that a human can be temporarily changed into a wolf through a **spell,** ingestion of certain substances, a curse, or simply from family disposition, but most often from the bite of another such creature.

The belief is very old. Greek sorceress Circe in Homer's *Odyssey* changed men into swine. Plato and Pliny the Elder referred to werewolves, and Virgil wrote about one person:

> By means of these [toxic plants] I often saw him turned into a wolf.

King John of England (1167-1216) was a far-from-excellent ruler whose body was dug up by superstitious folks who believed he was a werewolf, and in sixteenth-century France, serious laws were passed against those who were involved in such evil stuff.

Various cultures have elected other animals in place of the wolf.

In Greece we hear of a wereboar, in Romania a weredog, and in China a werefox. In Malaysia and other parts of the Orient, a very similar mythology is taught, but the animal into which the afflicted person changes is a tiger, leopard, eagle, or serpent. In Africa and India, the belief is that men change into hyenas, leopards, and tigers. In Chile it's a vulture and in Iceland they become bears. The American Plains Indians feared the werebuffalo.

The condition of being a werewolf is properly known as "lycanthropy." *See also* **vampire**.

Weyer, Johannes (Also Wier, 1515-1588) Born in Basel, Switzerland, Weyer was a sixteenth-century physician also known as Piscinarius, and a pupil of **Agrippa**.

The enlightened physician Johannes Weyer at age sixty.

In 1564, his book *De Praestigiis Daemonum* (*"On the Activities of Demons"*) tried to perform the same service as Reginald Scot's book *The Discouerie of Witchcraft*, which was published twenty years later, by denying that witchcraft was a genuine power or a threat to Christianity. In any case, both books were essentially ignored, and persecution of supposed **witches** continued. He was very enlightened on his subject when he observed:

> The uninformed and the unskilled physicians relegate all the incurable diseases, or all the diseases the remedy for which they overlook, to witchcraft. When they do this, they are talking about disease like a blind man does about color. Like many surgeons with their quackery, they cover their ignorance of our Sacred Art [medicine] with the playthings of magic malefactors and they themselves are the real malefactors.

Weyer vigorously pursued various claims of **magic** and witchcraft, showing that they had no basis in fact. He met the claimants on their own terms and defeated them. He investigated one of the most famous of all demon **"possession"** cases, that of the Nuns of Cologne in 1564. He solved that matter by determining that certain rather robust convulsions entered into by these virtuous ladies had been brought about, not by religious visions, but by visitations of neighborhood dandies who had favored them with their attentions and subsequently induced various raptures in the women by their very efforts at negotiating the walls of the convent. The ladies had turned heavy romance into religious exultation.

For his labors, Weyer was castigated by the church and his own profession. Complained one well-known physician of the time:

> Oh, if only such a man had never been born, or at least had not written anything! Instead of which, he gives many people through his books the opportunity to sin and to enhance the Kingdom of Satan.

Weyer managed to survive this criticism, lived to the then-surprising age of seventy-three, and was accorded a proper Christian church burial.

To many modern historians of medicine, he is looked upon as one of the founders of modern psychiatry; he is certainly one of the first philosophers to record a rational view of various human mental aberrations, many of which are believed even today, by the uneducated, to be caused by demons, witches, and other fanciful inventions. Weyer knew better and had the good common sense, intelligence, and fortitude to say so.

Strangely enough, Weyer also published *Pseudomonarchia Daemonum,* a catalog of demons and their attributes, in 1563. It was an inventory of devils, of which he said there were exactly 7,405,926, in 1,111 divisions of 6,666 each. (Modern Lutherans claim that there are 2,665,866,746,664 devils or demons, but demons are lively folks and very difficult to get to stand still during a count.)

White, Ellen G. — *see* Millerites.

wicca
Early English term for **witch.** Derived from a German root word meaning "to twist or to bend." Also used to denote the witch religion.

Willard, Frances — *see* Davenport brothers.

witch
According to *Malleus Maleficarum,* witches, men or women who have entered into pacts with **Satan,** are capable of changing themselves into other creatures, raising storms, bringing sickness to humans and animals, causing sterility, and **flying.** They consort carnally with **demons** and even with Satan himself.

The belief in witches brought about the persecution and prosecution of many unpopular persons in medieval times. *See* **witchcraft** *and* **Salem.**

A male witch is now often referred to as a warlock, though not strictly correctly. The term should more properly be applied to males of monstrous appearance who perform **magic.** "Warlockry" is the practice of infernal magic specifically by males.

witch of Endor
In the *Bible,* in book I Samuel 28, the witch of Endor was said to have called up the **ghost** of the prophet

Samuel at the command of King Saul. The ghost angrily predicted Saul's downfall. The original story was written about 1000 B.C.

witchcraft In **Reginald Scot's** book *The Discouerie of Witchcraft* (1584) appears one of the earliest descriptions:

> Witchcraft is in troth a cosening [deceiving] Art, wherein the Name of God is abused, prophaned, and blasphemed, and his power attributed to a vile creature. In estimation of the vulgar people, it is a supernatural work, contrived between a corporeal old Woman and a spiritual Divel [Devil]. The manner thereof is so secret, mystical, and strange, that to this day there hath never been any credible witness thereof. It is incomprehensible to the wise, learned or faithful, a probable matter to children, fools, melanchollick persons and Papists.

In modern times, witchcraft has been construed as a naturalistic religion of sorts, attributing **spirits** of all sorts to trees, rocks, clouds, and almost all "natural" objects. **Incantations** are used to try to bring about desired events, and in general it is a harmless distraction for otherwise idle persons to embrace.

The reputation for naked orgies, sacrifices, and other often odious practices that the public often attributes to witches is undeserved. Those habits are more properly assigned to followers of **Satanism**.

St. Thomas Aquinas, who accepted every myth of evil, lent his validation

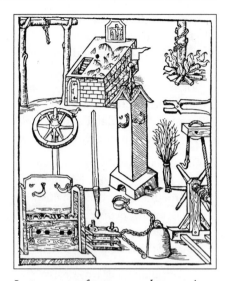

Instruments of torture used to convince those accused as witches to confess their misdeeds. The process was usually quite successful.

to witchcraft. It is interesting to note that the first woman ever burned alive for accusations of having intercourse with a devil died the year after Aquinas did (1274).

Penalties for practicing witchcraft have varied greatly over the ages. In ancient Egypt, Greece, and Rome, witches and magicians were prosecuted severely, and Plato approved punishment for the practice of magic of all kinds. The Romans set up special councils to punish witches, and in 139 B.C. all **sorcerers** were commanded to leave Italy within ten days. The Emperor Augustus ordered all books on magic to be burned publicly, and Tiberius again ordered witches exiled. Subsequent rulers (Constantius, Valentinian I, Valens) decreed death for witchcraft.

However, certain rulers such as Caracalla, Julian the Apostate, and Alexander Severus (third century

A.D.) consulted and employed witches.

Henry VIII of England, in 1542, passed a law against "conjurations and witchcrafts and sorcery and enchantments." In 1563, Elizabeth I forbade witchcraft and when James I succeeded her to the throne he was very severe in his condemnation and pursuit of witches. His Act of 1604 put to death some seventy thousand accused witches, according to one estimate, a grossly inaccurate figure. An even stronger act was passed in 1649.

In 1692, the town of **Salem,** Massachusetts, began hunting down witches and the absurdity took root in America.

One account says that the last witch executed in England was Alice Molland, condemned in 1685 for killing three persons with **spells.** However, two women were hanged at Northampton in 1705 and five more in 1712, and the death penalty for witchcraft was in effect until 1736. The prohibition of witchcraft in England continued up to 1951. The last known execution in Scotland for witchcraft took place in 1722, and a woman was burned as a witch in Germany, at Würtzburg, in June 1749.

See also **conjuring, Reginald Scot, Johann Weyer.**

witch doctors This term is usually applied to a native healer who practices among rural people in his or her own country. The modern witch doctor in Africa applies primitive psychology when he "pulls the thorn" by applying his mouth to a wound or the ailing portion of the body, producing by sleight of hand a thorn, stone, or sliver that is said to be either the actual cause of pain or a material representation of a **demon** or **devil.**

Anthropologists have spent much time examining these methods, and one of them has favorably compared these primitive methods to those used by today's more civilized practitioners. There may be a lot of information in these practices that can benefit medical science; much of today's medical knowledge came from similar sources.

witch's garland Known in Italy as the *Ghirlanda della Streghe,* this is a series of knots with the feathers of a black hen inserted at intervals. It is used to cast **spells.** It is a popular item for the local cottage trade and is sold to tourists who have no more success with it than the witches ever did.

witch's mark — *see* Devil's mark.

witches' sabbat — *see* sabbat.

Y

Yeti — *see* **Abominable Snowman.**

yin and yang In Chinese philosophy, these are two kinds of **qi** (*which see*). Yin is the Earth/negative/passive/wet/dark/feminine form, yang is the Sun/positive/active/dry/light/male form. Yin and yang are philosophical concepts, rather in line with outdated, chauvinist notions, with no objective existence. A circle with a bisecting pair of half circles, each half of the circle colored respectively black and white, is a symbol representing the concept.

The yin & yang symbols surrounded by trigrams, components of hexagrams.

yoga/yogi Yoga is an ancient Hindu teaching that is very much concerned with meditation, body postures, and proper breathing as methods to achieve "liberation" and "union with the universal soul." A yogi (also yogin) is a practitioner of these exercises.

A great number of incredible contortions of the human body and spirit go along with the process of enlightenment, and yoga is (often falsely) identified with street **fakirs** who mutilate themselves and perform various **conjuring** tricks.

There are a great variety of quite different yogic schools.

Zancig, Julius & Agnes (J. Jörgensen & A. Claussen; 1857-1929 & ?-1916; also Ada) The Zancigs were a married Danish couple who performed a two-person act which was basically an advanced development of the "**second sight**" act. Agnes was a hunchback with black, piercing eyes and Julius was tall and darkly handsome. They billed the act as "Two Minds with but One Single Thought," which was a clever dodge that did not, strictly speaking, claim **telepathy**.

Julius Zancig, with his wife, performed a superb two-person mental act at the turn of the century. They were seen by audiences around the world.

In their time, the Zancigs caused as much excitement and controversy with the press, scientists, and the public as any claimed **psychic** matter has ever enjoyed. A major British newspaper publisher, Lord Northcliffe, used the power of the *Daily Mail* to influence opinion in favor of telepathy that he believed took place between Julius and Agnes. He was totally convinced that they possessed mysterious psychic powers.

As with most such two-person acts, the "receiver" (Agnes) would sit on the stage blindfolded, while the "sender" (Julius) wandered about the audience accepting objects, written words, and small documents from members of the audience. Agnes would describe, apparently by telepathy, the appearance of the objects and details from the written material handled by Julius. A great deal of training, study, and practice was necessary in order to do this act, which had nothing to do with ESP of any sort.

Sir Oliver Lodge, the very prominent British scientist, and **Sir Arthur Conan Doyle,** the equally famous creator of the fictional Sherlock Holmes, witnessed the Zancig team in operation and declared them genuine because they had no idea of how the trick might have been worked. These two gentlemen also believed in the popular **spirit mediums** of their day, for essentially the same reason.

Just as the Zancigs were at the

top of their form, Agnes died. Julius was genuinely attached to her, and his grief at losing the mate who had spent so many long years developing the very difficult and sophisticated methods by which they communicated, was profound. He eventually remarried, this time to a Brooklyn schoolteacher named Ada. She was a confirmed **spiritualist,** and though she managed to learn the rudiments of the act, she was extremely shy and ashamed to face the audience with a blatantly fake act. For that reason, she performed with her head down and in a barely audible voice.

Seeing that Ada was unsuitable as a partner, Julius sought for another, and found Paul Vucci, a young man who was to eventually become an outstanding sleight-of-hand nightclub performer under the name Paul Rosini. Though Paul (who was called Henry in the act) was very proficient as a partner, the problem was that he was just draft age in 1917 and was about to become Uncle Sam's involuntary partner. Julius was fortunate enough to happen upon a thirteen-year-old youth named David Bamberg, who dropped into the position neatly for a while. (Bamberg went on to become a famous **conjuror,** touring with an oriental act in South America as Fu Manchu.)

Eventually Ada went back into service with Julius, but in his later years he, too, apparently began to accept **spiritualism** and spent much time at séances. The public enthusiasm for the Zancigs faded, and the act was soon working at carnivals and in cheap tent shows. To the dis-

may of his colleagues, Julius dedicated more and more of his time to belief in "real" psychic claims, and finally died in very impoverished circumstances in 1929.

Zener, Dr. Karl (1903-1963) In the early 1930s, a Swiss psychologist named Zener, a partner of **Dr. Joseph Banks Rhine,** designed a set of cards bearing five symbols which he felt were sufficiently different from one another that they would be ideal for conducting certain tests, among them **extrasensory perception (ESP)** tests. These symbols are: circle, plus sign, wavy lines, square, and star.

The five symbols developed by Dr. Karl Zener for use in tests of extrasensory perception.

These are normally used in a deck of twenty-five cards, five of each symbol. For decades, Zener cards have been employed in **parapsychological** laboratories in the search for the ever-elusive powers called **telepathy** and **clairvoyance.** So far, in spite of millions of bits of data gathered through that extensive exploration, experiments with Zener cards—or any other devices—have failed to yield convincing, replicable results.

After a few years of association with Dr. Rhine, Zener began efforts to have him removed from the campus of Duke University, fearing the burden that the university would have to bear for being connected with parapsychology.

zodiac The part of the sky through which the Sun, Moon, and planets move relative to the starry background. The zodiac consists of the twelve **astrological** signs as well as several other constellations that are ignored by the astrologers. Each sign is itself divided into twelve "houses," which are said to determine a human characteristic or prospect such as love, home, travel, death, health, and employment.

The idea of the zodiac appears to date from the fifth century B.C. There is a tablet in the Louvre Museum, Paris, dated at about 300 B.C., which is the earliest known listing of the signs.

Parts of the human body were assigned to be governed by each of the twelve signs, and the signs were used as a method of diagnosis by early physicians. An analysis of the positions of the planets against the zodiac, along with their attributes, was believed to indicate the appropriate treatment.

zombie In Haitian **voodoo**, a deceased human who is resurrected minus soul and can be made to perform simple tasks as a laborer. Some anthropologists have attempted to explain the legend by invoking the possible use of special drugs that they believe might simulate death and enslave the victim.

The fact that the idea of real zombies has been taken seriously in Haiti can be seen in their old penal code, where it is stated that "the use of substances whereby a person is not killed but reduced to a state of lethargy, more or less prolonged," falls under the category of "intention to kill by poisoning."

APPENDIX I

Curse of the Pharaoh Personnel

Name	Died	Age	Years after Opening	Function	Comments
Adamson, Sergeant Richard	1980+	—	57+	Guarded burial chamber day and night for seven years.	Closest person to Tutankhamen's remains.
Bénédite, Georges	1926	69	3	Louvre representative.	Died of heat stroke.
Breasted, Professor J. H.	1935	70	12	Archaeologist, University of Chicago.	
Bruyère, Bernard	1965+	80+	42+	Archaeologist.	
Burton, Harry	1939+	—	16+	Official expedition photographer.	Intimately involved in all operations.
Callender, A. R.	1939	—	16	Assistant to Carter.	Present at all tomb operations.
Capart, Jean	1947	70	24	Belgian archaeologist.	
Carnavon, Lord	1923	57	4 months	Expedition patron.	One of three persons present at opening of actual burial chamber, but died before mummy was uncovered.
Carter, Howard	1939	66	16	Chief of operations.	Most totally involved of all persons, and one of three present at opening of actual burial chamber.

Name	Died	Age	Years after Opening	Function	Comments
Derry, Dr. Douglas	1939	80+	16	Cairo University anatomist.	Dissected and examined mummy.
Engelbach, Reginald	1946	58	23	Cairo Museum representative.	
Gardiner, Sir Alan	1965+	80+	42+	Philologist.	Handled all written material.
Hall, Lindsley F.	1939+	—	16+	Project draftsman.	Present at all tomb operations.
Hauser, Walter	1939+	—	16+	Project draftsman.	Present at all tomb operations.
Herbert, Lady Evelyn	1980	78	57	Carnavon's daughter.	One of three present at opening of actual burial chamber.
Kuentz, Charles	1939+	—	16+		
Lacau, Pierre	1965	92	42	Egyptologist, Louvre Museum.	Intimately involved in all operations.
Lefèbvre, Gustave	1957	78	34	Cairo Museum.	
Lucas, Alfred	1950+	79	27+	Egyptian Government chemist.	Did analysis of mummy tissues, dust and foodstuffs.
Lythgoe, A.M.	1934	66	11	Metropolitan Museum New York City	
Mace, Arthur C.	1928	—	5	Metropolitan Museum New York City	Very ill when signed on, left project early by prior agreement.
Winlock, Herbert E.	1950	66	27	Metropolitan Museum New York City	

NOTE: Where a dash appears, data are not presently available. Where a date such as 1939+ is shown, it indicates that the person is known to have been alive as of that date, and possibly longer.

From the table, we see that the *average life span* of those involved, where we can determine that information, was seventy-three-plus years. This beats the life span expectation in actuarial tables for persons of that period and social class, by just one year. The average *duration of life* for these persons after the opening of the tomb, when the "curse" was supposed to become effective, was twenty-three-plus years. Particularly notable is the fact that Adamson, Carter, Burton, Derry, and Lucas—those who actually *opened* the burial chamber and *removed and handled the remains*—lived an average of more than twenty-six years after their very intimate involvement with the mummy.

Also note that those who have analyzed the matter have chosen to ignore the *hundreds* of Egyptian laborers who were involved in the tomb operation, as if these persons were unimportant. One common laborer from the area recently died, just 70 years after he helped open the tomb, but his death was not reported as significant in the overall picture.

APPENDIX II

Forty-Nine End-of-the-World Prophecies—That Failed

Divine prophecies being of the nature of their Author, with whom a thousand years are but as one day, are not therefore fulfilled punctually at once, but have springing and germinant accomplishment, though the heightfulness of them may refer to some one age.

—SIR FRANCIS BACON (1561-1626)

A favorite subject of prophets has always been the end of mankind and/or the demise of our planet and/or the collapse of the entire universe. Part of the technique, for some, is to place the date far enough ahead that when The End fails to arrive, the oracle is no longer around to have to explain why. Others, often to encourage the surrender of property and other worldly chattels by the Believers, prepare excuses well in advance and manage to survive the great disappointment that often follows a failed prediction. In any case, the resilient fans never discredit the notion; they merely redesign the details and settle back once more to confidently await doom.

Here is a short list of some rather interesting end-of-the-world prognostications, beginning with biblical references and ending with some contemporary seers and their doomsayings. Judging from the record earned by the soothsayers in this matter, we may safely assume that our planet will continue very much the same as it has for some considerable period into the future.

B.C.-A.D. According to the New Testament, The End should have occurred before the death of the last Apostle. In Matthew 16:28, it says:

Verily, I say unto you, there be some standing here which shall not taste of death, till they see the Son of Man coming in his kingdom.

One by one, all the apostles died. And the world rolled on for everyone else. . . .

A.D. 992 In the year 960, scholar Bernard of Thuringia caused great alarm in Europe when he confidently announced that his calculations gave the world only thirty-two more years before The End. His own end, fortunately for him, occurred before that event was to have taken place.

December 31, A.D. 999 The biblical Apocrypha says that the Last Judgment (and therefore, one supposes, the end of the world) would occur one thousand years after the birth of Jesus Christ. When the day arrived, though it is doubtful that there was all the panic that was reported by later accounts, a certain degree of apprehension was probably experienced. It was said that land was left uncultivated in that final year, since there would obviously be no need for crops. According to the *Encyclopedia of Superstitions*, public documents of that era began, "As the world is now drawing to a close . . ." Modern authorities suspect that historians Voltaire and Gibbon may have created or at least embellished this tale to prove the credulous nature of medieval Christians.

Significantly, Pope Sylvester II and Emperor Otto III momentarily mended their considerable political differences in anticipation of a certain leveling of those matters.

A.D. 1033 Theorists pressed to explain the A.D. 999 bust decided that the one thousand years should have been figured from the death of Christ rather than from his birth. Bust number two followed.

September 1186 An astrologer known as John of Toledo in 1179 circulated pamphlets advertising the world's end when all the (known) planets were in Libra. (If the sun was included in this requirement, this should have occurred on September 23 at 16:15 GMT, or at that same hour on October 3 in the new calendar.) In Constantinople, the Byzantine emperor walled up his windows, and in England the Archbishop of Canterbury called for a day of atonement. Though the alignment of planets took place, The End did not.

A.D. 1260 Joaquim of Flore worked out a splendid calculation that definitely pinpointed A.D. 1260 as The Date. Joaquim had a bent pin.

February 1, 1524 This was one of the most pervasive Doomsday-by-Flood expectations ever recorded. In June of 1523, British astrologers predicted that The End would begin in London with a deluge. Some twenty thousand persons left their homes, and the prior of St. Bartholomew's built a fortress in which he stocked enough food and water for a two-month wait. When the dreaded date failed to provide even a rain shower in a city where precipitation is very much to be expected, the astrologers recalculated and discovered they'd been a mere one hundred years off. (On the same day in 1624, astrologers were again disappointed to discover that they were still dry and alive.)

The year 1524 was full of predicted disaster. Belief in this date was very strong throughout Europe. An astrologer impressively named Nicolaus Peranzonus de Monte Sancte Marie, found that a coming conjunction of major planets would occur in Pisces (a water sign) that year, and this strengthened the general belief in a universal final deluge.

George Tannstetter, an astrologer/mathematician at the University of Vienna, was one of very few at that time who denied The End would occur as predicted. He drew up his own horoscope, discovered that he would live beyond 1524, and denied the other calculations were correct. But George was considered a spoilsport and was ignored.

A "giant flood" was prophesied for February 20 (some say February 2) of 1524 by astrologer Johannes Stoeffler, who employed his skill to establish that date in 1499. Such was the belief in his ability that more than one hundred pamphlets were written and published on his prediction.

The planets involved in this dire conjunction were Mercury, Venus, Mars, Jupiter, and Saturn, along with the Sun. Neptune, unknown then, was also in the sign Pisces. Other major influences,

Uranus and the Moon, were not. Nor was Pluto, also unknown then. But the date of this conjunction was February 23 (old calendar), not the twentieth.

In response to the 1524 prophecies, in Germany people set about building boats, while one Count Von Iggleheim, obviously a devout believer in Stoeffler's ability, built a three-story ark. In Toulouse, French President Aurial also built himself a huge ark. In some European port cities, the populace took refuge on boats at anchor. When it only rained lightly on the predicted date where Von Iggleheim had his ark, the crowd awaiting the deluge ran amok and, with little better to do, stoned the count to death. Hundreds were killed in the resultant stampede. Stoeffler, who had survived the angry mob, reexamined his data and came up with a new date of 1528. This time there was no reaction to his declaration. Sometimes people actually get smart.

Incidentally, the 1878 *Encyclopaedia Britannica* described 1524 as "a year, as it turned out, distinguished for drought."

1532 A bishop of Vienna, Frederick Nausea, decided a major disaster was "near" when various strange events were reported to him. He was told that bloody crosses had been seen in the skies along with a comet, that black bread had fallen from midair, and that three suns and a flaming castle had been discerned in the heavens. The story of an eight-year-old girl of Rome whose breasts, he was told, spouted warm water finally convinced this scholar that the world was due to end, and he so declared to the faithful.

October 3, 1533, at Eight A.M. Mathematician and *Bible* student Michael Stifel (known as Stifelius) had calculated an exact date and time for Doomsday from scholarly perusal of the Book of Revelation. When they did not vaporize, the curiously ungrateful citizens of the German town of Lochau, where Stifel had announced the dreaded day, rewarded him with a thorough flogging. He also lost his ecclesiastical living as a result of his prophetic failure.

1533 Anabaptist Melchior Hoffmann announced in Strasbourg, France, a city which had been chosen by him as the New Jerusalem, that the world would be consumed by flames in 1533. He believed that in New Jerusalem exactly 144,000 persons would live on while two characters named Enoch and Elias would blast flames from their mouths over the rest of the world. The rich and pious who hoped to be included in that number saved destroyed their rent records, forgave their debtors, and gave away their money and goods to the poor. How those commodities were to be used among the flames was not explained, nor did anyone point out that such sacrifices so near The End were hardly meritorious.

The time of cataclysm by fire came and went, and a new apostle named Matthysz arose to encourage those who now expressed some doubts, telling them it had been slightly postponed. Thus, in February 1534, more than one hundred persons were baptized in Amsterdam in anticipation of the still-expected event. As it turned out, the years 1533 and 1534 were noted for their lack of conflagrations, a fact that might be explained by the public's suddenly increased awareness of danger from fire.

1537 (And also in 1544, 1801, and 1814) In Dijon, France, a list of prophecies by astrologer Pierre Turrel was published posthumously. His predictions of The End were spread over a period of 277 years, but all were fortunately wrong. He had used four different methods of computation to arrive at the four dates, while assuring his readers that he had strictly orthodox religious beliefs—a very wise move in his day.

1544 *See* **1537**.

1572 In Britain, a total solar eclipse and a few impressive novas seemed to signal something important. Considerable panic ensued, to no avail.

1584 Astrologer Cyprian Leowitz, who had the distinction in 1559 of being included in the official index of prohibited writers by Pope Paul IV, predicted the end of the world for 1584. Taking no chances, however, he then issued a set of astronomical tables covering celestial events all the way to the year 1614, in the unlikely event that the world would survive. It did.

1588 The sage Regiomontanus (Johann Müller, 1436-1476), posthumously a victim of enthusiastic crackpots who delighted in attributing occult and magical powers to him, was said to have predicted The End for the year 1588 in an obscure quatrain, but in 1587 Norfolk physician John Harvey reassured his readers that the calculations ascribed to the master were faulty, and the resulting prophecy false. Harvey was right.

1624 *See* **1524.**

1648 Rabbi Sabbati Zevi, in Smyrna, interpreted the kabala to show that he was the promised Messiah and that his advent, accompanied by spectacular miracles, was due in 1648. By 1665, regardless of the failure of the wonders to appear, Zevi had a huge following, and his date was now changed to 1666. Citizens of Smyrna abandoned their work and prepared to return to Jerusalem, all on the strength of reported miracles by Zevi. Meeting a sharp reversal when arrested by the sultan for an attempted coup and brought in fetters to Constantinople, the new Messiah sat in prison while followers as far away as Holland, Germany, and Hungary began packing up in anticipation of Armageddon. Unfortunately for these faithful, the sultan converted the capricious Zevi to Islam, and the movement ended.

1654 Consulting his ephemeris and considering the nova of 1572, physician Helisaeus Roeslin of Alsace decided in 1578 that the world would surely terminate in flames in another seventy-six years. He did not survive to see his prophecy fail. That should have been an evil year indeed. An eclipse of the sun was predicted for August 12 (it actually occurred on the eleventh) and that was also widely believed to bring about The End. Many conversions to the True Faith took place, physicians prescribed staying indoors, and the churches were filled.

1665 With the Black Plague in full force, Quaker Solomon Eccles terrorized the citizens of London yet further with his declaration that the resident pestilence was merely the beginning of The End. He was arrested and jailed when the plague began to abate rather than increase. Eccles fled to the West Indies upon his release from prison, whereupon he once again exercised his zeal for agitation by inciting the slaves there to revolt. The Crown fetched him back home as a troublemaker, and he died shortly thereafter.

1666 *See* **1648**.

1704 Cardinal Nicholas de Cusa, without Vatican endorsement, declared The End was to arrive in 1704.

May 19, 1719 Jacques (also Jakob I) Bernoulli, the first of a famous line of Swiss mathematicians who made their home in Basel, predicted the return of the comet of 1680 and earth-rending results therefrom. The comet did not come back, perhaps for astronomical reasons, but Bernoulli went on to discover a mathematical series now called the Bernoulli Numbers. He is renowned for this and for the eight exceptional mathematicians his line produced in three generations, but not for Doomsday nor for his astronomical calculations.

October 13, 1736 London was once again targeted for the "beginning of the end," this time by William Whiston. The Thames filled with waiting boatloads of citizens, but it didn't even rain. Another setback.

1757 Mystic/theologian/spiritist and supreme egocentric **Emanuel Swedenborg,** ever willing to be the center of attention for one reason or another, decided after one of his frequent consultations with angels that 1757 was the terminating date of the world. To his chagrin, he was not taken too seriously by anyone, including the angels.

April 5, 1761 When religious fanatic and soldier William Bell noticed that exactly twenty-eight days had elapsed between a February 8 and a March 8 earthquake in 1761, he naturally concluded that the entire world would crumble in another twenty-eight days, that is, on April 5. Most suggested that the date should have been four days earlier, in keeping with that special day, but many credulous Londoners believed him and snapped up every available boat, taking to the Thames or scurrying out of town as if those actions would save them. History records nothing more of Bell after April 6, when he was tossed into London's madhouse Bedlam by a disappointed public.

1774 English sect leader Joanna Southcott (1750-1814) had the notion that she was pregnant with the New Messiah, whom she proposed to name Shiloh. History records that her pregnancy "came to nothing," nor did the world end as she had prophesied. She left behind a box of mystical notes that were to be opened only after her death, with twenty-four bishops present. Perhaps because of a failure to interest that many ecclesiastics of high rank to attend the occasion, the box was not opened and vanished somewhere. She was succeeded by several minor would-be prophets, all of whom tried other End-of-the-World predictions, with the same result. One successor, John Turner, we will meet up ahead.

1801 Astrologer Pierre Turrel (*see* **1537**) chose this date, along with three others, for The End. His first two had already failed by this time. Again, no luck.

1814 Astrologer Pierre Turrel (remember him?) chose this last date for The End. His three others had already failed, and, again no luck! As author **Charles Mackay** wryly noted, "the world wagged as merrily as before."

October 14, 1820 Prophet John Turner was leader of the Southcottian movement in Bradford, England. The specialty of this sect was End-of-the-World prophecies, the first one having been made by the founder of the group, Joanna Southcott, whom we have already met back in 1774. His failed prediction turned his congregation against him, and John Wroe (*see* **1977**, up ahead) took over the movement.

April 3, 1843 (And also July 7, 1843; March 21 and October 22, 1844) William Miller, founder of the Millerite Church, spent fifteen years in careful study of the scriptures and determined that the world would conclude sometime in 1843. He announced this discovery of what he called "the midnight cry" in 1831. When there was a spectacular meteor shower in 1833, it seemed to his followers that his prediction was close to being fulfilled, and they celebrated their imminent demise. Then, as each date he named failed to produce Armageddon, Miller moved it up a bit. The faithful continued to gather by the thousands on hilltops all over America each time one of the new dates would dawn. Finally, on October 22, 1844, the last day that Miller had calculated for The End, the

Millerites relaxed their vigils. Five years later, Miller died, still revered and not at all concerned at his failed prophecies.

The movement eventually changed its name and broke up into a number of modern-day churches, among them the Seventh-Day Adventist Church, which today has over three million members.

1874 A date calculated by **Charles Taze Russell** of the **Jehovah's Witnesses** for The End.

1881 Those who delighted in measuring the various passages of the **Great Pyramid** at Giza, presumed to be the tomb of Cheops, calculated that all would be over in 1881. Careful remeasuring and some imagination gave a better (but not much better) date of 1936. That was improved upon by other students, who decided upon 1953 as the terminal year. Further refinements and improvements of technique are still being made. If we get a new date, we'll let you know.

1881 Mother Shipton is supposed to have written:

> The world to an end will come
> In eighteen hundred and eighty-one.

The prediction, as well as the rhyme, are faulted. A book titled *The Life and Death of Mother Shipton,* written in 1684 by Richard Head, was reprinted in a garbled and freely "improved" version in 1862 by Charles Hindley. In 1873 Hindley admitted having forged that rhyme and many others, but his confession caused no lessening of the great alarm in rural England when 1881 arrived.

The world not having ended in that year, the spurious verse has since been published in a refreshed version which substitutes "nineteen" for "eighteen" and "ninety" for "eighty." The world, according to most authorities, did not end then, either.

1936 One set of **Great Pyramid** measurers came up with this date.

1914 One of three dates the **Jehovah's Witnesses** promised The End. The others were 1874 and 1975.

1947 In 1889, "America's Greatest Prophet," John Ballou Newbrough, said that for sure in 1947:

all the present governments, religions and all monied monopolies are to be overthrown and go out of existence. . . . Our present form of so-called Christian religion will overrun America, tear down the American flag, and trample it underfoot. In Europe the disaster will be even more terrible. . . . Hundreds of thousands of people will be killed. . . . All nations will be demolished and the earth be thrown open to all people to go and come as they please.

It wasn't a *great* year, but it wasn't all *that* bad.

1953 Again, a group of **Great Pyramid** nuts with their tape measures figured out this year as the last. Back to the King's Chamber, guys.

1974 Interestingly enough, the conjunction of heavenly bodies that occurred back in 1524 was far, far more powerful than the more recent one described in a silly book titled *The Jupiter Effect,* written by two otherwise sensible astronomers who, in 1974, predicted dreadful effects on our planet as a result of a March 10, 1982, "alignment" of planets. Other astronomers denied that any effect would be felt, and when the date came and went, as you may have noticed, no one noticed. One of the authors reported that some earthquakes which had occurred in 1980 had been the "premature result of The Jupiter Effect," and the public yawned in amazement.

1975 One of the several dates promised by the **Jehovah's Witnesses** as The Date. Wrong.

1977 John Wroe, who is described by the kindliest historian we can find as a "foul-mouthed, ugly, dirty lecher," in 1823 inherited the leadership of the Southcottian sect in England when an End-of-the-World prophecy by John Turner failed. Learning from the example, Wroe took no chances. He made his Armageddon prophecy for 1977. A 1971 book, *Prophets Without Honor,* says of Wroe:

At a time when thermo-nuclear powers face each other across the Iron and Bamboo Curtains, it is well to remember that—as far as can be judged from the scanty records—John Wroe, indeed, was a true prophet!

1980 A very old Arabic astrological presage of doom specified that when the planets Saturn and Jupiter would be in conjunction in the sign Libra at 9 degrees, 29 minutes of that sign, we could kiss a big bye-bye to everything—camels, sand, mosques, the whole bag. That astronomical configuration *almost* took place at midnight of December 31 (new calendar), 1980, a date calculated by astrologers many years ago as the one spoken of. Jupiter was at 9 degrees, 24 minutes, and Saturn was at 9 degrees, 42 minutes, so the calculation was close to correct. However, nary a camel blinked an eye.

1980s The unsinkable Jeane Dixon, ever optimistic and daring, predicted in 1970 that a comet would strike the earth in the "mid-80s" at a place that she knew, but did not deign to tell. That information was to be held until a "future date." Perhaps she is *now* prepared to tell us? She said of this event that it "may well become known as one of the worst disasters of the 20th century." But then Jeane also said that "I feel it will surely be in the 1980s that [an unnamed person] will become the first woman president in the United States." Back to that ephemeris, Jeane.

1996 It has been reasoned by biblical scholars that since one day with God equals one thousand years for Man, and that God labored at the creation of the universe for six days, Man should labor for six thousand years and then take a rest. Thus, using other scripturally derived numbers, the world should end sometime in 1996. With any luck at all, we'll see. . . .

July 1999 In Quatrain X-72, Nostradamus declared:

> *L'an mil neuf cens nonante neuf sept mois*
> *Du ciel viendra grand Roy deffraieur*
> *Resusciter le grand Roy d'Angolmois.*
> *Auant apres Mars regner par bon heur.*

> The year 1999, seven months,
> From the sky will come a great King of Terror:
> To bring back to life the great King of the Mongols,
> Before and after Mars to reign by good luck.

Sure.

BIBLIOGRAPHY

Abell, George O., & Singer, Barry, (Edited). *Science and the Paranormal.* New York: Charles Scribner's Sons, 1981.

Armstrong, David and Elizabeth M. *The Great American Medicine Show.* New York: Prentice-Hall, 1991.

Ashley, Leonard R. N. *The Wonderful World of Superstition, Prophecy, and Luck.* New York: Dembner Books, 1984.

Berger, Arthur S., & Joyce Berger. *The Encyclopedia of Parapsychology and Psychical Research.* New York: Paragon House, 1991.

Blackmore, Dr. Susan. *Beyond the Body: An Investigation of Out-of-the-Body Experiences.* London: William Heinemann, 1982

Brewer, E. C., Rev. Dr. *Dictionary of Phrase and Fable.* Cassell & Company, 18??.

Campbell, Eileen, and J. H. Brennan. *The Aquarian Guide to the New Age.* U.K.: Aquarian Press, 1990.

Cavendish, Richard. *A History of Magic.* London: Weidenfeld & Nicolson, 1977.

de Camp, L. Sprague. *The Fringe of the Unknown.* Buffalo, N.Y.: Prometheus Books, 1983.

Evans, Dr. Christopher. *Cults of Unreason.* London: Harrap, 1973.

Frazier, Kendrick, (Edited). *Paranormal Borderlands of Science.* Buffalo, N.Y.: Prometheus Books, 1993.

Gardner, Martin. *The Healing Revelations of Mary Baker Eddy.* Buffalo, N.Y.: Prometheus Books, 1993.

———. *In the Name of Science.* New York: Putnam's, 1952. Expanded and reissued as *Fads & Fallacies in the Name of Science* by Dover, New York, 1957.

———. *Order and Surprise.* Buffalo, N.Y.: Prometheus Books, 1983.

Garrison, Omar V. *The Encyclopedia of Prophecy.* Secaucus, N.J.: Citadel Press, 1979.

Guiley, R. E. *Harper's Encyclopedia of Mystical & Paranormal Experience*. San Francisco: Harper, 1991.

Hall, Manly Palmer. *The Secret Teachings of All Ages*. San Francisco: Crocker, 1928. Reduced and reprinted by the Philosophical Research Society, Los Angeles, 1977.

Hall, Trevor H. *Search for Harry Price*. London: Duckworth, 1978.

———. *The Medium and the Scientist*. Buffalo, N.Y.: Prometheus Books, 1984.

Hansel, C. E. M. *ESP and Parapsychology*. Buffalo, N.Y.: Prometheus Books, 1980.

Harris, Melvin. *Investigating the Unexplained*. Buffalo, N.Y.: Prometheus Books, 1986.

Hines, Terence. *Pseudoscience and the Paranormal*. Buffalo, N.Y.: Prometheus Books, 1988.

Hyman, Dr. Ray. *The Elusive Quarry*. Buffalo, N.Y.: Prometheus Books, 1989.

Johnson, Martin. *Parapsychologie*. Holland: De Kern, 1982.

Kerr, Howard, and Charles L. Crow, eds. *The Occult in America*. Chicago: University of Illinois Press, 1983.

Klass, Philip J. *UFOs: The Public Deceived*. Buffalo, N.Y.: Prometheus Books, 1983.

Kurtz, Dr. Paul, (Edited). *A Skeptic's Handbook of Parapsychology*. Buffalo, N.Y.: Prometheus Books, 1985

Langer, W.L. *An Encyclopedia of World History*. Boston: Houghton Mifflin, 1940.

Littlefield, Henry W. *History of Europe, 1500-1848*. New York: Barnes & Noble, 1939.

Mackay, Dr. Charles. *Memoirs of Extraordinary Popular Delusions and the Madness of Crowds* (1841). Reprint. Avenel, N.J.: Crown, 1980.

Mishlove, Jeffrey. *The Roots of Consciousness*. New York: Random House, 1975.

Ord-Hume, Arthur W. J. G. *Perpetual Motion—The History of an Obsession*. New York: St. Martin's Press, 1977.

Robinson, H.R. *History of Western Europe*. Boston: Ginn, 1934.

Schultz, Ted. *The Fringes of Reason*. New York: Harmony Books, 1989.

Shepard, Leslie A., ed. *The Encyclopedia of Occultism and Parapsychology*. Detroit: Gale Research, 1985.

Sladek, John. *The New Apocrypha*. New York: Stein & Day, 1973.

Smith, Dr. Morton. *Jesus the Magician*. San Francisco: Harper and Row, 1978.

Spence, Lewis. *An Encyclopaedia of Occultism.* London: George Routledge & Sons, 1920. Reprinted by Citadel Press, New Jersey, 1960.

Stevenson, David L. *The Elizabethan Age.* New York: Fawcett, 1966.

Thorndike, Lynn. *History of Magic and Experimental Science.* New York: Columbia University Press, 1958.

Wilson, Colin, and John Grant. *The Directory of Possibilities.* New York: Rutledge Press, 1981.

———. *Mysteries.* London: Hodder and Stoughton, 1978.

———. *The Occult—A History.* New York: Random House, 1971.

INDEX

Please first refer directly to the subject in the text headings of the encyclopedia. Additional references are listed here, along with alternate titles and designation.

About the Author

JAMES RANDI is a professional magician (The Amazing Randi), author and lecturer, amateur archaeologist, and amateur astronomer. Born in 1928 in Toronto, Canada, he received his education there. He was naturalized as a U.S. citizen in 1987 and now lives in Florida with a mellow red cat named Charles, several untalented parrots, numerous other unnamed creatures, and the occasional visiting magus. Understandably, he is single.

Mr. Randi was host of *The Randi Show* on WOR-Radio (1966/67) and he has had his own TV specials in Italy, England, Belgium, Hungary, Canada, Japan, Australia, and the United States. He has appeared in a great many TV documentaries, interview shows, and variety productions in France, Germany, Japan, Italy, the U.K., and other countries. He appears frequently on U.S. television shows. He has done three world tours as a performer and lecturer through the Far East, Europe, Australia, and North and South America. In 1974 he performed at the White House. He spends much of his time traveling between performances and lectures all over the globe.

Mr. Randi's writings (articles, essays, stories, book reviews) have appeared in many periodicals. In 1986 Mr. Randi was made a fellow of the prestigious John D. & Catherine T. MacArthur Foundation, an honor awarded him for his work in investigating claims of supernatural, occult, and paranormal powers, in particular, his exposures of TV evangelists and "psychics."

For more than twenty-five years, Mr. Randi's prize offer of $10,000 for "the performance of any paranormal, occult, or supernatural event, under proper observing conditions" has gone unclaimed. (As of this writing, the $10,000 prize offer has presently been temporarily withdrawn due to financial limitations, which are the result of legal costs relating to current litigation being brought against Mr. Randi. It is anticipated that the offer will soon be reinstated upon successful resolution of this action.)

James Randi lectures all over the world on the theme "Search for the Chimera," dealing with his lifelong quest for genuine psychic phenomena. Since his work is ongoing, the presentation is updated regularly to accommodate the latest discoveries.

This book is Mr. Randi's tenth.